First published in Great Britain in 2019 by

Policy Press
University of Bristol
1-9 Old Park Hill
Bristol
BS2 8BB
UK
t: +44 (0)117 954 5940
pp-info@bristol.ac.uk
www.policypress.co.uk

North America office:
Policy Press
c/o The University of Chicago Press
1427 East 60th Street
Chicago, IL 60637, USA
t: +1 773 702 7700
f: +1 773 702 9756
sales@press.uchicago.edu
www.press.uchicago.edu

British Library Cataloguing in Publication Data
A catalogue record for this book is available from the British Library.

Library of Congress Cataloging-in-Publication Data
A catalog record for this book has been requested.

ISBN 978-1-4473-3726-3 paperback
ISBN 978-1-4473-3785-0 ePub
ISBN 978-1-4473-3786-7 Mobi
ISBN 978-1-4473-3784-3 ePdf

Oxfam contributed some funding and research time to the development of this book. The views contained in the book are those of the authors and do not necessarily represent Oxfam policy.

Cover design by blu inc, Bristol

"With their concept of 'Arriving', the authors provide fodder for exciting debate on humanity's most important project, the search for well-being alternatives that will help make peace with the earth."
Ashish Kothari, Kalpavriksh

"A compassionate guide to shifting gear, from an economy based on pursuit of growth to one that can discover the joy of what it has already achieved. We need this book."
Neva Goodwin, Tufts University

"With its invitation to make ourselves at home in the world, *The Economics of Arrival* celebrates the pioneers and projects that show the new world emerging through the cracks of the old."
Hunter Lovins, president and founder of Natural Capitalism Solutions

"A must read for anyone who cares about social justice, the future of the biosphere and our place in it. Trebeck and Williams challenge us to think about what we owe to future generations and raise serious questions about pursuing economic growth as an end goal. An important and timely book worthy of a broad audience and vibrant discussion."
Tim Di Muzio, University of Wollongong

Contents

List of figures, table and boxes

Figures

Table

Boxes

List of abbreviations

CEO	chief executive officer
EU	European Union
GDP	Gross Domestic Product
GHG	greenhouse gases
GPI	Genuine Progress Indicator
IMF	International Monetary Fund
NHS	National Health Service
OECD	Organisation for Economic Co-operation and Development
ONS	Office for National Statistics
PB	participatory budgeting
SDG	Sustainable Development Goal
SPI	Social Progress Index

About the authors

Jeremy Williams is an independent writer and campaigner. He studied journalism and international relations and specialises in communicating social and environmental issues to a mainstream audience. He has worked on projects for Oxfam, RSPB, WWF, Tearfund and many others, and is a co-founder of the Postgrowth Institute. His award-winning website (makewealthhistory.org) was ranked Britain's number one green blog in 2018.

Katherine Trebeck is a researcher and advocate for a new economic paradigm and is based in Scotland. She has many years' experience, including as Knowledge and Policy Lead for the Wellbeing Economy Alliance and over eight years for Oxfam GB. She has a PhD in Political Science from the Australian National University and honorary posts with the University of Strathclyde and the University of the West of Scotland. Her work has ranged from construction of a new measure of progress for Scotland to rapporteur for Club de Madrid's Shared Societies and Sustainability project.

Acknowledgements

We never really intended to write a book. Not at first. It happened almost by accident, one idea following another. But here it is, and we have many people to thank for pushing us a little further, asking us challenging questions and encouraging us to keep going.

Many of those people are at Oxfam, and we're particularly grateful to Emily Gillingham for her help in contacting publishers, to Deborah Hardoon for the charts and statistics in Chapter Nine, to Nick Byrer and Irene Guijt and all Oxfamers who believed in the importance of the book and its contribution to a debate that has enormous relevance to the lives of people living in poverty.

Thanks to all of those who read and commented on early drafts, including Andrew Cumbers, Lorenzo Fioramonti, Andrew Goudie, John Magarth, Franziska Mager, Ruth Mayne, Hayley Richards, Franchesca Rhodes, Alberto Sanz Martins, Rebecca Sutton, Nikki van der Gaag, Pearl Van-Dyck, and Kerry Willis. Huge gratitude to Tim Di Muzio and the several anonymous reviewers whose critique made the book stronger. Thanks especially to Cylvia Hayes and Mick Blowfield, whose work helped inform some of the case studies.

Like so many others, we owe a certain debt to Roanne Dods, a woman who spent her career supporting the creativity of others. Cancer took her before we finished the first draft, but her early enthusiasm for the idea gave us the confidence to expand our ambitions for the book.

The whole business of dealing with publishers is a little nerve wracking, but we feel like we landed on our feet with Policy Press. Our commissioning editor, Paul Stevens, was supportive and positive from the start, and we're grateful for his guidance through an unfamiliar process.

If we were to list all the many thinkers and scholars who have influenced us and led us to where we are, we'd be here a long time. But we should mention Gehan McLeod (who pointed Katherine to Max-Neef many, many years ago), Herman Daly, Peter Victor, Tim Jackson, Jason Hickel, Michael Marmot, Maja Gopel, Neva Goodwin, Richard Wilkinson, Kate Pickett, Ha-Joon Chang, E.F. Schumacher, Michael Braungart, William McDonough, Tim Kasser, Manfred Max-Neef, Kate Raworth, Chris Goodall, Samuel Alexander, Juliet Schor, J.K. Galbraith, Amartya Sen and Donella Meadows.

We ought to thank Donnie Maclurcan, who put us in touch in the first place and Kerry Willis for her visual translation of our ideas and ever-wonderful enthusiasm. And Greensmiths, La Bottega, Victoria Library, Sartis, the Fruit Market Gallery and the various other cafes in London, Glasgow and Edinburgh where we outstayed our welcome while tapping away on our laptops.

Jeremy: Thank you to the readers and commenters on my blog, who keep me sharp and are always introducing me to new ideas. Thanks to all at the Millyard, for bringing a sense of community to this otherwise solitary writer. My deepest gratitude to Zach and Eden, and most of all to Louise, for all the love and the patience and for putting up with me on the days when my mind is elsewhere.

Katherine: There are many people who have accompanied me on my intellectual journey over the last few decades. Whether by patient friendship, inspiration, collegiality, financial support, encouragement or love, the following people (and many more) have had a hand in this book: Stefan Bergheim, Stephen Boyd, Chik Collins, Mike Danson, Lorenzo Fioramonti, Lars Fogh Mortensen, David Gait, Maja Gopel, Andrew Goudie, Peter Kelly, Gerry McCartney, Tam McGarvey, the team at Oxfam Scotland, Annie Quick, Erinch Sahan, Andrew Simms, Julia Steinberger, Willie Sullivan and Jen Wallace. I'm thrilled at the prospect of putting some of these ideas into practice, working alongside the crew at the Wellbeing Economies Alliance, especially the 'amplification team' of Ana Gomez, Lisa Hough-Stewart, Stewart Wallis and Michael Weatherhead. And I'm even more excited at spending some Sunday mornings with Mark Bradley rather than my laptop …

Foreword

Kate Raworth, author of Doughnut Economics: Seven ways to think like a 21st-century economist

What is the shape of economic success? Odd though that question may sound, a very clear answer to it lay at the heart of 20th-century economics: an ever-rising line of endless growth.

Growth has long been a metaphor for progress in Western thought and culture, and it is not hard to understand why. People love to see their children grow, delight in watching their gardens grow and so associate the concept with health and success. No wonder, then, that economics so readily adopted growth as an implicit goal of its own. National income was first calculated as recently as the 1930s, but within a few decades its growth – measured in terms of gross domestic product, or GDP – had become the overriding target for policy makers, as well as a matter of intense competition between nations.

This notion of economic progress as GDP growth was powerfully reinforced in W.W. Rostow's 1960 classic book, *The Stages of Economic Growth*, which described five distinct phases that countries pass through in the process of economic development.

Rostow's economic journey starts with *Traditional Society*, in which a nation's economic output is limited by its artisanal and agricultural technologies. Change begins to take place only with the *Pre-conditions for Take-off*, such as the creation of a banking system, schooling tailored to producing efficient workers and the belief spreading through society that growth is necessary for something beyond itself, like national dignity or a better life for the children.

Then comes *Take-off* itself, during which, wrote Rostow, 'growth becomes the normal condition' and 'the march of compound interest begins to bear its blessings'. In the fourth stage, the *Drive to Maturity*, nations invest in building a range of industries, no matter what their natural resource base. And this leads to Rostow's fifth and final stage, *The Age of High Mass Consumption*, in which citizens can afford to buy the goods they desire, like bicycles, sewing machines and other consumer desirables of the 1960s.

It's impossible to miss the implicit airplane ride in this story, complete with its pre-flight checks and moment of take-off. However, Rostow's metaphorical plane turns out to be like no other because he never allows it to land, but leaves it flying forever into the sunset of mass consumerism.

Rostow himself knew that the story was incomplete. As he fleetingly enquired in the pages of his book, 'And then the question beyond, where history offers us only fragments: what to do when the increase in real income itself loses its charm?' He asked that question but he never answered it. Why? Because it was 1960 and he was about to become economic advisor to presidential candidate John F. Kennedy, who was running for election on the promise of a 5% growth rate. So Rostow's job was to figure out how to keep that plane in the air, not to ask if, when or how it could ever be allowed to land.

Over half a century on, the legacy of this thinking still has us flying into the sunset of mass consumerism, with economies that have come to expect, demand and depend upon endless GDP growth. And yet so much has changed between Rostow's era and our own. Just two years after his book was first published, Rachel Carson's *Silent Spring* alerted the world to the toxic effects of agricultural pesticides on North America's wildlife. A decade later, the Club of Rome's report on *Limits to Growth* warned that the world's current path of resource-intensive economic development was leading to catastrophic levels of pollution. And two decades after that, in 1992, the world's governments agreed, in a landmark commitment, to prevent dangerous climate change.

Today we know so much more about humanity's dependence upon this delicately balanced living planet, but the policy focus on economic growth remains. Even in the highest-income countries, governments believe that the solution to their nation's economic challenges – from public debt to trade deficits, from inequality to pollution, from unemployment to innovation – lies in yet more growth.

I often wonder what Rostow would think if he were alive today, travelling with us as a fellow passenger on this apparently endless economic flight. I'm sure he would readily admit that his five-stage story of growth had left things somewhat hanging in the air. Imagine, then, if he were to reach into the seat-back pocket in front of him and pull out a copy of *The Economics of Arrival*. He'd soon realise, I think, that in his hands he had an essential part of the next stage of the story for his economic airplane: learning to land. What's more, I'm sure he would feel quietly relieved to know that people had started to answer the question he barely dared to ask back in the growth-fuelled days of the 1960s.

Rather than attempt to define a fixed destination, Katherine Trebeck and Jeremy Williams wisely invite us to start imagining what economic progress might mean when it stops meaning growth. With engaging clarity, warm humour and a bold spirit of possibility, they blend radical insights from the founding fathers of economics with inspiring policies and action from a surprising array of countries.

Fascinatingly, rather than challenge the growth metaphor at the heart of Western culture, this thought-provoking book encourages readers to connect even more deeply with it. Yes, we do love to see our children grow, but eventually they grow up. We delight in watching plants and trees grow but they, too, finally mature. *The Economics of Arrival* carries this insight deep into the realm of economics with the intriguing idea of a grown-up economy in which everyone can make themselves at home. The time for exploring such economic futures has indeed arrived, so fasten your seatbelt and read on.

Preface

> *Writing, no matter what its subject, is an act of faith; the primary faith being that someone out there will read the results. I believe it's also an act of hope, the hope that things can be better than they are.* —*Margaret Atwood*[1]

Not many people start writing a book together on the day they meet for the first time. Inadvertently, that is what we appear to have done.

We met at a cafe on the Lower Marsh, London. Jeremy was on his lunch break from his part-time job at a nearby charity. Katherine was down from Glasgow. We were introduced over e-mail by our mutual friend Donnie Maclurcan, with whom Jeremy founded the Post Growth Institute and whom Katherine met by virtue of 'tweeting back and forth', which led to several Skype conversations. 'Lots of common interests for you to explore', Donnie had said, and indeed there were.

It was immediately obvious that we shared a passion for making the world a better place, an anger at injustice and greed and a holistic view that saw development and sustainability as interconnected. We were working with all of this in different ways – Katherine as a researcher and 'policy wonk' for Oxfam, Jeremy as a communicator and activist – but we had a similar curiosity about ideas, and a scepticism of easy answers.

Over lunch we talked about growth, and how consumer societies could shift away from an overarching narrative of endless upward progress. When Jeremy shared something he had been mulling over for a while – 'some countries need to recognise that they have arrived' – Katherine recognised the genesis of a metaphor worth exploring. So we finished lunch with the frequently uttered 'we should do something together on this'. But we actually did: while we didn't meet again for six months, we began to jot down some ideas to flesh out that idea of 'arrival'. What would it mean for economies if people took that possibility seriously? We each took a run at it. Jeremy sent over pages of notes on mythology and progress. Katherine wrote an outline for a paper investigating diminishing returns, failure demand and policy ideas for a new economic model. In the meeting of those two approaches was arrival – our central argument (supported by a range of evidence we set out below) that, beyond a certain point, economic increase ceases to be meaningful and that after this phase the growth agenda should give way to new priorities that are qualitative rather than quantitative.

Those rough notes became a discussion paper. Katherine talked about it with her colleagues at Oxfam, who supported further exploration. We e-mailed it back and forth, drawing on a wide range of different ideas from debates and discourses that have been raging and growing for some time: wellbeing, development, the limits of growth, critiques of GDP, inequality and human nature. In many respects our contribution is essentially stepping through a door that many others have opened. One of the first was Jean Charles de Sismondi – the 18th-century political economist whose work has been described as a humanitarian protest against the dominant orthodoxy of his time. His book *Nouveaux Principes d'Economie Politique*, published in 1819, was a powerful and poetic rage against an economy focused too much on increasing wealth and the idea of wealth accumulation as an end in itself. More recent names include Hazel Henderson, Neva Goodwin, Lorenzo Fioramonti, Tim Jackson, Clive Hamilton, Kate Raworth and many, many others. Organisations (too many to list fully, but including the New Economics Foundation, The Great Transition Project, India's Radical Ecological Democracy movement, Fundación Rosa Luxemburg and the Transnational Institute) have synthesised and promoted these critiques and issues, so they sit, to varying degrees of prominence, in the minds of many campaigners, activists and even one or two policy makers.

So we are certainly not the first to outline the inadequacy of economic growth as an overarching ambition. What we embarked upon is exploring what comes next. If not growth, how do we understand progress? Can we describe a society that has 'grown up', and can we now pursue more qualitative forms of improvement?

The months went by. It got longer. It began to look more like a book. Jeremy quit his job to give it more attention and Katherine carved out pockets of time in her Oxfam role and on many a Sunday morning.

We presented the ideas to staff at Oxfam HQ in 2016. There was excitement at opening up a debate on these topics. It seemed as if we were putting language to things that people had been thinking. We started circulating drafts and getting feedback from a range of people. Ideas were refined and expanded. Katherine's colleague Deborah Hardoon crunched some numbers across a range of variables – revealing a turning point after which many apparent benefits to growth tail off.

We teased out the distinction between arrival as a juncture but not yet a satisfactory realisation of good lives for everyone. And we began to set out some of the deliberate policy choices of making ourselves at home, gathering more real-world examples and policy ideas. Helpful comments from those first readers gave us a long to-do list of improvements and additions. We half expected somebody to raise an objection at some point that we couldn't answer, but even the most robust critics saw something worthwhile in what we were doing.

In February 2018 we met Paul Stevens in a pub near Kings Cross station in London. Paul was economics editor at Bristol University Press and saw in our now rather lengthy manuscript something that he would 'pick up off the shelf and read'. Borrowing Margaret Atwood's words, we have faith that Paul won't be the last to pick it up off the shelf, and that other readers will find it useful. We echo Atwood's hope that things can be better, and we hope that you, as one of those readers, will find our ideas useful, challenging and timely for a world where things can't stay as they are.

Katherine Trebeck and Jeremy Williams
April 2018

ONE

Introduction

> *The purpose of this journey could change. We could go from trying to own the world to trying to feel at home in it … And that's when you take off your shoes – prepared to stay a while.* —*Katrina Marçal*[1]

The last century has seen unprecedented economic and social progress. Many people in many places are richer and better educated than ever before, and can look forward to longer lives in a fairer and more tolerant world. Unfortunately, aspects of that progress are now threatened by climate change, inequality, extremist politics and environmental degradation. Much of this damage to people and planet is driven by the pursuit of a narrow definition of 'progress'. Having achieved so much, the next generation may see achievements begin to slip away. Others, who can only dream of the living standards of the rich world, find themselves shut out as competition for resources and the consequences of climate change erode economic gains as fast as development can proceed.

What a tragedy it would be if, in the rush for more, the fruits of progress rotted before everyone had a chance to enjoy them. There's no need to keep running, on and on. It is time to recognise that the richest countries have already Arrived in the world long hoped for. There are more than enough material and monetary resources. Yet most economies do not operate in a way that appreciates them or shares them very well. The priority now is to make ourselves at home – a very different task from that of pursuing more and more without regard to quality or distribution.

Gross Domestic Product (GDP) rich countries such as the UK have come a long way in the last century. From a position of relative affluence, it is easy to forget just how many people lived in grinding poverty just a couple of generations ago. There are still too many disadvantaged households and regions in Britain, but the type of widespread material destitution of the past is mercifully rare. Where it occurs people are often shocked and wonder what has gone wrong. How did they slip through the safety net? Does that safety net need mending? Many will go so far as to ask if those experiencing poverty are being exploited, paid too little or offered inadequate hours. As seen recently in the rise of food banks, poverty has certainly not been abolished. But it is no longer considered normal or inevitable. Many would recognise the persistence of poverty in rich countries as a matter of distribution: a consequence of resource allocation that reflects political choices rather than any scarcity facing society as a whole.

Over their lifetimes, our grandparents' generation saw the British National Health Service created and the rolling out of the welfare state. They witnessed electrification of homes and the spread of indoor plumbing. They benefited from big steps forward in workers' rights and health and safety.

Box 1.1: 'Third world' poverty at home

> *As a child, I remember hearing stories from my Grandmother's childhood. Her family were so poor that she walked to school barefoot. One day she found an orange peel discarded in the gutter. This was such a rare and exotic fruit at the time that she picked it up and took it with her, so that she could pretend to her school friends that she'd had an orange. That was Liverpool in the 1930s. —Jeremy*

The writer Helen Forrester was a contemporary of Jeremy's grandmother and lived in the same city. In her memoirs Forrester describes her family of nine sharing two beds between them, and making do with one meal a day. She called her book *Two Pence to Cross the Mersey*, because the defining dream of her childhood was to go and visit her grandmother on the Wirral, a peninsula just the other side of the river. The two pence that the ferry cost were an unaffordable luxury.

But by the time of her death in 2011, Forrester would have seen the advent of affordable air travel, mobile phones, free video calls with people the other side of the world and a doubling in the number of people surviving a cancer diagnosis.[2]

From the economic crash of 1929 to the 1970s, the industrialised world enjoyed a sustained period of economic equalisation as the gap between rich and poor declined. The trauma of war unified people around a common sense of shared interests, and many of the gains from increased prosperity were channelled to middle- and lower-income groups. The existence of a Communist alternative to the East kept the pressure on Western governments to deliver better lives for ordinary people, dismantling old elites and encouraging egalitarian policies (after all, in the face of a perceived enemy, you have to be nice to your friends). Union rights expanded, and gender inequality fell as women stepped into new roles in society and the economy. Workers enjoyed a higher share of the global economic pie via increased labour share. Education raised skill levels, boosting job quality and remuneration (and raising wages for low-skilled workers as their labour became more valuable). Some called it the 'Golden Age of Capitalism' and the idea that economic gains would 'trickle down' seemed to be working. The tax system became more progressive, and a lot of the revenue from taxation was spent on social welfare. As the 20th century unfolded, new technologies became available to a growing number of people, and global trade delivered an ever greater range of consumer goods.

In country after country, successive generations have seen similar advances. East across Europe and south across Latin America, people are escaping poverty. Hundreds of millions have joined the middle classes in China and India, and many African economies are growing fast. In the Western world, and in a growing number of other places, there is living vindication of John Maynard Keynes' hopes that subsistence would not be 'the permanent problem of the human race'.

It must have been hard to hope for such progress from the depths of the Great Depression, but Keynes did just that, offering a vision of abundance rather than scarcity. In his famous essay 'Economic Possibilities for Our Grandchildren', he let his imagination 'take wings into the future' and foresaw a time when absolute poverty would be over.[3] The struggle for subsistence – what he called 'the economic problem' – would be solved. Societies could then devote themselves to the challenge of living well.

Today's GDP-rich countries are the inheritors of that future – but, as we show below, they are also at grave risk of squandering this inheritance and blocking it for everyone else. Keynes thought that this might happen: he foresaw that people would find it hard to adapt. Survival has been a primary goal since time immemorial, biologically wired into us. Keynes was thinking 'with dread of the readjustment of the habits and instincts of the ordinary man [sic], bred into him for countless generations, which he may be asked to discard within a few decades'.[4] Robert Skidelsky (a biographer of Keynes), writing with his philosopher son Edward, offers a similar warning. 'The irony is', they write, 'that now that we have at last achieved abundance, the habits bred into us by capitalism have left us incapable of enjoying it properly'.[5]

Writing in 1930, Keynes knew that the drive for *more* could be mobilised to overcome the Great Depression, and to raise standards of living for everyone. 'The strenuous purposeful money-makers may carry all of us along with them into the lap of economic abundance,' he wrote. But once there, a new challenge would emerge, and the role of the money makers would take a back seat. 'It will be those peoples, who can keep alive, and cultivate into a fuller perfection, the art of life itself and do not sell themselves for the means of life, who will be able to enjoy the abundance when it comes'.[6]

Keynes made a distinction between the 'means' and the 'art' of life. The means are the basics, the survival priorities. These have been humanity's preoccupations throughout history – making ends meet, feeding the family, storing up enough to get through the winter. Beyond those immediate concerns there was always a more philosophical set of questions around what made a life worthwhile, what made it fulfilling and satisfying. Historically – and still in many places today – the only people who could ask that second set of questions were the privileged elite: those who had enough land and tenants, or slaves, or stocks and shares, or factories, to take their own material survival for granted. For everyone else, the choice was out of their hands.

Keynes recognised that he lived at the threshold of a new era. More and more people were stepping off the treadmill of subsistence. For the first time the majority of people would be able to legitimately ask themselves what they really wanted out of life – beyond mere survival and instead towards the art of life.

About this book

As those who live in that new era, our purpose here is to look at how societies can nurture, in Keynes' terminology, the art of life itself. How can *all* of humanity enjoy the world's abundance? What changes need to happen in everyday lives, in communities, in work, in technology and in the economy itself to appreciate, cultivate and – importantly – *share* that abundance?

This book goes beyond a false binary of painting all growth as either good or bad. Instead we recognise the benefits that growth has delivered thus far when it has been used well, but explain how many parts of the world are entering a period where growth is bringing a diminishing suite of benefits and often even increasing harm. The institutions and policies that once rendered growth positive are being eroded, leaving the benefits of growth to be enjoyed by fewer and fewer people. We first set out what might be seen as some of the 'fruits of growth' (Chapter Two), before showing how the pursuit of more poses ever greater risk for people and planet (Chapter Three) and examining the stranglehold that growth has on our political and economic systems (Chapter Four). Building on the insights of diverse schools of thought (from development to neuroscience, from economics to human geography) and weaving together the wisdom and ideas of a range of scholars and activists, we then propose two interrelated concepts as an alternative to perpetual striving for more growth: 'Arrival' and 'making ourselves at home'.

These will be explained and developed throughout the book, but for the time being let us clarify up front that Arrival is about adequacy, being able to meet basic needs. It is primarily a material notion, a matter of having the resources to deliver a good life. We could describe it as reaching a point of ample sufficiency. We use it as a deliberately provocative term that confronts the ostensibly forbidden question of whether development has a destination.

Crucially, however, having enough resources *collectively* obviously does not necessarily mean everyone *individually* has enough.

Failure to share the world's harvest, both within and between countries, is one of the most enduring frustrations and tragedies of our time. As we explain below, the benefits of growth are not only beginning to tail off in many respects, but pursuit of ever more growth is often driving more problems that require yet more resources to fix. This is called 'failure demand' in social policy terms. It also speaks to the notion of defensive expenditures used in ecological economies and underpins the concept of uneconomic growth in respect of the economy writ large. Failure demand and uneconomic growth are discussed in a little depth in Chapter Five, but they are recurring themes in this book and they show that pursuit of infinite growth risks unravelling the benefits that growth has brought.

The idea of Arrival does not imply that all problems are solved. It does not suggest that everything is resolved and everyone has what they need. Rather, it is the idea that a society collectively has *the means* for this. Growth has reached a point at which a decent standard of living could, theoretically, be universal. It is a possibility, not a promise. We're using a journey metaphor, but you could also consider Arrival to be a process of maturing or reaching full size. What does the economy want to be when it grows up?

Realising the possibility of Arrival demands a new project – using resources in a smarter, fairer way, rather than wasting or hoarding them. Diminishing marginal returns and failure demand show that while a society might have Arrived in the material sense, there is still a great task ahead: to cease the endless race for 'more' and instead focus on the quality and distribution of economic activity and material resources. We are in agreement with John Stuart Mill when he wrote:

> It is scarcely necessary to remark that a stationary condition of capital and population implies no

> stationary state of human improvement. There would be as much scope as ever for all kinds of mental culture, and moral and social progress, as much room for improving the Art of Living, and much more likelihood of its being improved, when minds ceased to be engrossed by the art of getting on.[7]

That is the task that we refer to as 'making ourselves at home'. The twin concepts of Arrival and making ourselves at home recognise that material progress matters and is indeed vital in meeting basic needs. Material goods are the foundation for a good life, but not the essence of it.

In Chapters Six and Seven we explain how, once the point of Arrival has been passed, this shift in purpose for the economy – to one that makes itself at home – constitutes a more useful, healthier and more satisfying mantra than that of more growth. Calling for 'growth' is like a child telling their parent that they want 'more'. It begs the follow-up question: 'more of what?' Perhaps more bread? Or is it more water? And perhaps what is needed is not more food, but the tools to benefit from what is already there (a spoon, for example). Further, as we discuss in Chapter Three, planetary limits raise the question of leaving enough for everyone in our global household. Do we really need more growth? Of what? And for whom? These are the sorts of questions inherent in the notion of Arrival and making ourselves at home.

We show how, once the delusion of growth as both an end in itself and the best of all possible means is discarded, discussion can then turn to what sort of economy we can create, what sort of life we can lead if GDP-rich societies pause to notice that, collectively, they have Arrived. This is the time to shift energy, intelligence and creativity to making better use of what has already been accumulated and, perhaps more than anything, ensuring it is fairly distributed. This is a recalibration of economic purpose: making ourselves at home, rather than endless running, growing, striving for more.

We show, in Chapter Eight, that many aspects of this grown-up economy are already in existence – and indeed flourishing. We describe how making ourselves at home means getting things right for people in the first place, rather than having to constantly repair the damage created by an economy set on growth at all costs. This means taking a long-term perspective and applying measures and goals that align the purpose of institutions and businesses with the needs of people and planet.

What we are proposing shouldn't be seen as an easy option. Aspects of it will be difficult, extremely difficult. Shifting gear, from an economy based on pursuit of growth to one making the most of what it already has, will encounter resistance. It will be susceptible to regression and mistakes. It will be an ongoing project. It seeks to transform a system built on an ideology that itself took several decades to emerge. Friedrich von Hayek was one of the key thinkers behind what became known as neoliberalism, and we share, at least, his perspective on taking a longer view. Describing the purpose of the Mont Pelerin Society, one of the early groups championing neoliberal thinking, Hayek explained that:

> It is from [a] long-run point of view that we must look at our task. It is the beliefs which must spread, if a free society is to be preserved, or restored, not what is practicable at the moment, which must be our concern.[8]

Neither should making ourselves at home be mistaken for a simple end point of some kind. This is an economy in which there is scope for continuous improvement. Science and technology will advance. Human creativity and imagination are boundless. Politics will evolve. The economy will remain dynamic. What changes is the ultimate goal. Making ourselves at home is an ethos of qualitative improvement that is a very different system-wide goal to the sometimes meaningless, sometimes harmful and sometimes unnecessary pursuit of *more*.

Chapter Nine examines ways in which the point of Arrival might be determined. It is not our place to dictate a definite line in the sand, so instead we consider some alternative notions that we hope will enable a conversation and debate.

In Chapter Ten the thorny, but ubiquitous question of 'how?' is tackled. We do not pretend to have all – or even most! – of the answers as to how this far-reaching shift will come about. Instead we offer some insights from systems thinking, from political science, from behavioural science and from movements and change agents themselves. We finish by exploring the sorts of policies that making ourselves at home entails – by no means a comprehensive set of changes, but some ideas for those who want to be at home sooner rather than later.

The book will refer to the global context throughout, particularly when drawing practical examples from all around the world – good ideas can come from anywhere. However, we both live in the UK and are writing from a rich-world perspective. It is in mature consumer economies that the concept of 'Arrival' applies most immediately and urgently, so most of our examples and statistics pertain to GDP-rich countries. Ours is first and foremost a message for the GDP-rich world.

When we consider the abundance in the world around us, the tyranny of averages might imply that the world at large has Arrived. But the many stark inequalities suggest that there is much more to do to make ourselves at home. In fact, many in the poorest countries (let alone the majority of the nine billion people expected to live on the planet by 2050) may never reach that point of Arrival, if economies and people in countries that industrialised first leave nothing for them.

For those countries that do not yet have the ability to meet the basic needs of their citizens, we offer more of a cautionary tale. If development is taken to be a linear and one-size-fits-all process, then these countries risk following in the dirty and alienating footsteps of the GDP-rich nations. But if the world can imagine that other routes to development are possible, then there is no need to follow. As we discuss at the end of Chapter Seven, there is an opportunity to 'leapfrog' instead, learning from the failures of GDP-rich nations and bypassing them altogether. This means pioneering a better path to Arrival – a gentler path that is more conducive to making oneself at home when the time comes, and one that is less harmful for people and planet on the way. That doesn't diminish the role of growth – poorer countries do need *more* in order to boost the standard of living of their citizens in a material sense. Like laying the foundations of a house, growth is necessary here, and of course it needs to be good quality and shared well.

Importantly though, for this growth to happen in places and communities where it is needed, GDP-rich countries need to make room – quite literally in an ecological sense – for countries that have not yet Arrived. GDP-rich countries shifting towards making themselves at home can facilitate the Arrival of others. The call for an economy that makes itself at home speaks to that change of purpose necessary in GDP-rich countries, but also points to what a gentler path might look like for those who have the opportunity to choose it.

'A people are as healthy and confident as the stories they tell about themselves,' wrote Nigerian poet Ben Okri. 'Sick storytellers can make nations sick'.[9] The story of infinite growth on a finite planet is a sick story. So is trickle-down economics, or the rising tide that lifts all boats. But these dead-end stories must be countered with another story, a better story. Drawing on diverse schools of thought that have emerged in recent decades, from the limits to growth, to scholarship around the determinants of wellbeing; from analysis of the drivers of inequality, to literature exploring pro-social business models, Arrival and making ourselves at home offers such a narrative. We believe it is compelling because it is fundamentally a success story – it's about the end of striving and the possibility of the fulfilment of our ancestors' hopes. The agenda of fighting for survival could be over if the economy were to engage with a new challenge: that of building ourselves a lasting home in this place of plenty.

TWO

The fruits of growth

This is the best time in human history to be born, for you are more likely than ever before to be literate, to be healthy, and to be free to pursue your dreams. —*Barack Obama*[1]

The International Geosphere-Biosphere Programme identifies a series of socio-economic trends that exponentially rose from around 1950 onwards. Collectively known as 'the Great Acceleration', (see Figures 1a and 1b) they demonstrate how far material progress has come, and how fast.[2] For example, between 1950 and 2010:

- global GDP grew by a factor of ten;
- total energy use grew by a factor of five;
- the number of cars passed 1 billion in 2010;
- international tourism rose from fewer than 50 million visits a year to over 900 million;
- the number of phone subscriptions (landline and mobile) rocketed to over 6 billion.

One could look at other datasets and see the following that have taken place.

- Globally, the number of people living in very extreme poverty has declined by more than half, falling from 1.9 billion in 1990 to 836 million in 2015, with most progress being realised since 2000.[3]

Figure 1a: The Great Acceleration: earth system trends. Accelerating environmental impacts.

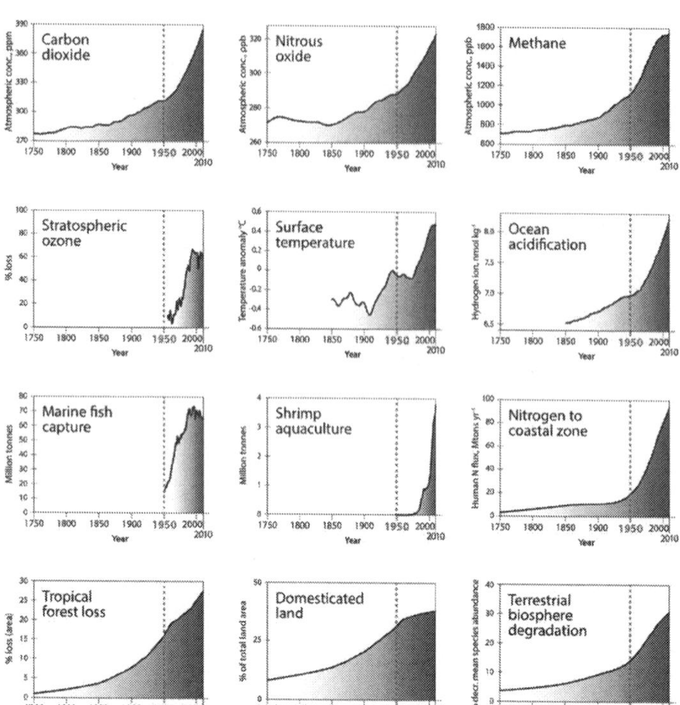

Source: International Geosphere-Biosphere Programme and Stockholm Resilience Centre

- The number of children who will die before they turn five has fallen from 90 in every thousand births in 1990 to 42 in every thousand in 2015.[4] Over the same time period, the number of mothers who die in childbirth has fallen by almost 44%.[5]
- Previously common diseases are being controlled, with smallpox eradicated, polio cases down by 99%,[6] and progress on many other diseases as vaccination programmes are extended. These efforts, along with new treatments for AIDS, malaria and other diseases, have added 10 years to global life expectancy since 1980.[7]
- In the decade to 2012 all countries accelerated their achievement in the Human Development Index (education, health and income).

Figure 1b: The Great Acceleration: socio-economic trends. Accelerating growth trends.

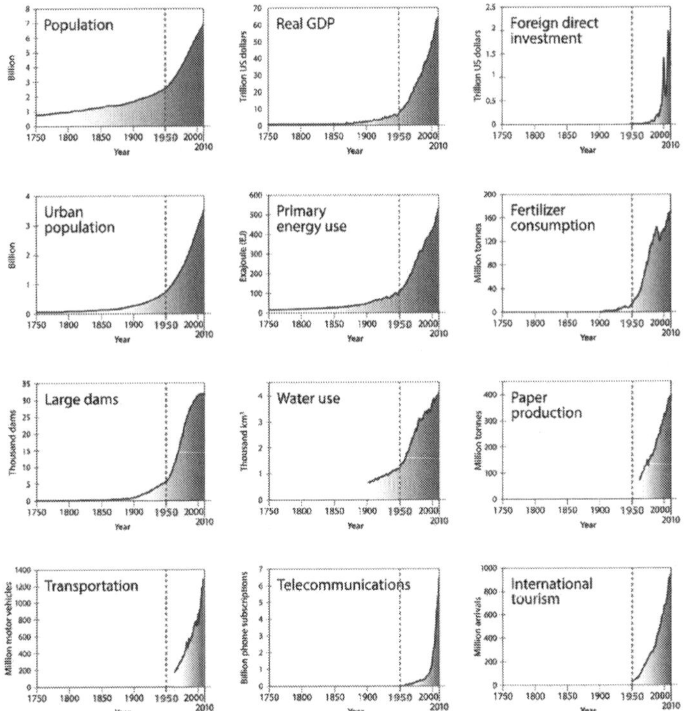

Source: International Geosphere-Biosphere Programme and Stockholm Resilience Centre, reproduced with permission.

- Around the world, the number of primary school-age children who do not attend school has almost halved (it is now 57 million, compared to 100 million in 2000).[8] By 2013, the adult literacy rate was 85%.[9]
- There has been a fall in interpersonal violence around the world. Between 2000 and 2012 global homicide rates fell by an estimated 16%.[10]
- From a low base, women's empowerment in politics and in the workplace has increased. Global female literacy rates at least are well on their way towards gender parity – by 2016, young women were only 4% less likely to be literate than young men.[11]

- We have seen a spread of various tenets of democracy: representation, more people able to vote, political decentralisation and more participatory processes.[12]

By any measure, that is a remarkable list of human achievements. The world, in the aggregate at least, has come a long way in a short period of time.

It was not so long ago that people in places like Britain and the US had their work clothes and their 'Sunday best' as their two choices of outfit. Today, across the Western world we can have an array of functional and beautiful clothes to choose from. 'Magic lantern' slide shows portraying life in distant lands used to be a form of entertainment. Those early 19th-century audiences would have been astonished to know that future generations of ordinary people would be able to visit those exotic locations for themselves. They would go there on holiday, because it no longer took months at sea to reach India or China, or even Australia. Many people in GDP-rich countries are able to fly there in a day. When Samuel Pepys died in 1703, he left behind one of the finest private book collections of his time. It was bequeathed to Magdalene College in Cambridge and amounts to some 3,000 volumes. Today you could fit the whole library onto a single e-reader and carry it in your pocket. With an internet connection, you have access to millions more books within seconds.

The examples are endless, and most people would be able to name a favourite aspect of modern living. We live in an extraordinary age. Much has been achieved and it is appropriate to acknowledge these successes. While too many are still out in the cold, it is an incontrovertible fact that never before have so many of us lived so well, for so long.

Good growth and bad growth

> *It's strange that we have this lust for endless economic growth without wondering whether it could ultimately be disruptive of society and the living world.* —*Kate Raworth*[13]

Economic growth is the increase in economic activity in a given region.* Material progress is very difficult without growth of this kind, but growth per se does not automatically help people to move out of poverty. As Britain's Department for International Development has cautioned: 'the extent to which growth reduces poverty depends on the degree to which the poor participate in the growth process and share in its proceeds'.[14] Growth translates into real progress when resources are shared, including via investment in collective institutions and socially constructive purposes, education and useful infrastructure – such as the National Health Service in the United Kingdom, or the 'Bolsa Familia' cash transfer programme in Brazil.

Growth that is not inclusive is easily wasted or becomes counterproductive, even in countries that need more growth. For example, after Hosni Mubarak's free market reforms, Egypt regularly posted growth figures of 6% or 7% a year, attracting international admiration and investment. Unfortunately, 90% of the population never benefited from this growth, with the number of people living on less than $2 a dollar a day rising from 20% to 44% in the years prior to the revolution in 2011.[15] Egypt is a dramatic example, but not a unique one. A recent study noted that sub-Saharan Africa has a number of countries that 'have experienced very rapid rates of growth, but have been unable to efficiently translate this growth into poverty reduction'.[16]

The United Nations Development Programme identifies different forms of negative growth, including 'jobless growth' that does not create employment, 'ruthless growth' in which the rich get richer and the poor get poorer, and 'futureless growth' that comes at the expense of the environment.[17] In many respects

* GDP is the most-used measure of economic activity – it tallies up the amount of money changing hands via consumer spending, investment and government spending, and is bounded by domestic activities, so that exports are included, but imports are deducted. The inadequacy of GDP in a technical sense to measure economic activity (missing, for example, non-market activity and many aspects of the information technology revolution, many of which improve people's quality of life) – let alone national success – is increasingly recognised.

it seems that many parts of the GDP-rich world are seeing all three at once.*

Instead, rising quality of life depends on deliberate steps to ensure that the economy works for everyone – as seen in the spread of education or the raising of the minimum wage and formalising of the labour market in Brazil. Vietnam's combination of market reform and land reform throughout the 1990s ensured that the rural poor were included in new growth opportunities.[18] Improvements in health in developing countries are often due to public health interventions such as water, sanitation or immunisation. They represent the concerted use of growth to invest in collective provision and improve the lot of many people, rather than simply chasing growth for its own sake.

In other words, many of the apparent fruits of growth reflect deliberate investment in public institutions and purposeful structuring of the economy in a way that provides for more people than just the wealthy. They were not a result of growth on its own. Indeed, taking the income component out of the Human Development Index reveals that there is no statistically significant correlation between per capita GDP and attainment in health and education.[19] At the risk of stretching the metaphor, it is not a matter of waiting for trickle down, but of strategically building reservoirs, channels and aqueducts.

'Growth' is an abstract term, like 'activity' or 'motion'. Nobody would say that all activity or motion was welcome. They would want to know what activity we were talking about. Motion in which direction? So it is with growth, making it a meaningless statement to be 'pro-growth' or 'anti-growth'. Vital questions need to be asked: what is growing? Who is benefiting? What are the costs and who bears them? And where is this growth taking us?

Robert and Edward Skidelsky (economist and philosopher, respectively) have similarly written that 'we may reasonably

* The other two forms of negative growth that the UNDP warns of are 'voiceless' growth (growth without improvement in democracy or social inclusion) and 'rootless' growth (growth that comes at the expense of cultural identity or the loss of minority identity).

ask not just growth *for* what, but growth *of* what. We want leisure to grow and pollution to decline'.[20] They suggest that rather than seeing GDP growth as a goal in itself, it should be 'treated as a by-product of policies aimed at realising the good life. Only experience will show whether the GDP outcome is positive, negative or stationary'.[21] Kate Raworth suggests that 21st-century economists should be 'agnostic about growth', and focus on how to 'create economies that make us thrive, whether or not they grow'.[22] We agree: some of the changes outlined below and the policy shifts that we recommend may in fact increase GDP; others will not. The point is that they are pursued for their positive impact on people and planet, rather than for their boost to the GDP ledger.

THREE

Are the fruits of growth beginning to rot?

I believe that, in any society, as conviviality is reduced below a certain level, no amount of industrial productivity can effectively satisfy the needs it creates among society's members. —*Ivan Illich*[1]

In the GDP-rich world we may be living through an age of prosperity, but it doesn't necessarily feel like it. When comedian Louis CK commented in an interview that 'everything's amazing right now, and nobody's happy', it struck a chord and the clip was viewed millions of times online.[2] Life has its worries and preoccupations. Small victories are short lived – the iPad 4 came out just eight months after the iPad 3. 'Do more', say the American Express billboards. 'Keep up', says Virgin Media. Advertisers, from cleaning products to beauticians, tell us that the route to wellbeing and happiness is as simple as a clean house and a pedicure, and always just one more purchase away. Not only is this a false promise, it is an agenda that marginalises the many families and individuals who, even in GDP-rich countries, cannot afford to participate in consumerism.

If, in the rush for more, society failed to notice the abundance of the world humanity has created, that would be tragedy enough. But there is a bigger risk. By pursuing the goals of the 19th and 20th centuries into the 21st, despite their being ostensibly realised, the economic models of developed countries may begin to undo the hard work of previous generations. To abuse that abundance, and in so doing pass on a poorer future to future generations – not to mention the ongoing injustice of so poorly sharing the benefits around the world today – constitutes a huge betrayal of the opportunities and possibilities of today's world.

Some commentators spotted this risk decades ago. 'To furnish a barren room is one thing,' wrote John Kenneth Galbraith in 1958; 'To continue to crowd in furniture until the foundation buckles is quite another'. Like Keynes, Galbraith saw an end to the 'economic problem', and that in its place a new challenge was emerging:

> To have failed to solve the problem of producing goods would have been to continue man [sic] in his oldest and most grievous misfortune. But to fail to see that we have solved it and fail to proceed hence to the next task would be fully as tragic.[3]

To borrow Galbraith's furniture metaphor, what if the house is full? It has a full complement of appliances and Scandinavian storage solutions. Pack in any more, and there'll be no room left for its occupants. Counter to the usual narrative of 'onwards and upwards', there *is* such a thing as too much progress – at least when it is defined in material terms and when no heed is paid to its distribution.

Growth can be a trap. In nature, endless growth is pathological or cancerous. Yet the logic of progress as growth dictates that the next step is inevitably better, and always desirable – until we take a step too far and are overtaken by the unforeseen consequences. Conventional wisdom tells us that the farmer who gets two chickens per square metre is running a more efficient farm than their neighbour with just one per square metre. But what about six hens per square metre, eight, or ten? When European law allows 19 chickens per square metre, less than a sheet of A4 per bird, is that still progress? Or is there now such a high price in animal suffering, low-quality meat and higher risk of disease that such developments can no longer be called progress?

Amartya Sen and Jean Dreze point to 'unaimed opulence' – countries that prioritise growth rather than security for their populations.[4] Friends of the Earth warn that in the future we will see a higher incidence of the 'diseases of affluence': heart disease, obesity, cancer and mental health disorders.[5] Across the world, the wellbeing of many people has fallen since the early 2000s due to environmental degradation and increasing droughts, barriers to use of public services, HIV, and economic crises and fluctuations in commodity prices.[6] In some communities, even in GDP-rich countries, life expectancy is stalling, or even falling.[7]

Unfortunately, mainstream economic debates rarely question the goal of 'growth' (usually conflated with GDP, but often booming markets for certain goods). Consequently, expansion goes unchallenged: the business media celebrate a rising housing market, despite the growing numbers of people, particularly younger generations, who are priced out. Record new car sales are reported as good news, regardless of the implications for traffic, pollution and personal debt. Supermarket firms open new branches and celebrate their increased market share, but in GDP metrics no heed is paid to dying town centres or bankrupt farmers. The media rarely voice such concerns, and whatever the private views of some politicians, these views remain private for fear of the accusation of economic heresy. The underlying assumption is that growth is always good, with little regard to its quality or distribution. One of former British prime minister David Cameron's favourite phrases was 'the global race' – but a race to where? A race implies a finishing line. Without an end, such a race sounds more like The Runners in Paul Auster's dystopian novel *In the Country of Last Things* – a suicide cult whose members train themselves to the peak of their fitness, and then run until they die of exhaustion. It is unlikely that David Cameron would welcome the comparison.

The problem is that at both micro and macro levels GDP-rich countries are pursuing something that is only a means to an end, but as if it is an end in itself. Worse than that, it is all-too-often an unsuccessful and harmful means to the ends that we really want. For individuals, once basic needs are met, more consumption is a poor means to greater wellbeing – it is, according to Chilean economist Manfred Max-Neef, a 'pseudo-satisfier' that does not truly meet people's needs. For example, a football fan might go out and buy a new television because their team has made the final. But what they are really looking for is someone to share their sense of excitement. The purchase is a substitute for the real need, which is for a sense of social affiliation and inclusion. A more direct route to that need would be to get some friends and neighbours together to watch the game, regardless of how high-definition the screen might be. Other examples are all around us: from the purchase of status goods in an effort to attain social acceptance, to the pursuit of 'likes' on social media in the pursuit of affirmation and affection. Pseudo-satisfiers can generate a false sense of satisfaction of a given need. At their worst, they 'may on occasion annul, in the not too long term, the possibility of satisfying the need they were originally aimed at fulfilling'.[8]

These pseudo-satisfiers are evident at the macro level too, where growth seems to have become the central objective in and of itself. Others, more thoughtfully and often well-intentioned, call for growth as a way of delivering other objectives – claiming that it will bring jobs, deliver high standards of living, pay for better health systems and lead to better lives. But just as consumption becomes a 'pseudo-satisfier' of fundamental human needs after basic needs have been met for individuals, so too at the macro level does GDP growth become a rather unreliable means to the ends really sought. As the following sections suggest, it risks compromising the scope to meet the needs that people are, deep down, most interested in. Society, politics and the economy need to find other ways of satisfying those needs – and this is where the process of making ourselves at home comes in.

Unsafe growth

> *Economic growth hides the poverty it creates through the destruction of nature, which in turn leads to communities lacking the capacity to provide for themselves.* —*Vandana Shiva*[9]

In 1972 the Club of Rome published its 'World Model' ('World3'), which mapped trends in resource use, pollution, population, food and the industrial system.[10] World3 warned of 'overshoot and collapse' by the mid to later part of the 21st century.* Economic growth was identified by the Club of Rome authors as a key leverage point to bring about change.[11] But the world did not take its foot off the pedal of economic growth, and real-world trends have followed the World3 projections surprisingly closely. Graham Turner, of the Melbourne Sustainable Society Institute in Australia, found that World3's 'business as usual' (standard run) scenario has, thus far, been close to reality.[12] In 2016 Professor Tim Jackson's analysis for the UK's All-Party Parliamentary Group on Limits to Growth similarly revealed that what the Club of Rome predicted in 1972 was holding up.[13]

Blindness to the downsides of growth has already had consequences at a planetary scale. For example, unlocking hydrocarbon energy was an incalculable boost to human civilisation. But any apparent 'progress' in tapping new sources, from tar sands, to underground rocks, to Arctic oil, has led to a destabilised climate.[14] Nobody set out to do that. The fossil fuel industry just advanced, step by inevitable step, applauded all the way by rising stock prices. As historian Ronald Wright says, 'progress has an internal logic to it that can lead beyond reason to catastrophe'.[15] Naomi Klein is more explicit in describing 'extractivist economies' (those based on removing raw materials) as operating from a 'nonreciprocal, dominance-based relationship with the earth, one purely of taking ... It is the reduction of life into objects for the use of others'.[16]

Growth as a means for poverty reduction ignores the failure of wealth accumulated at the top to 'trickle down' to the rest of society (as we will discuss shortly), but it also ignores planetary boundaries. While depreciation of the ecosystem is not measured in most national accounts, much economic growth is underpinned by the natural world, relying either on the input of natural resources or on natural systems to process waste. Economies draw on the earth's resources of timber, fish, topsoil, metals, fresh water, sand and gravel, and a thousand other

* It is often repeated that the *Limits to Growth* report predicted collapse by the year 2000 and is therefore discredited. This is an easy way to tell whether or not an author has bothered to glance at the original report – the graphs all run to 2100.

materials. But these environmental stocks are being exhausted. Both the non-renewable resources and the capacity of the earth to absorb economic effluent are wearing out. For over 40 years the demand on nature from human activity has been greater than the replenishing capacity of the planet. This has taken the global economy into overshoot as trees are cut down faster than they mature, more fish are caught than the ocean can replenish and so on.[17]

Extractive growth is the primary driver of a host of environmental problems, from climate change and ocean acidification, to soil erosion, to the growing number of marine dead zones and collapsing fish stocks. According to the Intergovernmental Panel on Climate Change, emissions of greenhouse gases (GHG) due to human activity have multiplied since the Industrial Revolution, and in particular since the mid-1990s. The increase in CO2 levels in the atmosphere has gone from 280 parts per million (ppm) before the Industrial Revolution to over 400ppm today.[18] The number of weather-related disasters has tripled in the last 30 years, with climate change shown to be a key factor.[19] Humanity currently uses the biocapacity of 1.6 earths every year, an ecological 'overshoot' that can be sustained only for so long.[20] The UN Food and Agriculture Organization reports that almost 60% of fish stocks are 'fully fished',[21] and land-based wildlife is faring little better. The crisis in biodiversity is serious enough that some scientists describe it as the 'sixth mass extinction' in Earth's history.[22] Looking specifically at the UK, we see that wildlife numbers are declining,[23] the sustainability of fish stocks is under threat* and the UK exceeds its 'share' of carbon emissions by 410%.**

It is not just flora and fauna that are impacted: DARA International estimates that 5 million lives are lost each year as a result of climate change and a carbon-based economy.[24] Worse estimates come from the International Energy Agency, which

* Sixty-four per cent of UK fish were harvested unsustainably in 2012 (Defra, 2014: 180; and Joint Nature Conservation Committee, nd).

** The 2015 Oxfam report (Sayers and Trebeck, 2015) assessed the UK's consumption of CO2 (MtCO2) against a (per capita) boundary drawn from a Stockholm Resilience Centre (SRC)-based UK boundary, revealing that in 2011 the UK exceeded the boundary by 410%.

suggests that every year approximately 6.5 million deaths are caused by air pollution.[25] Projections suggest that drought could increase by more than 20% in most of the world by 2080, with the number of people exposed to droughts increasing by 9–17% by 2030.[26] Simultaneously, the number of people exposed to river floods could increase by 4–15% by 2030.

Of the many and intertwined environmental problems, climate change stands out. July 2016 was the warmest month globally since modern record keeping began in 1880 (albeit with around 20% of the heat attributed to a strong El Niño climatic event), until it was equalled by July 2017.[27] Climate scientist Gavin Schmidt warns that it is 'very unlikely' that the world will be able to remain within the 1.5 degrees temperature limit named in the 2015 Paris Agreement.[28] For some, climate change is thought to be serious enough to put the whole future of humanity at risk: in an interview in 2016 President Obama identified it as an 'existential threat'.[29] And yet, when it comes to addressing this danger, growth remains the non-negotiable priority. In the G20 statement from the Hangzhou summit, 'growth' was mentioned over 60 times and 'climate' just four times.[30] If an existential threat gets only passing mention when world leaders meet, it is hardly surprising that other environmental issues aren't on the agenda at all.

Of course, responsibility for this environmental abuse is not equally shared. High-income countries, with 16% of the world's population, account for over 75% of global consumption and 41% of global CO2 emissions.[31] The top 10% of emitters account for about 45% of all emissions (and they live on all continents, with one third living in emerging economies).[32]

In a consumer economy, strategies that drive spending sometimes result in social and environmental harm. For example, planned obsolescence compels customers to replace their goods quickly, because they no longer work or are not able to perform the services they were once meant to. This can simply be a matter of perception, if advertising or changing fashions have rendered something 'old' or 'inferior'. The design of a product (along with the way labour is priced, skills are taught and passed on and so on) can make it more expensive to fix a product than to replace it. But this cost assessment is partial – many new items are apparently cheap to the consumer, but only on the proviso that they do not take into account the true costs of their fabrication: they are made in other countries where labour is cheap, and in most instances the cost in environmental terms is disregarded.[33]

Planned obsolescence and disregard of environmental impacts highlight the importance of casting an eye to the way businesses operate when considering unsafe growth. Many businesses make hefty profits by extracting value from nature, but without paying for it, nor being responsible for any resulting damage (so-called 'environmental externalities'). The extent to which this happens is enormous: a report for the UN Environment Programme calculated that very few of the biggest agricultural industries* would turn a profit if they had to account for the environmental costs associated with their operations.[34] Unpriced environmental impacts (such as land use, water consumption, GHG, air pollution, waste) are estimated to be equivalent to $7.3 trillion – a figure that was equivalent to 13% of global economic output at the time. Fioramonti puts it graphically: 'large corporations ... have to thank GDP for having washed away all their negative externalities (whether in the form of environmental degradation or social distress) through the statistical "laundromat"'.[35] Other evidence** suggests an imbalance between the impact of big and small firms: one estimate is that approximately one third of all damage to the environment can be traced to the top 3,000 companies in the world.[36] Focusing just on carbon emissions, Richard Heede calculates that just 90 companies and government-run enterprises are responsible for two-thirds of human-induced global warming.[37]

Whichever measure of impact is used, it is clear that ecological damage is disproportionately caused by those who have experienced the most growth and benefited the most from it. Because the wealthy are insulated from the effects of environmental damage, it is easy for them to ignore it. 'The

* Such as soybean and other oilseed processing; animal slaughtering and rendering processes; poultry processing; wet corn milling; and beet sugar processing.

** This is contested, with some attributing more environmental impact to small and medium-sized enterprises (SMEs). Many SMEs of course supply larger firms, making it difficult to disentangle.

lifestyle of the rich prevents them from sensing what surrounds them,' writes French environmentalist Hervé Kempf. They are 'cut off from the environment, where the fissures in the biosphere are beginning to show'.[38] Instead, it is at the margins that the problems are most visible. And it will be those least responsible who bear the brunt of environmental degradation. It is to such inequalities that we now turn.

An unevenly shared harvest

> *If they find a tremendous accumulation of riches, an improved agriculture, a prosperous business community, manufactures which multiply without end all products of human industry ... they call the nation opulent that has all of these things, without stopping to inquire whether all those who work with their hands, all those who create this wealth, are not reduced to mere subsistence.*—*Jean Charles de Sismondi, 1819*[39]

Our world is terrible at sharing. The 2018 World Inequality Report* revealed that in recent decades income inequality, measured by the top 10%'s share, is getting worse in almost all parts of the world.[40] In 2016 the richest 1% owned as much wealth as the rest of the world[41] and the gap between the real incomes of people in the global North compared to those in the global South has expanded by approximately three times since 1960.[42] Over a more recent period, the last 25 years, the average annual income of the poorest 10% of people in the world has risen by less than $3 each year,[43] with 700 million people living on less than $1.90 a day.[44] If we take a broader definition of poverty and consider the Ethical Poverty Line[45] (which identifies the income threshold where life expectancy rapidly falls, currently $7.40 a day), then as many as 4.3 billion people live in poverty.[**, 46] The Overseas Development Institute has

* The World Inequality Report is built on data collection work carried out by more than 100 researchers located across every continent.

** Jason Hickel points out that this is three and a half times more than the numbers reported by the UN and World Bank, and that 'Poverty has been shown that *if* growth in developing countries between 1990 and 2010 had benefited the poorest 40% by just 2% more than the average, we would be looking at (extreme) poverty rates in the region of 5.6% in 2010 – in other words, hundreds of millions of people would be living free of poverty.[47]

This is a world where some use toilets that flush when you wave your hand in front of them, while almost a billion people have to defecate in the open air.[48] A world where an investor was prepared to pay over $450 million for a single painting,[*,49] while 1.1 billion people do not have access to electricity.[50] A world where Rolls Royce imagines driverless cars with silk 'thrones',[51] while a billion people have no access to an all-weather road.[52] Divide global food production by population and you get 2,870 kcal per person per day – more than enough to feed everyone, but one in nine of us is still undernourished,[53] not least due to the amount of waste throughout the food system.[54]

Even within the GDP-rich countries that may have Arrived overall, there are many people who patently do not have enough. In the UK, for example, the use of food banks has risen dramatically since the financial crisis in 2008 , with 7% of people not able to afford an adequate diet.[55] Evidence from the US shows the toll that this kind of exclusion takes on the mental health of young people: 'concentrated disadvantage' is associated with more mental health problems (even once factors such as family demographics, maternal depression and childhood mental health are taken into account).[56] Anne Case and her husband (Nobel laureate) Angus Deaton have shared findings of their research that points to reduced life expectancy among white American men – what they call 'deaths of despair', attributing them to 'cumulative disadvantage' in labour market fortunes.[57] Writing in 1819, Jean Charles de Sismondi[58] would have cautioned us against calling such a nation wealthy at all. How could it be, when destitution and poverty are still so prevalent?

getting worse, not better ... Around 500 million more people have been added to the ranks of the poor since 1981'.

* Ironically, the most expensive painting ever auctioned was a painting of Christ, who told his followers 'do not lay up treasures for yourselves on earth'.

Such nations certainly have not made good use of their wealth and are yet to make themselves at home with their prosperity.

Instead, it seems that in holding out for growth to solve collective problems, the world has to tolerate extraordinary levels of inequality, as well as environmental harm. A variety of social problems can be glossed over by the growth agenda: when progress is measured through GDP per capita, the tyranny of averages means that, as the designer of GDP himself warned, 'luxury at the top offsets poverty at the bottom'.[60]

More than that, it often seems as if growth is relied on as a substitute for greater equality – indeed, former governor of the Federal Reserve Henry Wallich admitted as much in 1972: 'Growth is a substitute for equality of income ... So long as there is growth there is hope, and that makes large income differentials tolerable'.[61] Professor of Economics Richard Holden observed that it's only when growth stalls that people turn their attention to distribution (which he deems to be a bad thing).[62] Growth is often used as a way to avoid an apparently too difficult or unwanted conversation about redistribution. Unfortunately, in pushing that conversation onto the back burner we ignore a host of important related issues, because inequality is a multifaceted problem. Behind the straightforward income categories lies a legacy of division along race lines and class, across genders and between generations. If it is simplistically assumed that growth will eventually filter down to disenfranchised minorities, then persistent injustices remain unresolved. Redistribution isn't about taking from the rich and giving to the envious poor. It is about bringing people in from the margins, supporting the disadvantaged and, in some cases, making up for past oppression.

The equity question cannot be postponed forever. Not only is growth as a means to reduce poverty environmentally unsustainable (indeed inequality has been shown to harm the environment[63]), it has proved itself to be ineffective.[64] With rising inequality have come static or falling living standards for many, and growing alienation and anger. Let us briefly look at some of the explanations offered for the extent of the world's unequally shared harvest and then turn to how such inequalities harm people and communities.

The drivers of inequality

There are a range of causes of such inequality – and others have written detailed explanations and offered compelling hypotheses as to why various dimensions of inequality persist and get worse.[65] There is not scope to do justice to that body of work here, but it is important to note the extent to which substantial benefits of growth accrue to the wealthy owners of capital – the so-called 'rentier class'.

Often, the owners of capital are not the same as those actually doing the work: they are (already relatively well-off) investors and director shareholders. Piketty highlighted the inequality-reinforcing impact of such returns to wealth, explaining that money makes more for people who already have it than others can earn through their labour effort.[66] Even within the population of those who own shares, we are looking at a narrow demographic of investors from overseas, unit trusts and wealthy individuals (in the UK, for example, pension funds directly constitute only about 3% of the UK share market[67]).

We saw previously how a lot of profit is derived by ignoring environmental inputs and damages (the process of creating externalities). In a similar vein, the work of Mariana Mazzucato and William Lazonick points to the extent to which public investment underpins much innovation, yet a few actors reap shares of financial rewards from the innovation process; rewards that do not reflect their contribution.[68] They conclude that a few manage to

> position themselves along the process of innovation to extract more value than they create, while others get out much less than that which they put in ... [A] major source of inequality is the ability of economic actors to appropriate returns from the innovation processes that are not warranted by their investments of capital and/or labour in it.[69]

The benefits of productivity are often captured by those at the top. In the US in the 30 years following 1980, productivity increases accrued to upper-income groups, whereas real median wages and salaries did not increase.[70] In the UK, the economy grew rapidly in the five years running up to the 2008 financial crisis, but while productivity gains and economic growth fed corporate surpluses and high salaries at the top, those on middle and low salaries saw little benefit from the boom years.[71]

At the same time, the number of middle income jobs in countries such as Britain has fallen, partly as manufacturing jobs have moved overseas and partly as work has been streamlined by computing. This concentrates employment at the top and at the bottom, 'hollowing out' the middle and driving inequality.[72] The McKinsey Global Institute has mapped the consequences of such trends and reports that 81% of the US population is in an income bracket that experienced flat or declining income,[73] between 2005 and 2014. The figure in Italy is 97%; in Britain 70%; and in France 63%.[74]

Again there are a range of explanations for this, but the structure and purpose of certain businesses constitutes a key concern and hence a barrier to making ourselves at home. Allen White from the US-based Tellus Institute puts it rather starkly: 'shareholder primacy is the single greatest obstacle to corporate evolution toward a more equitable, humane, and socially beneficial institution'.[75] Those firms that operate to pursue short-term shareholder value often pick the option that serves shareholders when there is a tension between the interests of, say, workers and shareholders, or between suppliers and shareholders or between the natural environment and shareholders.

There are plenty of arguments that a short-termist view of how to deliver shareholder value fails to recognise the relevance and impact on the firm of other factors, such as healthy staff whose fundamental needs are met, company reputation and ecosystem health. There are also arguments that this perspective is not one compelled by legal mandates,* but is instead a reflection of social norms[76] and the nature of the stock market and its changing dynamics, and, related to this, the increasing tendency for

* The Sustainable Companies Project at the University of Oslo, an initiative that draws on the work of 40 legal scholars looking at 26 jurisdictions around the world, found that no company law system demands that directors pursue maximum shareholder profits at all costs.

executive remuneration and other incentives to be tied to share price rises.[77] The idea that 'the overriding purpose of companies should be the pursuit of shareholder value gained ever-wider acceptance, both among government and regulators, investors and indeed companies themselves'.[78] Of course the UK and the US are particularly acute in this interpretation of managerial duties and the associated structures of the business: its internal governance architecture, if you like.[79] Cambridge economist Ha-Joon Chang suggests that an 'unholy alliance between the professional managers and the shareholders was all financed by squeezing the other stakeholders in the company (which is why it has spread much more slowly to other rich countries where the other stakeholders have greater relative strength)'.[80] Chang's comment in parentheses – added almost as a throwaway thought – speaks to the existence of alternatives to the (Anglo-Saxon) model of shareholder-orientated companies. As we explore later, there are a range of scenarios already in existence that elevate the interests of a diversity of stakeholders and change the purpose and architecture of business.

Nonetheless, it remains the case that economic models are configured in such a way that only a small proportion of GDP growth trickles down to the wages of the bottom half of the working population.[81] Looking at the UK, if we take out tax and if welfare transfers are factored out, Britain's inequality is higher than that of the US. In other words, markets and firms in the UK produce more unequal outcomes, which then require substantial state intervention to mitigate.[82] So in the UK the state makes more of an effort to equalise market outcomes than it does in the US – but the result is still an economy that is one of the most unequal in the developed world. We have just seen that part of this is due to the decisions about how value and financial flows are allocated within firms. But ultimately the levels of inequality prevalent in the UK and other parts of the world reflect political choices – a culmination of decisions taken over many years by successive governments. The results can be seen in the level of the minimum wage; the relatively low (compared to other Organisation for Economic Co-operation and Development countries) rate of top income tax rates; loopholes inserted into legislation that enable tax avoidance; the scope for unions to collectively bargain and fight for workers' pay and conditions; and the adequacy and accessibility of benefits.

Politics is also at play when the returns from *wealth* ('financial capital') are taxed more favourably than earned income. Inheritance tax and capital gains tax impinge on wealth only a little, and are themselves subject to avoidance and exemptions, raising only 1.2% of taxes in the UK.[83] There are warnings that the regressive nature of UK company taxes 'favour[s] rent seeking and financial activities; [and] acts as a bias against the substantially productive' activities.[84] In other words, the current political process, particularly around business decisions, holds back countries such as the UK and the US from making themselves at home – despite levels of wealth that would suggest that they have Arrived.

One of the big problems with inequality in places like the UK and the US is that it can become self-reinforcing, driving a wedge between rich and poor. This happens because inequalities of income and wealth translate into inequalities of power – and vice versa.[85] The richest can donate to political parties and hire lobbyists to promote their interests, leading to the under-representation of lower-income groups in government. Take one stark example: according to the Center for Responsive Politics, US business interests overwhelm labour interests in terms of their respective financial involvement in politics by 15 to 1.[86] Certain industries are more culpable than others: in 2013 US and European Union (EU) decision makers were lobbied by fossil fuel industries who spent an estimated $213 million doing so (roughly $4 million a week),[87] while the British finance sector is the biggest of all British lobbyists active in Europe.[88] Soft power is also used: the threat of moving business abroad, playing governments off against one another, or influencing within public institutions via the 'revolving door' of politics and business employment. As we have just noted, the economy becomes configured in the interests of the richest, with institutional arrangements that further shift flows of resources to those at the top. Donella Meadows describes this situation as one in which there

> are many reinforcing feedback loops in society that reward the winners of a competition with the resources to win even bigger next time—the 'success to the successful' trap. Rich people collect interest; poor people pay it. Rich people pay accountants and lean on politicians to reduce their taxes; poor people can't. Rich people give their kids inheritances and good educations ... the government itself ... [becomes] one that reinforces success to the successful![89]

Inequalities of income and influence also lead to inequalities of government priorities for spending. In a round of budget cuts in 2012, for example, many of the deepest were implemented in the most deprived areas of the UK, with some councils forced to cut six times more per head of population than the wealthiest boroughs.[90] These inequalities of power and political attention compound the problem and create a vicious circle.

When the wealthiest are able to bend the rules in their favour while the poorest are unable to change their circumstances, democracy and trust are eroded. As a former managing director of the International Monetary Fund (IMF) warned: inequitable distribution of wealth 'can wear down the social fabric ... and it can lead to instability, a breakdown in democracy, and even war'.[91] The hierarchical structures of unequal societies generate mistrust, crime, violence and other social ills.[92] Anger stems from a sense of unfairness – the Skidelskys warn that 'the coexistence of great wealth and great poverty, especially in societies in which there is enough or everyone, offends our sense of justice'.[93] Britain may have experienced something of this in the 2016 vote to leave the EU, and the same could be said of America's election of President Trump. There are multiple reasons for such decisions and it would be wrong to over-simplify, but many commentators saw these outcomes as a protest vote from regions and communities that had been left behind by the political establishment and the prevailing economic model.

Distribution is also profoundly skewed between men and women, and this is something that will not be addressed by a bigger economic pie. Recent research from the Institute of Development Studies found that 'there is no guarantee that growth on its own will address critical dimensions of gender equality'.[94] Gender norms are embedded in labour markets (with women often performing the lowest-paid, lowest-status, least secure work and so on[95]), and the growth imperative can foster competition that can perpetuate gender inequality. The current paradigm is one in which the market value is paramount. This compels women into the workforce, where they are more likely to be in low-paid, insecure work under bad conditions, while still undertaking the lion's share of unpaid work in what Neva Goodwin termed the 'core economy' (or care economy) – that realm of work which takes place outside the formal market.[96] A disproportionate number of women work in low-paid jobs and make up the majority of workers without formal labour rights.[97] In Asia and Africa, for example, three-quarters of the work that women undertake is in the informal sector, so they are unlikely to have access to benefits such as sick pay, maternity leave or pensions.[98] When they do enter the formal labour market, women are often paid less than men, on the assumption that they are dependent on a male earner. Such inequality enables the more powerful and rich – most often men – to make increased profits by suppressing wages and creating low-paid jobs that women often fill.

Inequality's impact on individuals

Whatever the nature of inequality, it affects health and wellbeing. Robert Manchin, the managing director of Gallup Organisation Europe, observes that at the individual level 'income differentials that opened up in the last eight years ... created a general backward trend in subjective wellbeing'.[99] Humans are social animals and feel anxiety when at risk of exclusion from their group.[100] With extreme inequality, people feel more anxiety about their status and worry about threats to their self-esteem.[101] The European Social Survey finds an association between income inequality and status anxiety: 'people are, on average, more concerned about their position in social hierarchy in unequal contexts ... both the poor and the rich feel more anxious about their status in unequal societies'.[102] Other research confirms that in countries with lower levels of inequality people of all levels of income report less status anxiety than those living in countries with higher inequality.[103] In short, status anxiety affects every level of income. It is not just a matter of the poor envying the rich: the rich worry about their relative position too.

Fear of inferiority and ostracisation affects individuals so much that it can influence health outcomes. Inequality shapes health outcomes by intensifying relative deprivation and psychological stress at both the community and personal levels. Together these dynamics mean that it is 'the width of, and place within, the social hierarchy which is more important than any particular mechanism in determining individual health'.[104] Epidemiologists Kate Pickett and Richard Wilkinson compared different GDP-rich countries and found that income seems to be an important predictor of health within societies, but is meaningless between them, suggesting that it is *relative* social status that matters for health.[105] Analysis from the US found that socioeconomic factors have the largest impact on health – 40% of all influences.[*, 106]

Whether it is via the tangible everyday struggle associated with life at the bottom of the socioeconomic pile or the stress of lack of status, respect, and the fear of shame and exclusion, inequality creates anxiety. Anxiety results in increased levels of the stress hormone cortisol. This in turn raises blood sugar, suppresses the immune system and in the long term damages health. As explained by another epidemiologist, Michael Marmot, the lower you are in the social hierarchy, the less control you are able to exercise over your life, which in turn undermines physical and mental health.[107] People who live with chronic stress also suffer cell loss in their hippocampus, which causes a loss of memory (especially memories of good things). They have fewer minerals in their bones and accumulate body fat more easily.[108]

Pervasive inequalities have wider impacts too: they make it difficult for people of all incomes to feel that they have 'enough'. Many feel that they face a scarcity of chances and choices in a world that seems to offer unprecedented opportunities to everyone else. Relative poverty matters because it impacts on

* The other influences on health are: clinical care and the quality of care (20%); health behaviours (30%; and of course many of these are spurred by socioeconomic circumstances); and physical environment (10%).

participation in society. Without money to participate in socially defined 'normal' activities, people cannot afford to be involved. There are many dimensions to this – there are the literal costs, and then there are those motivated by the fear of being noticeably poor, outlays to 'keep up appearances' and to avoid standing out for the wrong reasons. These are not new concerns: centuries ago Adam Smith talked about the importance of the 'ability to appear in public without shame'. Often expenditure is undertaken to maintain a sense of social position, often not out of envy of the rich but because of the necessity to maintain self-respect.[109] Thorstein Veblen, an early observer of consumerism, noted almost a hundred years ago that:

> No class of society, not even the most abjectly poor, forgoes all customary conspicuous consumption ... Very much squalor and discomfort will be endured before the last trinket or the last pretence of pecuniary decency is put away.[110]

Box 3.1: Debt: a mirage of growth?

> *[W]hat real redistribution failed to provide, fake redistribution in the form of greater access to consumer credit helped to supply instead.*
> *— Tamara Lothian and Robert Unger*[111]

By fixating on the quantity of growth and not its quality or distribution, flattering GDP figures have hidden a hollowing-out of the economy, leaving a fragile edifice of debt and derivatives. As discussed earlier, a lot of 'growth' has been on the back of the environment, but it has also been founded on growing personal indebtedness. Credit has been cheap and widely available, even for those on low incomes, and debt has expanded accordingly. US consumers, for example, collectively owe over a trillion dollars in student loans, another trillion in auto loans and yet another trillion in outstanding credit card debt.[112] The result has been described as 'privatised Keynesianism', as individuals and families have taken on more and more debt.[113] Greater access to consumer credit allowed consumption to rise, despite weak incomes – a kind of 'fake redistribution' based on the 'fake wealth' of cheap debt.[114] Spending power ran ahead of incomes, breaking the connection between what one earned and what one could afford. Stephen Green, chairman of HSBC, admitted that 'banks have chased short-term profits by introducing complex products of no real use to humanity'.[115] Greece offers a dramatic example of how this can unravel, revealing that what looked like growth and redistribution was in fact an unsustainable credit boom.[116]

Despite GDP growth, the share going to workers through their wages has fallen in the UK since the 1970s.[117] But those who could afford homes at least still *felt* they were getting richer, due to the rising housing market.[118] Consumption (which showed up as increases in GDP) was made possible by the use of housing stock as collateral.[119] This also drives inequality, because banks will lend more generously to people who already have assets. 'People born without any assets other than their ability to work for a salary are disadvantaged for loans,' say Di Muzio and Robbins. 'It is the opposite for the wealthy because they already have assets accumulated from previous generations of privilege that they can borrow against'.[120]

While some forms of credit are needed to enable investments and so on, it is a sign of harmful growth when credit becomes predatory and disconnected from societal needs. Indebtedness – and associated 'assetisation'[121] – has been driven by financialisation, a process that boosts GDP and, as some argue, reinforces the need for growth in order to pay interest.[122]

Growth that hurts

> *[We live in a] curious mixture of liberalism and despotism …We barely notice that we live schizophrenic economic lives, in which half our waking hours are spent being indulged and obeyed as sovereign consumers, while the other half is spent being ordered around as employees.* —*Will Davies*[123]

Despite GDP growth, social progress and improvement in people's quality of life are clearly not on an endless upward curve. Instead, there is another, less desirable form of decoupling underway: the decoupling of social progress from GDP growth as diminishing marginal returns to growth set in. We examine this in more depth in Chapters Five and Nine, but it is worth looking at one example here: life expectancy. Preston has shown that the relationship between mean national income and life expectancy is curvilinear. This means that there is a direct relationship between the income of a country and the average life expectancy of its people up to around $10,000 per capita (Purchasing Power Parity in 1990) per year. After that level there is little or no additional improvement in life expectancy with increased national income.[124] This can be seen by comparing life expectancy in Cuba with that in the US, UK, Singapore or Australia. All have similar life expectancies, despite Cuba being considerably poorer in GDP per capita terms. Japan has been able to achieve an improved life expectancy since 1990, but this was a period during which it saw little growth in its GDP per capita.[125] Several scholars have concluded that improvements in nutrition, social infrastructure, education or scientific progress seem to matter most for improved health of the population, but these are not necessarily related to economic growth.[126]

At the macro level, these trends are reflected in the flat-lining of collective measures of prosperity. For example, the Genuine Progress Indicator (GPI) draws on a range of factors, not just the output of marketable commodities, to measure human welfare.* This assessment shows that at 'the global level, the decrease [in Genuine Progress] begins to occur around 1978. This decrease has occurred while global GDP/capita has steadily increased ... [A]lthough GDP growth is increasing benefits, they are being outweighed by rising inequality of income and increases in costs'.[127] A more recent entrant to the pool of alternatives to GDP is the Social Progress Index (SPI), which aggregates over fifty social and environmental indicators across three dimensions: basic human needs, foundations of wellbeing,

* In its construction, the GPI effectively takes account of impacts that are otherwise disregarded (externalities). For example, it encompasses crime, GHG emissions, pollution and resource extraction. When families spend their money on filters and bottled water this is deemed a cost because it is a defensive expenditure. In contrast, wetlands, rivers, lakes are valued as a positive impact.

and opportunity.[128] The SPI reveals that several Scandinavian countries rank higher than the US, even though their GDP per capita is lower. It also shows that Costa Rica has a GDP per capita less than half that of South Korea, but that the two countries are similar in terms of social progress.[129] The *Economist* magazine concludes that the SPI results demonstrate that the gains 'in social progress appear to slow when a country enters middle-income status. It also becomes harder to improve at a high-income level as countries face rich-world problems such as obesity'.[130] Such 'rich world' problems feed demand for more expenditure, which can be termed 'failure demand' (or 'defensive expenditures'). We will return to this later.

At the micro level, we see that the benefits of money are only a one-for-one improvement for those on low incomes.[131] We can easily imagine that £10 is worth a great deal to a homeless person, but very little to someone who owns 10 houses. This suggests that once an individual, a household (and indeed a country) is out of poverty, more income is not particularly effective in raising wellbeing or quality of life. So, while people experiencing poverty *do* of course benefit from higher incomes and the consumption they enable, rich countries like the US and the UK experienced little change in average (subjective self-reported) wellbeing from the 1950s onwards.[132] It has been estimated that, globally, a plateau in wellbeing emerges after incomes of around £26,000.[133] A different study, by Kahneman and Deaton, found that it is income over $70,000 that does nothing to improve how much people enjoy their daily lives.[134] Whatever the exact figure, the point is that after a certain threshold there are diminishing returns to increases in income in terms of personal wellbeing.

It is often claimed that self-reported happiness does not correlate with economic growth – the phenomenon is known as the Easterlin Paradox, after being described by economist Richard Easterlin in the 1970s.[135] Eye-catching graphs notwithstanding, self-reported happiness surveys are problematic for a range of reasons (both methodological and regarding the appropriateness of 'happiness' as a life goal or development objective*). So we should not rely on them too much. Plenty of other indicators reinforce the argument that prosperity is not translating into fulfilling lives in the way we are told to expect. Instead there are signs of alienation, distress and despair.**

- The World Health Organization describes depression as 'the leading cause of disability worldwide, and … a major contributor to the overall global burden of disease'.[136] Rates of clinical depression have been rising in America, and in 2015 an estimated 16.2 million adults in the US had at least one major depressive episode in the past year.[137] The US Centers for Disease Control report that about four out of 10 Americans feel that they lack a satisfying life purpose and almost a quarter of Americans feel neutral or do not have a strong sense of what makes their lives meaningful.[138] Use of antidepressants among young people has risen in the UK by 54% from 2005 to 2012 (and by over 60% in Denmark, 18% in the Netherlands and almost 50% in Germany).[139] In the six years since 2012, the number of patients being admitted to English hospitals with potentially life-threatening eating disorders almost doubled[140] – an affliction often attributed to a sense of lacking control.
- The mental health of young people, especially young women, is a growing concern. Marjorie Wallace, chief executive officer (CEO) of the British mental health charity Sane, describes the situation as 'a slow-growing epidemic'.[141] Trends include: one third of 14-year-old girls report symptoms of psychological distress;[142] young women are deemed a high-risk group for common mental health disorders;[143] and eight out of 10 schools have seen an increase in pupils self-harming or having suicidal thoughts.[144]

* Not least because of the different and sometimes almost contradictory conceptions and definitions of happiness and their tendency to present fixed scale in comparison with an open-ended scale.

** Each on its own might be an artefact of reporting, but when seen as part of a suite of alarming trends, they paint a picture of something going seriously wrong in our society.

- Time pressures are encroaching more on people's relationships with family and friends. In the US, full-time workers with one paid job worked an average of 46 hours a week.[145] A survey across Europe asked people to agree or disagree with the statement that they 'seldom had time to do things they really enjoyed in daily life': only 45% of people were able to disagree or strongly disagree, suggesting that the majority suffer from 'time poverty' to some degree.[146] Data on work hours in 10 countries from 1963 to 1998 shows that greater economic inequality leads to longer work hours.[147]
- In the US 40% of people over the age of 45 say they are lonely, up from 20% in the 1980s.[148] One quarter of people in the UK worry about feeling lonely, and, perhaps surprisingly, this is more common among young people (36% of people aged 18–34, compared to 17% of those over 55).[149] British people are less likely to have strong friendships or know their neighbours than inhabitants of any other country in the EU.[150]

The individual impacts, such as those listed above, sit alongside the erosion of community (or the rise of negative communities, such as neofascists). Commentator David Brooks suggests that individualised societies create an atomisation. This can lead to crime and reduced wellbeing: family and friends are no longer supporting each other to the degree that they once did.[151] Juliet Schor observes how 'economic growth undermine[s] the need for community interdependence. When people can afford to purchase goods, they ask for favours less often ... Prosperity itself can corrode community, by undermining our need for one another'.[152] The decline of social capital – whether due to reduced interdependence as Schor suggests, or simply less time to invest in relationships – leads to a weakening of reciprocal relations.

So the important things in life – control over your life, and social relationships – correspond to health inequalities, and even to how and when we die.[153] We have to ask ourselves: what good is growth that damages the things we value most – community, relationships and our own health?

Workplace hazards

Moving from the community to the workplace, we again see how the division and commodification of labour risks subordinating society to the requirements of the market economy and its growth agenda. Under Taylorist and then Fordist modes of production, the increasing intensity of work left many with no time for recuperation during the working day. Coupled with the menial nature of a lot of work, many people have found themselves under-stimulated, exhausted and treated almost as machines.[154] Much of the early theory around labour in an industrial economy can be applied to those in the modern service industry too, with increasing demands for worker 'flexibility' and the growing use of freelance agents to reduce staffing costs – the so-called 'gig economy'. As long ago as 1944 Karl Polanyi warned of the human impact of treating labour as a commodity in this way:

> the alleged commodity 'labour power' cannot be shoved about, used indiscriminately, or even left unused, without affecting also the human individual who happens to be the bearer of this particular commodity ... human beings would perish from the effects of social exposure; they would die as victims of acute social dislocation through vice, perversion, crime and starvation.[155]

More recently, Marxist urban geographer David Harvey warned of the deleterious impact of people working in ways that do not respect their needs and which instead treat them as just another input to the profit-making process. He described how people go into the labour market with character, embedded in their networks of social relations and socialised, with skills, tastes, dreams, desires, hopes and fears. For their capitalist employers however, 'such individuals are a mere factor of production ... hired on contract'.[156] One needs only to look at the dark underbelly of the 'gig economy', in which workers with little power and few enforceable rights are treated as disposable – at the beck and call of an app. Tellingly, the UK's Mental Health

Foundation has suggested that the biggest challenge to the mental health of the UK population is the increasingly pressured work culture.[157] Not everyone has this experience of work of course, and it is more common for lower-skilled workers. Nevertheless, news stories demonstrating the problem are commonplace, from care workers on 24-hour call, to delivery drivers paid less than the minimum wage. Working conditions at Sports Direct provide a high-profile example. An investigation by the UK Parliament's Business, Innovation and Skills Committee reported, in language resembling that of Polanyi and Harvey, that the company's business model 'involves treating workers as commodities rather than as human beings with rights, responsibilities and aspirations'.[158]

In such a work culture, it is perhaps unsurprising that 60% of people in both the UK and the US report feeling unhappy at work.[159] A quarter of UK employees are thinking of leaving their job because of management failures;[160] 37% feel their jobs are meaningless;[161] and 19% of British people lack satisfying work.[162] The polling agency Gallup tracks worker engagement, a measure of whether or not employees feel involved in and committed to their work. If we were to take 10 employees from the average US firm, just three would feel engaged and enthusiastic in this way. Five would be disengaged and uncaring about their work, and at least one of the 10 would be 'actively disengaged' – negative, unproductive and maybe even undermining their colleagues.[163] From a global perspective, US engagement rates are in fact relatively healthy. After all, many in developing countries are trapped in informal or subsistence labour. But it is disappointing that even the world's so-called advanced economies are unable to deliver satisfying work to the majority of citizens – a clear testament to an apparent ongoing unwillingness to make themselves at home.

In his book *The Happiness Industry*, William Davies wonders 'if capitalism is being ground down by the chronic, unspecifiable alienation of those it depends on'.[164] Perhaps concepts such as 'engagement' and worker satisfaction are indeed unspecifiable and a little nebulous, but there are changes in the labour market that have negatively impacted on people's lives in more measurable ways. Among those changes are the decline in union membership since the 1980s in the UK[165] and beyond (partly the result of deliberate government policy to reduce trade union power), which removed a once-effective check on wage disparities and constituted a means to improve work conditions in many workplaces. A similar trend can be observed in the US, where the number of male workers in unions fell from one in three in the early 1970s to less than one in 10 by 2007.[166] In both countries it is estimated that the reform of labour market institutions accounts for one fifth of the increase in inequality during the 1980s,[167] while the abolition of wage councils and trade union reforms is likely to have resulted in the rising proportion of people on low pay.[168]

It is not only the commodification of low-paid work that gives cause for concern, but the insecure nature of work. The UK is one of the biggest users of zero-hours contracts in Europe,[169] and since 2010 the growth of the UK's jobs market has been largely driven by burgeoning self-employment. Four in 10 of the jobs created between 2010 and the beginning of 2013 were self-employed roles, and by 2014 the total number of self-employed reached 15% of the workforce, or 4.5 million people.[170] Since 2007, women have accounted for 60% of self-employed workers.[171] Galloway and Danson found evidence of 'hidden enterprise', in which self-employment is used as an alternative to unemployment (often to avoid benefit sanctions), but where rates of pay are below minimum or living wage levels and the 'firms' create low value and are likely to cause harm to health and wellbeing.[172] The Resolution Foundation estimates that the median salary of self-employed workers is only slightly higher than the minimum wage, and 'typical self-employed earnings in 2014–15 were lower than they were 20 years earlier'.[173] Observing such trends, Bernard Maris warns that for those who earn wages, it is not a case of 'the end of work, as the underlying reduction in the number of hours worked would appear to show, but work without end, job insecurity, isolation, stress, fear and the certainty that they will have to leave their workplace quite quickly'.[174] Unsurprising then, is evidence of a link between how long a worker is on a flexible employment contract and their chance of falling into ill health.*[175]

A pernicious paradox emerges from such employment relationships that treat workers as 'just in time inventory' – the same way that a factory orders exactly the parts it needs, or a cafe calculates the milk it needs for each day.[176] Strong family relationships and social networks are an important asset in vulnerable communities, allowing people to rally around and help each other out as fortunes fluctuate and circumstances change. Yet in its desire for cost savings the prevailing economic model favours cheap, flexible labour: available when business needs it; expendable when it does not. This approach works only when individuals have community support networks to lean on – think of the networks of friends, neighbours or grandparents who might step up to do the school pick-up so that a mother can accept a three-hour shift at a call centre, for example. Paradoxically, in its pursuit of growth, the economy relies on these networks of reciprocity and social solidarity (often provided, unpaid, by women) while simultaneously eroding them through time pressures, consumerism and inequality.

Box 3.2: Expanding the market-places

> *Each tree cut down and made into paper, each idea captured and made into intellectual property, each child who uses video games instead of creating worlds of the imagination, each human relationship turned into a paid service, depletes a bit of the natural, cultural, spiritual, and social commons and converts it into money.*
> *—Charles Eisenstein*[177]

One of the surest ways to drive economic growth is to create markets for goods and services that had previously been free. This is known as marketisation – bringing non-monetary economic activity into the market-place and trading them as goods and services. Thus, GDP gives an indication of how marketised a society is[178] – something which is not necessarily desirable.

* This holds for a variety of health conditions and for various types of contract: seasonal, temporary jobs or a fixed time.

Many scholars have noted this.[179] Karl Marx explained how the crisis of capital is delayed by developing new industries and new markets, and finding new realms of social, natural, cultural capital to convert into money. Karl Polanyi wrote about *The Great Transformation* in the 1940s, observing the commodification of land, labour and money. More recently, Jorgen Norgaard, from the University of Technology in Denmark, has reflected that 'much of the growth in GDP over the last years can be ascribed to pulling activities like child care, health care, cooking, entertainment, maintaining houses ... from the non-paid amateur economy into the professional economy'.[180] For example, a woman might choose to breastfeed a new-born baby – a natural act of human care that is widely considered to be best for a child's development, but that contributes nothing to GDP. If a mother chooses to bottle-feed the baby, she will need to buy bottles, sterilisers and formula milk. Feeding the baby becomes part of the formal economy. Nobel laureate Paul Samuelson famously offered another example in early editions of his economics textbook, observing that GDP falls when a man marries his maid.

Or consider cooking. As work pressure increases, time and energy for cooking at the end of the day declines. For those of us living in wealthy urban areas, the options to order food to be delivered have duly expanded (taking advantage of the gig economy, such as Deliveroo and Uber Food). With only a few clicks on an app, busy people can have food at their doorstep – an extension of the market into eating at home, where take-out was once a special treat. The UK's *Sunday Times* ran an article celebrating the kitchen design opportunities that this trend yields, asking 'Could meals on mopeds kill off the kitchen cupboard as we know it?'[181] But the serious side is that cooking is becoming marketised, moving from a household chore (mostly done by women) to a paid service (again mostly done by women, often receiving low wages). The result is economic growth, saving time for users of the delivery services, and perhaps higher-quality food (not least compared to the scant nutritional value of frozen pizza!). The follow-on is that people's cooking skills might decline, and in turn cooking skills may not be passed on in families, so the next generation has no choice other than to turn to the market for meals.

Of course, marketisation is not always a problem. Those who have enough money to do so feel no great need to sew their own clothes, churn their own butter or carry out the many other household tasks that are now delegated to the market. There are possible benefits from extensions to marketisation in some key areas, too. For example, it could be used to price in the costs of externalities, helping to tackle pollution or creating a market for carbon. Take the example of charging for plastic bags in shops. Research has found that a 'five pence charge has been effective in reducing plastic bag use across the [UK]. Not only that, it has also made people think more about the environment, and as a result they have become more supportive of other environmental policies'.[182]

But there is always a trade-off to marketisation, and sometimes the effects aren't clear in advance. Not everything that can be bought and sold should be bought and sold. The bestselling book *What Money Can't Buy: The Moral Limits of Markets* (by Harvard philosopher Michael Sandel) has a list of examples of marketisation that would boost GDP but are questionable in terms of social progress: from purchasing citizenship to buying a place in a queue to meet with US members of Congress.[183] Sandel argues that societies such as the US and UK's have shifted from utilising a market economy to being market societies. In such societies, people without money are vulnerable to coercion, and intrinsic goods or relationships are corrupted by their exchange for money.

Marketisation, and the way growth is measured, is also problematic from a gender perspective. With its orientation towards production and consumption, GDP growth not only damages the planet but also focuses on one type of production: that which takes place in the market. The production that happens, largely by women, in the 'care' or 'core economy' (that human network of families and neighbourhoods where most work activity actually happens) is disregarded. A woman serving food in a cafe is being paid, and thus plays a role in the market. When that same woman goes home and cooks for her family, that contribution is invisible, even though other members of the household may depend on those meals to get them to work. Activities in the home underpin those in the market-place: cooking, caring for children and housework are necessary for the marketised economy to function (not least via reproduction of the workforce). But they are not valued or accorded the same status – and too often it is because care work is seen as 'women's work'. Marilyn Waring's book *Counting for Nothing* critiqued mainstream economics and the UN System of National Accounts for 'excluding the great bulk of women's work – reproduction, raising children, domestic work and subsistence production'.[184] Ignoring this contribution makes women appear to be less productive and more dependent than they actually are, which in turn exacerbates problematic gender norms that produce gender inequalities in the first place.

Over-development

> *Our modern society is engaged in polishing and decorating the cage in which man [sic] is kept imprisoned.* —*Swami Nirmalananda*[185]

Expanding the capacity to meet human needs can reasonably be described as progress but not only is growth hurting, it is often disconnected from meeting fundamental human needs and protecting the planet. We have seen above how a lot of growth has been premised on extraction from the natural world (unsafe growth) and has been siphoned off by those who already have access to more than enough resources (an unevenly shared harvest). We have also seen that the mode in which this growth is generated has put great strain on people's wellbeing – it is, quite literally, growth that hurts. But there is another reason to question the pursuit of growth as manifested in GDP-rich countries: what if it simply facilitates (and indeed relies on) endless rounds of identity construction through fashion and novelty? This would be all the more futile if the motivation for this consumption was anxiety and competition – driven by structural inequalities and insecurity of livelihoods and identity – rather than true self-expression.

For relatively well-off consumers, plenty of the purchases they make are no longer about meeting basic material needs. Instead, products act as symbolic communicators: conveying social status, constructing an identity for the owner, and enabling differentiation from or association with others.[186] Belk's notion of the 'extended self' highlights the role of consumer goods or activities as tools with which to create identity.[187] Creation of identities and how we are seen by others matters to us social beings – even Adam Smith recognised this. He writes in the *Theory of Moral Sentiments* that 'Nature, when she formed man for society, endowed him with an original desire to please, and an original aversion to offend his brethren. She taught him to feel pleasure in their favourable, and pain in their unfavourable, regard'.[188]

As discussed already, experimental evidence shows that the greatest effect on people's levels of stress hormones is from 'social evaluative threats'.[189] We saw how these harm health directly, but they also drive consumption and unhealthy behaviours. People buy things for all sorts of reasons, and it's easy to get caught up in theories of consumerism that don't reflect how people make decisions. But we do know from neuroscience and psychology that people are vulnerable to damaging social comparisons, which can lead to rivalry, competition and the pursuit of positional goods.[190] Status anxiety is a natural human emotion, across cultures,[191] as reflected in several of Max-Neef's fundamental human needs such as affection, participation and identity (see Table 1 in Chapter Six). Status anxiety, exacerbated by inequality, is often exploited by advertisers and has been pointed to as a 'trigger for higher levels of consumption'.[192] How much of what people spend on clothes, cars and homes is actually needed and wanted? How much is motivated by status anxiety? And how much of that status anxiety is spawned by inequality and played upon by advertisers in their pursuit of ever more growth?

Part of the answer can be found by looking at the process of wealth at the top racing away, pushing ever higher notions of what is ostensibly 'necessary' – for example, off-street parking, a guest bedroom, a certain brand of fridge, the right colour of wall paint, the biggest television screen available. The same applies to phones, cars, shoes, holiday destinations and so on. Economist Robert Frank talks of a 'positional arms race' that results from people's concerns about relative consumption and positional goods.[193] Even in his day, John Stuart Mill saw conspicuous consumption and found it problematic: 'I know not why it should be matter of congratulation that persons who are already richer than anyone needs to be, should have doubled their means of consuming things which give little or no pleasure except as representative of wealth'.[194] Status anxiety puts people on a hedonic treadmill: not only does consumption for these purposes have associated costs (time, effort, environment),[195] but any benefit in terms of boost to positive emotions that is derived from the consumption seems to quickly wear off.

This amounts to a scenario where increased consumption is important for wellbeing only when meeting basic needs; after which point the benefits of consumption decrease and may become negative, due to psychological adaptation, and psycho-social impacts on health. Scholars have come up with an explanation for the consequent impact on society writ large: the 'social rank hypothesis'. This captures how health and wellbeing in a society deteriorate when people prioritise their social status over other aspects of their lives, such as their family, traditions or maintenance of supportive relationships.[196] The psychologist Tim Kasser's synthesis of his own and others' research reveals that a materialist focus (money, image, possessions, looks and fame) is associated with a range of harmful effects: susceptibility to narcissism, depression, lower life satisfaction, less investment in relationships and even physical symptoms such as headaches, backaches and sore muscles.[197]

We have seen how such consumerist pressures are particularly acute in more unequal GDP-rich societies: money is not valued for what it can buy, but for the status it confirms. The nature of the economic system and the extent to which it generates inequality, which in turn inflames status anxiety, thus goes a long way to explaining harmful consumerism. For example, Walasek and Brown used Google Trends to examine internet searches in 99 countries. They found that more people search for what they refer to as 'positional brand names' in countries that have more income inequality.[198] Other, often related factors that spur consumption include the design of cities and privatisation of public space – making non-consumptive activities difficult. Advertising too is often pointed to as a driver of unnecessary consumption – turning wants into perceived needs, creating a sense that what one has is insufficient or out of date and conflating happiness with consumption.[199] The reach of advertising is staggering: the British public see an average of 1,400 advertisements every month,[200] and in total British businesses spend £22.2 billion a year on advertising.[201]

A dramatic example of these processes and how they interact can be seen in the fashion industry, where the days of four fashion seasons a year have long since passed. Retailers such as Zara, H&M and Mango can now deliver a new collection every two weeks, ditching printed catalogues and traditional advertising in favour of social media buzz.[202] 'This is the way the world works,' says designer Jonathan Anderson in defence of this speed: 'It is about the chase against boredom'.[203] Others disagree, arguing that pressure to deliver ideas quickly has devalued the creative process, making it less likely that genuinely 'new' ideas emerge.[204] This is 'innovation' that doesn't necessarily represent progress or improvement, but simply change for the sake of driving consumption. It is emblematic of a pursuit of novelty that accelerates the hamster wheel of buying and discarding, a manufactured sense of scarcity that is hardly geared towards meeting fundamental needs.

What makes fast fashion all the more concerning is that it relies on underpaid garment workers in developing countries, working long hours in poor conditions for low pay.[205] Their misery is implicitly scorned when rich-world consumers do not even wear all the clothes and accessories we acquire. The average British adult has £4,000 worth of clothes, 30% of them unworn in a given year.[206] Consider the potential legacy of social and environmental waste behind a fast-fashion garment: made in sweatshop conditions for poverty wages, shipped across the world and paid for with consumer debt, only for that item to remain unworn at the back of a wardrobe. And it's not just clothes, of course. Altogether, Britons 'waste a staggering £80 billion a year' on goods that are never used or used rarely.[207]

Fitting all the possessions people own into their homes can be a challenge too, as J.K. Galbraith predicted. In the US a 2016 survey of over 1,300 adults showed that most report being burdened with material objects they no longer want or need – and one in seven say that they have a room in their house so full of junk that it is unusable.[208] The rise of consumerism in

America coincided with a boom in self-storage facilities. The self-storage industry has been one of the fastest-growing sectors of the United States commercial real estate industry since the late 1970s (total self-storage rentable space in the US is roughly 2.5 billion square feet, more than 210 million square metres).[209] These vast warehouses are a sort of consumerist netherworld, full of half-remembered things. They are 'laid out like mausoleums' as Hank Steuver points out: 'Your stuff is resting in peace'.[210]

As they fill their self-storage, people are transferring an increasing proportion of their time into market activity (see Box 3.2) – working more hours; purchasing goods and services at later stages of processing; committing less unpaid time to community work; and instead taking part in more commodified leisure as spectators, rather than as participants.[211] This can backfire in other ways, not only on the planet, but on communities. People who have lots of expensive possessions may come to fear losing them. They may spend more on security, or move somewhere safer, perhaps eventually into a gated community. Social trust declines, and this has an impact on the next generation. Children are too afraid to go out, or are not allowed to go out, and end up living sedentary, indoor lives. That has consequences for physical and mental health, which of course requires further spending to address. For example, take the rise in the number of indoor 'soft play' areas. These padded, primary-coloured play gyms were almost unknown a generation ago, and are now very popular. The industry is new and hasn't been studied much, but it is interesting that the rise of indoor play areas coincides with the decline of outdoor play among children.[212] Fun as it may be to fall about in the ball pool, this might be another example of 'failure demand' (something we discuss more in Chapter Five): parents don't let their children play in the woods any more, so now they need to build them indoor, commercialised playgrounds.

For others, perhaps even simultaneously, consumption is used to fill the family- and community-shaped gap in people's lives. Serge Latouche refers to 'consolation goods' – things we buy in order to console ourselves in the face of a stressful, anxious life.[213] One can imagine the bottle of wine to 'deal with' a hard day at work, the mindfulness classes for CEOs and overworked employees alike, or the 'pamper weekends' for women pressured to do 'it all'. As Latouche notes, 'one of the objectives of the system is to create needs and then to satisfy them by producing goods to mend what has been broken and to compensate and console us for what we have lost'.[214]

These dynamics suggest an 'over-development' in which people work and consume without developing in the true sense of meeting what Max-Neef identified as fundamental human needs, without enjoying a greater quality of life beyond material sufficiency, nor feeling more fulfilled. Consumption becomes a substitute for what individuals and communities really need.[215] But as people grasp for pseudo-satisfiers, they only make the meeting of needs more elusive. Figure 2 shows how increases in levels of consumption have enabled people to move up a curve of fulfilment. This is a shift from survival to comfort, at which point people have 'enough'. If income, and hence consumption, continues to rise, they then progress through to luxury and even extravagance, where more and more consumption fails to increase fulfilment. Instead, the additional costs of more and more consumption exceed any marginal satisfaction people might gain (for example, the constant work or debt to pay for additional consumption). In many ways this is an individual-level form of the 'uneconomic growth' that we mentioned above.

At the macro level, societies are developing in the conventional sense – more economic growth, more consumption, more income – but not in terms of what really contributes to a good life. Instead, more and more growth, consumption and income can end up harming those things that make life most worthwhile. This sort of growth has become unsafe, unevenly shared and detrimental.

To return to J.K. Galbraith: 'we are guided, in part, by ideas that are relevant to another world', he wrote of a collective failure to adjust to affluence. He continued: 'as a result we do many things that are unnecessary, some that are unwise, and a few that are insane. We enhance substantially the risk of depression and thereby the threat to our own affluence itself'.[216]

Figure 2: Fulfilment curve 1. The fulfilment curve shows flattening fulfilment as spending delivers survival, comforts and then luxuries.

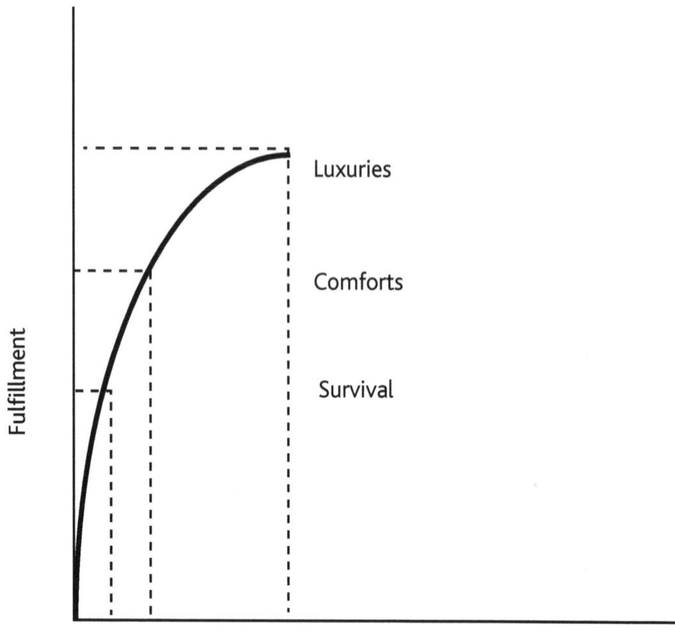

Source: Financial Integrity, reproduced with permission

Box 3.3: Considering population

There are various ways to expand an economy, and one of the simplest is to grow the population – the more people, the more economic activity. As Helen Kopnina writes, 'a growing population serves capitalist, industrial, and expansionist interests as population creates a "demographic dividend" which is good for the growth economy'.[217] Conversely, Morgan Stanley's chief global strategist describes a slowing population growth rate as 'toxic for economic growth'.[218] For some countries, this has become a critical dependency.[219]

Certain countries have turned to migration; others have encouraged citizens to have more children (such as Australia, Russia and Singapore). Either way, population growth is deemed an integral part of the growth complex.

Every ecosystem has a carrying capacity. The earth is no different, but where the limit lies depends on consumerist lifestyles. In his book *How Many People Can the Earth Support?* biologist and mathematician Joel E. Cohen refuses to answer his own question: 'Support with what kind of life? With what technology? For how long? Leaving what kind of Earth for the future?'[220] In other words, the issue of 'how many?' is inseparable from 'how much?'

In many ways the latter is the more pressing question. Population growth is highest in low-income countries, where ecological footprints are far lower. At current consumption rates, an Eritrean mother would need to have six children to match the ecological impact of one new American.[221] Where children are born and the lifestyle they are born into is as much of an issue as the actual number of children being born. In assessing the impact on the planet, the lifestyle and consumption patterns that each new child inherits are by far the biggest factor.

However, 'at current consumption rates' is a key phrase – Eritreans may have a low ecological footprint at present, but it will rise. The more Eritreans that are born, the more resources they will need later, particularly if they are to move out of poverty, which is surely their right. But if the world were to hit a global resource or climate crisis before Eritrea reached that middle-income band, its citizens might find themselves shut out of a higher standard of living. They would be locked out by the levels of consumption of the richest consumers elsewhere – one of the reasons why addressing this *over-development* and the cost of failure demand and uneconomic growth is one of the key messages of this book.

Globally, population growth serves GDP-rich countries in the short term, but is potentially devastating for everyone in the long term. Fortunately, all the research shows that the most effective ways to achieve an earlier peaking of global population[222] are education for girls, rights for women and universal access to contraception – things that many people would agree are good things in their own right and key aspects of making ourselves at home. There is also scope to dramatically cut the amount of waste in the system – in the sense of food and raw materials wasted to the avoidable burdens on the state driven by failure demand. Reducing the amount of resources that are lost and hence not available to those who need them would also alleviate pressure on the planet and ensure that more people have enough.

FOUR

Stockholm Syndrome? How the economy fell in love with its captor

> *[I]n the negotiation of trade-offs between economic, environmental and social policy objectives, it is economic objectives that still trump others … there is a bias in policy making towards prioritizing GDP growth and efficient markets. —Alistair Whitby*[1]

From the vantage point of the 21st century, one can look back with raised eyebrows at the beliefs that people held in the past – a flat world, or the sun going around the earth. One day the conviction that endless growth is possible, let alone desirable, may belong in the same category.

For the time being, all kinds of interrelated forces and dynamics entrench the position of growth-based economic models, and spur political decision makers to seek more GDP. Countries such as the UK and the US have constructed economic systems that are structured in a way that crisis ensues when growth stalls. There is panic and the fear of 'recession'. Latouche also observes such a reaction to a lack of growth:

> As soon as growth slows down or comes to a halt, there is a crisis, or even panic …The need to accumulate means that growth is an 'iron corset'. Jobs, retirement pensions and increased public spending … all presuppose a constant rise in Gross Domestic Product.[2]

This panic is real and well placed: current economic models are totally dependent on growth in order to function (despite the downsides of 'functioning' as we have outlined in Chapter Three). In such a configuration, many institutions will become unstable without growth. This reality prevents people from looking beyond the current model – it closes down the political imagination and confines apparent progress to surviving in the current system. To paraphrase Henry Ford, you can have any kind of economy you like as long as it grows.

It is important to remember that GDP is simply a measure of the market value of flows of things and services that are made and purchased in each year. It does not count capital stocks, let alone environmental stocks, nor most real sources of prosperity (be they natural, social or economic). Yet in the decades following the Second World War such growth came to be seen as the solution to poverty and to class struggle, and the very essence of development. As the Organisation for Economic Co-operation and Development (OECD) observes: 'for a good proportion of the 20th century there was an implicit assumption that economic growth was synonymous with progress: an assumption that a growing GDP meant life must be getting better'.[3] Certainly, nowadays GDP is used as a proxy for not only economic health but national success, in a way that far exceeds the function that its creator envisaged. GDP is used in a 'maximalist' way, with a 'bias in policy making towards prioritizing GDP growth above other objectives'.[4] Labour prime minister Gordon Brown declared in 2010 that 'going for growth' was the government's 'number one priority'.[5] A few months later his Conservative successor, David Cameron, promised that a 'relentless focus on growth is what you will get from this government'.[6]

The prevailing – desperate and sometimes rather pathetic – clinging to economic growth is evident in efforts to humanise it. Adjectives are attached to growth: 'sustainable growth'; 'inclusive growth'; 'green growth'; 'shared growth'; 'low carbon growth'; and so on. To an extent, the addition of these adjectives is indicative of some recognition that growth in its prevailing mode has not helped everyone's flourishing and that growth needs to become more environmentally friendly. Equally, however, the stubborn refusal to consider any economic model other than one with growth at its core shows just how entrenched the mental association of growth with progress is. Professor Tim Jackson's seminal *Prosperity Without Growth* points to the three pillars on which the current economic model rests. They explain the interlocking dependence between the current economic model and growth. First, flourishing is deemed to be contingent on material wealth. Second, GDP growth is assumed to deliver key social goods such as health or education. And third, without growth the economy will collapse, taking social stability with it.[7] These are beliefs – despite growing evidence that suggests their validity is wearing thin – on which institutions and structures such as pensions, the banking system and the labour market are founded. Any vision for change is up against this formidable structural dependence. As David Harvey notes, 'a corner stone of capitalism's ideology [is] that growth is both inevitable and good. *Crisis* is then defined as a lack of growth'.[8]

Efforts to forge a new system also confront a 'hegemony of the common sense'.[9] This creates a context in which questioning the merits of endless economic growth is to risk appearing naive, romantic or delusional. Eric Assadourian calls growth 'one of the fundamental sacred myths of modern culture', and few commentators want to risk the taboo of growth scepticism.[10] Tim Jackson was told that the prime minister and his office had 'gone ballistic' over the title of his report *Prosperity Without Growth?*[11]

Structural dependence and a 'hegemony of common sense', as Gramsci might recognise, are mutually reinforcing because, under its current configuration, a lack of growth is indeed deleterious. Harvard economist Sendhil Mullainathan and his co-author Eldar Shafir have shown that when something is seen as scarce, this limits people's mental capacity, imposing what they call a 'bandwidth tax'. This causes people to focus on what is scarce at the expense of paying attention to other concerns.[12] Extrapolating Mullainathan and Shafir's work to the societal and political level suggests that times of low GDP growth may reinforce obsession with growth, to the exclusion of other concerns and needs.

However, just because the current economic model relies on economic growth, that does not make economic growth worthy of being an end in itself, nor a pre-eminent political goal. A coffee addict might rely on coffee to be functional (or even just polite!) before 10am, but that does not mean that more and more caffeine is unilaterally a good thing. A drug addict might fear terrible withdrawal symptoms in a process of going 'clean', but that does not mean that they should carry on using indefinitely. The seemingly paradoxical dependence on growth – something that we have shown is causing harm to society and to the planet – resembles the concept of the 'Stockholm Syndrome'. Stockholm Syndrome describes the identification with and affection for their captor that a hostage can come to feel. Sometimes the hostage is unaware of the effect, but it can also be a conscious mechanism to cope and to distil some hope in a situation that is, ostensibly, hopeless.[13]

How did today's economies become hostage to growth? How did so many leaders become blind to its dangerous hold on the economy and on society? Why did the world of politics and economics become so enamoured with growth as a solution to all problems, and how did growth become the main signifier of success?

Some scholars point back to the Industrial Revolution as the beginning of a growth-focused economy, with its associated use of fossil fuels. As a measurement, however, it was not until the post-war period that GDP (or Gross National Product as it was initially) emerged and began to influence political and economic decision making.* Nation-states were asserting themselves geopolitically, and also taking a more active role in providing for their citizens' welfare, and this drove the need for national accounting. This was accentuated by Cold War rivalry: GDP could be touted as a measure of national achievement and thus useful evidence of the merits of one economic system vis-à-vis another.[14]

What eventually became GDP arrived on the scene a few years earlier: in 1932 the US Congress tasked economist Simon Kuznets with constructing a mechanism for measuring the nation's output. National accounting was born – essentially

* See Diane Coyle (2013) *GDP: A Brief but Affectionate History* for an explanation of the longer history of national accounts and a fulsome account of the ascendance of GDP as an economic benchmark.

a tally of economic activity via exchange value. The use of GDP expanded as it was deployed to measure the impact of US President Roosevelt's New Deal, and then later as a tool for economic planning during the Second World War. Despite Kuznets' warning that GDP should not be used as a measure of progress,[15] the first international guidelines for national accounting, which focused on production, were issued in 1947.[16] They shaped the UN System of National Accounts, which, to this day, has GDP at its core.[17]

Around the world we see growth-orientated policies adopted, regardless of the cautionary tale that the GDP-rich world could tell:

> Developing countries have adopted remarkably similar macroeconomic policies since the 1980s, in large part due to the influence of the World Bank and IMF. Those policies have included a reduced role for the state in directing investment, fiscal austerity, inflation-targeting, coupled with trade, investment, and financial liberalization.[18]

Faith in progress as accumulation also led to a de facto GDP meritocracy: those countries with bigger GDP per capita assumed more power in global politics, with admission to many global governance institutions being based on a country's GDP. Seats at the G7 or the G20 go to those with the biggest GDP. Voting rights at the IMF are based on economic power. As Fioramonti explains, 'GDP has been instituted (via international financial institutions) in the governance processes of virtually all countries around the world; it has become the global parameter for success and prestige'.[19]

As GDP was becoming entrenched in political and statistical affections, the structure of the economic system stepped in line. This was a period of Keynesian policy making, in which harnessing GDP growth – as a proxy for aggregate demand – was a vital element of any effort to achieve full employment.*

* Of course, this is counter to subsequent neoliberal arguments for more flexibility on the part of workers.

Still today, high national debt has to be serviced somehow (for example, through taxes or income from the sale of public assets). As with loans to individuals, additional revenue is necessary to pay back the capital plus interest. This agenda was paralleled in the private sphere, where advertising was used to drive demand for the outputs of factory production. Interest-bearing debt – which flourished as credit became more widely available – means that borrowers need to make the capital and an additional amount to pay back the debt. Moreover, many developed countries have experienced a housing-market boom as people took on mortgages to buy a home. Whereas loans with an expectation of interest were once seen as sinful 'usury', they seemingly now form a key plank of the economy.

Box 4.1: Political pursuit of growth

> Creating growth is the goal of our government. —Angela Merkel, German Chancellor[20]

> We also need a plan to drive growth up and down the country – from rural areas to our great cities. —Theresa May, British Prime Minister[21]

> My key message to global policy makers: they need to upgrade their policy recipes to reinvigorate growth and reduce global uncertainty. —Christine Lagarde, IMF Managing Director[22]

> I am crossing every time zone – and at each stop, we're working to boost economic growth that's inclusive, that benefits all people. —Barack Obama, then US President[23]

> [Human rights are] not one of our top priorities ... the prosperity agenda is further up the list. —Sir Simon McDonald, Permanent Under-Secretary at the UK Foreign and Commonwealth Office and Head of the UK Diplomatic Service[24]

> What Australians want to see from their government is strong leadership, in particular strong economic growth ... —Malcolm Turnbull, then Australian Prime Minister[25]

At the micro level, rising incomes and growing profits were needed to buy products and pay debt. The imperative to grow – to hasten the flows that add to GDP – has led to a culture of consumerism, and underpins the profit motive at the firm level, both with harmful consequences. That GDP is often taken as a gauge of economic welfare at the macro level explains, in part, the pursuit of consumption at the micro level. There's a big assumption behind the ascent of GDP as a measure of societal wellbeing: that preferences are best satisfied by consumption. Or, to put it another way, when a good or service is introduced and someone pays for it, this is considered inherently beneficial (regardless of whether they really needed it, if they could afford it and how harmful its production was).[26] From this assumption flow the privatisation of public spaces, the processes of marketisation and the promotion of a 'consumer as king' mentality. To spur consumption, advertising has flourished – much of which plays on a very natural human sense of status anxiety, a need to belong and fear of shame.

Profit can be seen as the firm-level equivalent of GDP. Growth in profit is often predicated on a gap between what labour receives and what it creates.[27] Expanding this gap by driving down wages (and similarly payments to suppliers) not only exacerbates inequality but creates a divide between employees' effort and their reward. Pursuit of short-term profit also creates blind spots – environmental impacts, for example, invariably do not feature in a short-term conception of profit and are hence dismissed as externalities. As previously discussed (see Box 3.2), economic growth is also founded on transformation of the natural world into goods for sale.

The results of the pernicious but seemingly intractable dependence on growth are increasingly apparent – much harm is rendered in the name of growth. Austerity, marketisation of family and community life, faster exploitation of the environment and aggressive business practices all have roots in the pursuit of GDP growth. Strategies and policies that drive growth often damage workers, communities and individuals, and they wreck the environment. In some respects it is not the growth itself that is the problem beyond the point of Arrival, but the steps taken in pursuit of it. There is inevitably a web of interlinked causes that flow in several directions. The point is that inequality, consumerist culture, marketisation and environmental exploitation are all counter to making ourselves at home – and are symptoms of the failure to recognise that GDP-rich countries have Arrived and need to re-orient around a new purpose. The resulting precariousness (both in livelihood terms and in terms of people's sense of autonomy and identity), coupled with materialism and neglect of the environment, undermine the ability to make ourselves at home. Transfixed by the vision of growth and passionately committed to the very thing that is tearing society and the environment apart, wealthy countries risk losing the prosperity they already have. The fruits of growth are rotting.

FIVE

Rushing past our stop: failure demand, uneconomic growth and consolation goods

> *Just when we need it least from the point of view of human or environmental wellbeing, we are committed to an economic system that can only flourish if people keep spending – which means they must keep working, which means they have less time to do things for themselves, which means they have to buy more goods and services to make up for the time deficit … consumer society is dependent on a collective preparedness to spend the money we earn by working too hard and too long on provision to compensate for the more diverse, enriching and lasting satisfactions we have sacrificed through overwork and overproduction.* —*Kate Soper*[1]

Can we legitimately claim that economic growth is still delivering better lives in GDP-rich countries? There is a weight of evidence, as just outlined, of dissatisfaction, inequality, waste, over-development and failure demand. These are 'externalities', to use economic terminology, of the growth-orientated economic model.

There have been warnings that 'however affluent the economy, it will always produce unhappiness, frustration and dissatisfaction because the unlimited production of goods is intimately tied to the unlimited production of needs'.[2] Henk Molenaar (executive director at WOTRO Science for Development), in similar terms to Max-Neef's notion of pseudo-satisfiers, explains that the allure of growth

> is based on a distortion of our perception. We feel that growth allows us to satisfy our needs, and we fail to see that growth compulsion leads to the continuous multiplication of needs, the general spreading of scarcity, and the increase in inequality.[3]

We have just considered the reasons for this growth compulsion: the extent to which society has fallen in love with something that is holding it captive. But the need to question this model of the economy could not be more urgent. As failure demand and defensive expenditure spurs more government spending to deal with the harm of the growth model, as much growth itself becomes 'uneconomic' and as individuals turn to consolation goods, many of the fruits of growth are beginning to rot. The time has come to move away from an economy that is increasingly uneconomic and unsafe, with the unevenly shared bounties from growth being spent on things that do not meet fundamental human needs.

Let us look a little deeper at some of these costs. The term 'failure demand' was coined by John Seddon[4] in relation to manufacturing and corporate systems. He sought to critique the rise in demand for a service as often reflecting a problem, rather than constituting a sign of success.* It was used in relation to public services in a 2011 report for the Scottish Government that warned that demand for public services will rise, driven by an ageing population, but also 'because of our failure up to now to tackle the causes of disadvantage and vulnerability, with the result that huge sums have to be expended dealing with their consequences'.[5] In 2013 health experts gave evidence to the Scottish Government in which they explained this dynamic in a bit more detail:

> Societies which have greater inequalities in health and the consequent burdens on health and social

* Seddon first observed failure demand in call centres. Lots of people calling a telephone helpline doesn't mean that you have a good helpline. It means that there's a failure somewhere else in the business. A rise in demand for helpline services is therefore failure demand.

> services; and which have greater levels of social harms (e.g. crime) due to greater disenfranchisement and socioeconomic and educational inequality, spend a far greater proportion of public spending on dealing with problems and mitigation, rather than the goods and services that are more desirable and positive.[6]

Failure demand is thus expenditure that not only could have been avoided by earlier preventative measures, but is reactive spending. It is a response to the consequences, as opposed to the causes, of inequalities. This is an inefficient and ineffective way of seeking to deliver a goal – in this case, good lives for all. It's also an approach that runs counter to both the scientific evidence and the lived experience of the resource limits to growth. In the depressingly circular logic of failure demand, growth is required in order to pay for fixing the harm done in the creation of the growth, but this growth is, of course, pursued while disregarding the environmental consequences. In ecological economics there is the concept of defensive expenditure: spending driven by the need to clean up damage to the environment. And for individuals, as already seen, the idea of 'consolation goods' captures the expenditure individuals undertake to compensate for meaningless or lonely or stressed lives.

Examples of such inefficient and costly expenditure driven by failure to make ourselves at home are not hard to find. Think about the huge sums of government money spent on topping up the incomes of those whose wages are insufficient for a decent livelihood; or the money spent cleaning up after oil spills; or cyclists buying face masks so that they can breathe when riding on polluted streets. Here are some of the figures.

- In 2012 it was estimated that 40% of what local authorities in Scotland spend was driven by 'failure demand'.[7]
- The Joseph Rowntree Foundation estimates that poverty costs Britain £78 billion every year, and that 'a large proportion of what we spend publicly (about £1 in every £5 spent on public services) is making up for the way that poverty damages people's lives'.[8]

- Loneliness (or 'disconnected communities') carries a cost of £5.2 billion in terms of demand on health services and £205 million in demand on policing, according to the Centre for Economics and Business Research analysis.[9]
- Jules Pretty and his colleagues have estimated that what they call 'negative consumption externalities' in the UK equate to £62 billion for the National Health Service and £184 billion for the economy as a whole. These are driven by mental ill-health, dementia, obesity, physical inactivity, diabetes, loneliness and cardiovascular disease.[10]
- Others have estimated that if the UK does not address its failure to deliver good and secure livelihoods for people, the cost of addressing social problems over the 20 years to 2040 will amount to £4 trillion; a preventative approach could mean £486 billion returned to the UK economy instead.[11]
- In the US, alcohol misuse problems cost $249 billion* in 2010[12] and the estimated annual medical cost of obesity was $147 billion in 2008.[13]
- Also in the US, the rise of 'guard labour' could be deemed another example of failure demand. In 2011 Samuel Bowles and Arjun Jayadeve (professors of behavioural science and economics, respectively) estimated that 5.2 million US workers could be described as performing guard labour – as private security guards, police officers, members of the armed forces, prison and court officials, civilian employees of the military and those producing weapons.[14]
- *The Economist* magazine recently ran a story on homelessness in New York, in which it explained that the cost of renting had risen by more than the increase in wages.[15] Over a similar period, the number of people living in shelters had increased, with the mayor planning on opening another 90 shelters. Such spending on homeless shelters must be one of the clearest examples of failure demand.
- Coming to our ecosystems, there are a plethora of examples of 'defensive expenditure' whereby people or governments have had to spend to clean up, adapt to or treat the consequences

* This includes direct costs such as medical, police and justice costs, and indirect costs such as absenteeism.

of environmental damage. Take just one example: before 2017 was finished, the US had spent over $2 billion fighting wildfires, according to the then Secretary of Agriculture Sonny Perdue, who noted that with the fire season getting longer, this has increased in recent years.[16]

- Turning to the causes of such climate-related demands on state funding, in 2015 the IMF revealed that effective subsidies to fossil fuel companies (taking account of the expenditure due to harm caused to local populations due to pollution, as well as the impacts of floods, droughts and storms being driven by climate change) equated to $5.3 trillion (£3.4 trillion) a year. That is $10 million a minute every day.[17] Downstream actions such as carbon capture and storage or geo-engineering are more expensive than upstream initiatives such as zero-carbon technology investment, renewable energy and waste recycling. As the World Bank observes, 'downstream arrangements for dealing with risk are wasteful and often counter-productive'.[18]
- Some forms of failure demand are almost impossible to quantify, but are nevertheless clear. For example, there is no demand for wildlife conservation unless wildlife is threatened. With no disrespect implied, the whole conservation sector could be considered an example of defensive expenditure.

Many of these costs of growth (and avoidable demands on various levels of government) count as an addition to the ledger of national 'success'. Herman Daly's concept of 'uneconomic growth' captures the perversity of this bizarre tally. Daly explained that there comes a point – which he terms 'the futility limit' – where the marginal utility of production hits zero.[19] Max-Neef (and his co-author Phillip Smith) similarly pointed to the existence of a threshold beyond which the benefits of growth taper off: 'in every society there is a period in which economic growth contributes to an improvement of the quality of life, but only up to a point, the threshold point, beyond which if there is more economic growth, quality of life may begin to deteriorate'.[20] After that point (see Chapter Nine), often GDP will record the economy as growing, due in part to increased expenditure on solving problems that this particular sort of growth has created. From this point on, the costs of growth outweigh the benefits. Forms of spending intended to correct the downsides of growth start to dominate – 'failure demand' at the societal level, 'defensive expenditures' in terms of the environment, and 'consolation goods' at the individual level.

GDP growth that comprises spending due to failure demand, defensive expenditure and purchase of consolation goods is a self-reinforcing process as it 'produces negative externalities that, in turn, force people to further contribute to growth'.[21] J.K. Galbraith put it rather succinctly when he wrote: 'One cannot defend production as satisfying wants if that production creates the wants'.[22]

Have GDP-rich countries reached that point, like a dog chasing its tail, where the consequences of over-development are now a source of growth? We examine this more specifically in Chapter Nine, but for now, let us note that examples of economic perversity abound. Rising house prices boost the economy by encouraging consumer spending, but they simultaneously spur state spending on Housing Benefit for those struggling to keep up. Working in the opposite direction, ever-lower food prices drive farmers to the brink of bankruptcy, leading to spending on farming subsidies. The financial industry encourages people to live beyond their means with cheap loans, and then sells them payment protection too. Big corporations hold both fast-food and slimming brands in their portfolios. In airport bookshops, self-help books about mindfulness and meditation sit alongside books urging readers to win at all costs. In a bizarre way, abundance has led to catastrophe as society and policy makers design and plan further exploitation of the environment, and reactionary spending to address problems created in pursuit of more growth.

SIX

Embracing Arrival and making ourselves at home

[We need an economy characterised by a] subtle and complex economics of maintenance, qualitative improvements, sharing, frugality, and adaptation to natural limits. It is an economy of better not bigger. —*Herman Daly*[1]

Instead of rushing calamitously onwards, embracing Arrival and making ourselves at home demands a profound shift in the purpose of our economies. Of course growth up to a certain point is important – and countries and people below their respective threshold points need more of it, as long as it is good quality and distributed well. After that point, however, societies need to become better at focusing on the quality of the economy instead of its size. This is an acknowledgement that material goods are the foundation of a good life, but not the finished article. Nobody lives in the foundations, but in the home that is built on them, and a good life is constructed on the solid base of material provision.

Bricks and mortar are the material foundations of a house, but they are not what constitutes the warmth, welcome and comfort of a home – that stems from relationships, security and personalisation. Once the foundations and the shell of the house are in place, the builders move on and it's up to the inhabitants to make it into a home that people enjoy living in.

Similarly, growth provides the material foundation for prosperity, and then attention should turn to other priorities to deliver quality of life. Once growth has served its purpose of providing the material foundations of a good life, economies can become post-growth. This is what we refer to as economies making themselves at home – and it is to this task that our discussion now turns.

The necessity of such a shift stems from two realities that we have set out in the previous chapters: the declining relevance of growth to social progress and good lives once an economy has Arrived, and the risk that pursuit of further growth threatens undoing the achievements already realised. As John Stuart Mill explains, growth is necessary up to the point when everyone enjoys a reasonable standard of living: beyond that we need a 'stationary state', to move past the 'trampling, crushing, elbowing, and treading on each other's heels'.[2] In later discussion (Chapter Nine) we explore locating the point at which more growth stops delivering the goods and even starts to undo progress. Of course 'enough' is impossible to define precisely, but many nations have certainly arrived in a place where they have, in aggregate if not with current distributional arrangements, more than enough to meet basic material needs and secure a good life for everyone. Uruguayan scholar Eduardo Gudynas talks of a 'field of sustainability' that lies between the poverty threshold and an opulence threshold, but under the appropriation threshold in terms of use of nature.[3] Lorenzo Fioramonti and the Wellbeing Economy Alliance advocate for a 'wellbeing economy'[4] and UK columnist George Monbiot has called for 'private sufficiency and public luxury'.[5] Scholars such as Julia Steinberger and Dan O'Neill are researching the energy and other biophysical inputs required for a good life, taking into account resource constraints – 'living well within limits'.[6]

A useful way of visualising concepts such as living well within limits, a wellbeing economy or a field of sustainability is the 'doughnut', developed by economist Kate Raworth (Figure 3). The doughnut is a combination of the ecological ceiling the economy should not breach, and a 'social foundation' that society should not fall below.[7] Between these two limits is the 'safe and just' operating space for the economy. Operating inside the doughnut demands a profound repurposing of the economy towards the needs of people and planet. This depends on the quality and distribution of economic activity, rather than growth

Figure 3: Doughnut. Between a social floor below which we should not drop, and environmental limits that we should not exceed, lies a doughnut-shaped 'safe space for humanity'.

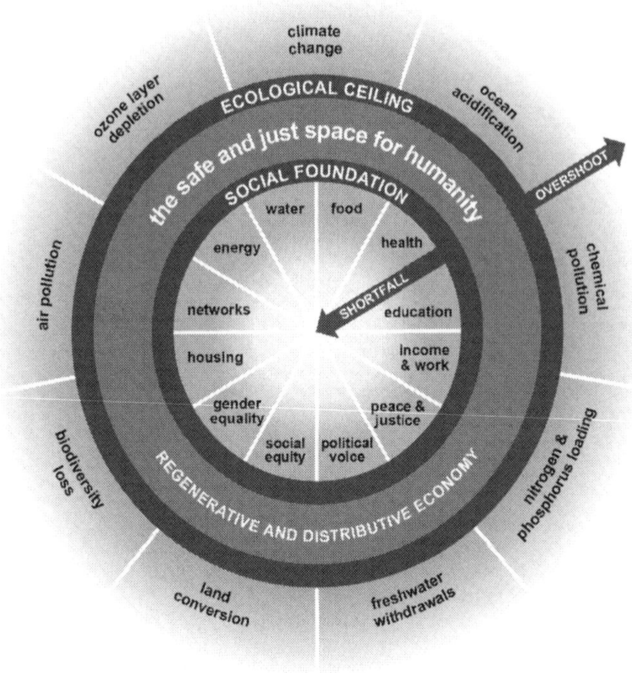

Source: Kate Raworth, reproduced with permission

per se. It is, of course, the task of an economy that seeks to make itself at home.

So, whether there is a need for growth or not depends on context, and, no matter what, quality matters. Later we discuss the scope – and indeed the need – for countries not yet Arrived to 'leapfrog' to a place where they can make themselves at home. Not by proceeding with ever more pace down the same path that GDP-rich countries have so heavily trodden, but by charting a different course – one that benefits from both wisdom and technology, and so is gentler on the planet and places less strain on people.

The terms 'developed' and 'developing' are common parlance when describing different countries, but in reality we should call all countries developing, since growth is currently pursued and expected in rich and poor countries alike. Similarly, in accordance with a reclaimed notion of development, few could be deemed to operate within the doughnut – they may have Arrived in the sense of having enough collectively, but this has not been recognised in policy or national goals. This has been shown through the work of Dan O'Neill, Andrew Fanning and Julia Steinberger, which concluded that no country has an economy located inside the doughnut.[8] As we have noted above, material wealth has not translated into prosperity for everyone, as poverty persists in all of the wealthiest economies. Analysis published in 2015 of how OECD countries meet the Sustainable Development Goals (SDGs) found that only Sweden, Norway, Denmark, Finland and Switzerland were 'ready' (let alone having attained or delivered) for the SDGs: the UK was ranked 15th out of 34 in the OECD in SDG performance, and the US 29th.[9] The author of this analysis warned that

> Their inability to fight the growing social divide combined with their overuse of resources therefore shows that today's high income countries in their current shape can no longer serve as role models for the developing world. In terms of sustainable development, all countries are now developing countries.[10]

But what if it was possible to own that 'developed' term more literally? To take a second look at what might be considered genuinely developed, and to change the focus from quantity to quality of economic activity? This would enable a dialogue about improving the economy, rather than just inflating it in an endless game of 'mine's bigger than yours'.

Another way of thinking about this is the language of modernity. History recognises the Modern Era as beginning during the Renaissance as scientific and rational ways of understanding the world emerged and slowly began to eclipse tradition and theology. Codified science and empirical argument laid the foundations for progress, and expansion followed – expansion in knowledge, in the human population, in technology and in economic advancement, and in ecological impact too. Alongside much else of course, expansion became a fundamental characteristic of modernity.

Many of the central tenets of modernity are now being revisited, and it would be quite possible to position Arrival as part of the wider story of postmodernism. Indeed, theorists such as Wolfgang Sachs have written about 'post-development' in this way. 'Development has become outdated,' wrote Sachs. 'Above all, the hopes and desires which made the idea fly are now exhausted: development has grown obsolete'.[11] While Sachs is most concerned with a perceived Western imperialism that lies behind the idea of development, we would also argue that development (in the traditional sense of the term) is obsolete because in many parts of the world its work is done. If the developed world is actually developed in the material and wealth sense, if not the distributional and quality-of-life sense, then it's time for a new challenge – a more nuanced, more human, more postmodern understanding of the future, founded on an economy that is not growing so much as fully grown. Or, to use our term, an economy that has Arrived.

The idea of development with a destination is not new. Back in 1776 Adam Smith imagined a future country that had acquired a 'full complement of riches'[12] – and a small subset of economists have entertained similar ideas ever since. The notion of a 'steady state economy' was rediscovered in the 1970s as the environmental sector emerged, and it has enjoyed more attention in the 2010s under a variety of names – post-growth, degrowth (or 'décroissance' in the Francophone world),* a grown-up economy,[13] and even 'a-growth' as in 'atheism'.[14]

The idea of a post-growth economy has yet to break through to the mainstream, mainly because when growth per se is universally considered a good thing, being perceived as anti-growth is a non-starter. When post-growth ideas are referenced, it is often only for a snap dismissal that often repeats common misconceptions. Among those common misunderstandings is

* Professor Josef Senft has suggested that the coming post-growth age should be called the 'Adultum'. This draws on the German translation of degrowth as 'ausgewachsen', which means 'grown up'.

the false idea that a steady-state economy would be a static and constrained world without change or improvement, or that it would represent permanent recession.

Box 6.1: Permanent recession?

Their recession is not our degrowth. —Serge Latouche[15]

There are a number of common questions that arise the moment that a post-growth economy is suggested in anything less than dismissive terms. How will jobs be created? How will public services be paid for? Won't it just lead to economic collapse? There are a couple of things to say about this.

First, tough questions are no reason to write off an idea. If they were, then we would have walked away from the idea of economic growth long ago. If the main objection to post-growth thinking is an inability to imagine how it would all work, then the same problem is surely evident in the current state of affairs. Among the tough questions we could level at the status quo: how can infinite growth proceed on a finite planet? How can we protect people from the havoc caused by the recessions that are ostensibly a normal part of the growth economy? How can democracy be protected in an age of vast global corporations? How can inequality be curbed in a system that inherently rewards the richest first? Growth has failed to deliver on many such counts, and is unlikely to do so in the future. Jobs created have too often been bad quality, and automation raises the prospect of a jobless future. Demand for public services is often accentuated or even created by policies pursued in the name of growth, and experiences of the financial crash of 2008 tell us that the current structure of the economy is far from immune from economic collapse.

The second thing to say is that a post-growth economy is not a simply a growth economy without the growth. It is an economy that functions in a different way, driven by a different purpose (that of making ourselves at home) and is not *dependent* on growth in the first place. In the same way that an electric car is not threatened by a petrol shortage, a steady-state economy is not threatened by recession. Among many other things, that requires new business models, ways of raising finance without interest, sharing to end poverty rather than relying on 'growing the pie', recasting notions of productivity and a focus on cooperation as well as competition. We will look at some of these things in more detail later. In an economy making itself at home, innovators will still come up with new ideas, jobs will be created, quality of infrastructure will improve (including being more efficient with resources so that there is more to go around), and yes, there may even be GDP growth – although the economy will not go into meltdown if there is not. GDP will not be the key measure of success and will instead be incidental to more important economic goals. It will be a side-effect rather than a primary (and sometimes counter-productive) ambition, and in time statisticians may even conclude there is little point tallying it up at all.

Finally, post-growth economics is not a fully fleshed-out system waiting in the wings for some big future switchover. Nor are our own notions of Arrival and making ourselves at home. Moving towards these alternatives will be an evolutionary process, driven partly by new ideas and partly by the failure of old ones. Everything is up for discussion, within the normal (and ideally enhanced) procedures of democratic government.

Indeed, we should be wary of those who demand a fully articulated alternative. 'Alternatives,' writes Larry Lohman, 'are usually imagined to be comprehensive, well-thought-out blueprints formulated by a few smart people for political leaders to execute, rather than unpredictable, ever-evolving processes'.[16] There is no 'alternative model', but *alternatives plural* – varying by place and by time. Nor are there neatly ordered master plans ready to be taken off the shelf and applied. The reality is much more messy, more open ended. It will be hard work, and grounded just as much in grassroots movements as in political theory or expert analysis. Far from ducking the question, we would suggest that declining to articulate a comprehensive alternative is actually quite important, because it rejects the idea of grand, top-down visions. We can help people to imagine alternatives (which is our intention in writing this book) and make policy recommendations, but the future is not ours to plan and then impose. The alternatives will be something people and communities discover together.

One of the things that hold back post-growth narratives is that they are frequently negative: they call for a halt; they declare 'enough!' Most contentious of all is the term 'degrowth', which calls for society to stop and go backwards in material input terms, to deliberately shrink the economy of rich countries. However reasonable the arguments behind such an idea of contraction (and convergence at a global level), degrowth in the rich world is not a frame that captures the imagination and it is unlikely to get a sufficient hearing.

As well as being a non-starter in mainstream political debates, degrowth as a term is philosophically challenging too. There is reason to be careful of painting growth in entirely negative terms: 'in a sense, everybody believes in growth, and rightly so, because growth is an essential feature of life', said E.F. Schumacher. 'The whole point, however, is to give to the idea of growth a qualitative determination; for there are always many things that ought to be growing and many things that ought to be diminishing'.[17] Nor is degrowth a long-term alternative – after all, presumably the plan is not to contract to nothing; it is a means to an end, a way of rebalancing. Ultimately, degrowth still aims for a place of sufficiency, perhaps approaching Arrival from the other side, from a point of overdevelopment. Arrival and making ourselves at home cut to the chase and talk about the end we have in mind, the destination instead of the journey, and what we do when we get there – replacing quantity with quality as the economy's goal.

Drawing lines around who is pro-growth or anti-growth in a black and white way can become a distraction. We need language that opens up these questions without alienating more traditional views and that doesn't throw the development baby out with the economic growth bathwater. This means a more nuanced conversation about what different contexts need more of and what they need less of. It means asking who needs more and who could actually benefit from less.

This is why we propose the idea of 'Arrival' as the successor to the 'more equals progress' narrative that currently underpins an unhealthy and unsafe obsession with material growth. To *Arrive* as a society is to be in a position to recognise and celebrate the wealth that an economy and society already has. Making ourselves at home means sharing wealth more widely, rather than permitting a few to pathologically hoard it. Sharing is key in making ourselves at home, and in this sense Arrival counters the obsolete mindset of scarcity. Arrival does not say that growth is bad, but that growth can lead to a place of economic maturity where more is no longer necessary. Instead of being forever on the road to somewhere, Arrival recognises that as a society we *are* somewhere, and in the grand scheme of history this can be a place of remarkable prosperity. Writ large, society has Arrived and now needs to turn its attention, ingenuity and effort to making ourselves at home. Instead of growing more and more fruit, regardless of need, this is about savouring what is already grown and ensuring that it is shared with those who still don't have enough. In the next sections we explore what this might look like, by reflecting on what a good life could mean. We then discuss how designing our economies for making ourselves at home enables us to get things right in the first place and hence avoid the harm and costs that come with a blinkered focus on more.

What is a good life anyway?

> *The ache for home lives in all of us, the safe place where we can go as we are and not be questioned.* —*Maya Angelou*[18]

Shifting to a focus on making ourselves at home sounds to us like a positive vision, but it would represent a deep cultural shift, let alone an economic and political one. The progress narrative runs deep and is constantly reinforced. Mainstream, marketised and corporate conceptions of a good life are currently defined by a capitalist system that defaults to constant expansion. Dominant Western institutions and ideology have come to suggest that this is even inherent in human nature. Through a blend of free market doctrine and misappropriated Darwinism, 'greed and laziness have been enthroned as basic human motivations'.[19] But that is a reductionist philosophy, a modern construct premised on the discredited notion of 'rational economic man'.[*, 20]

Instead, society, supported by an economy geared to making itself at home, can cultivate new, different and more authentic conceptions of a good life – building on innate instincts and knowledge of what development might entail if we broke out of the growth mindset. Let's delve into some non-GDP-based understandings of what a good life might be, and what they might mean for the economic model.

Building on Amartya Sen's work on freedoms and capabilities, Martha Nussbaum offers a useful take. She describes the purpose of development as to 'enable people to live full and creative lives, developing their potential and fashioning a meaningful existence commensurate with their equal human dignity'.[*, 21] A little more specifically, human-scale development, popularised by the Chilean economist Manfred Max-Neef, identifies 'needs' as subsistence, protection, affection, understanding, participation, leisure, creation, identity and freedom.[22] For Max-Neef, it is the purpose of every political, social and economic system to generate the conditions for people to adequately satisfy their fundamental human needs. These needs are satisfied in three contexts: with regard to oneself, with regard to the social group or community and with regard to the environment.[23] Skidelsky and Skidelsky focus on the basic goods that people everywhere need to have a good life.[24]

As Table 1 shows there are clear commonalities across these diverse contributions from different corners of scholarship. But in another sense we do not really need to draw on renowned development theorists or economists or philosophers. To build a definition of a good life we find that the answer is within

* Among other things, this assumption is undermined by insights from psychology that point to, inter alia: cognitive myopia, loss aversion, the influence of social norms, cultural cognition, adaptive preferences, lack of information and instinct- and emotion-led 'fast' decisions.

* This differs from the self-reported wellbeing agenda that often seems to prioritise an increase in average and often narrow conceptions of wellbeing. As Nussbaum explains, her approach focuses on freedom and choice: societies should be promoting a set of opportunities/substantial freedoms that people 'may or may not exercise in action: the choice is theirs'.

Table 1: Components and underpinnings of a good life according to Nussbaum, Max-Neef and Skidelsky and Skidelsky. There are many other such lists, but these three are a sample of the different approaches taken.

Nussbaum's 'core capabilities'	Max-Neef's 'fundamental human needs' (being; having; doing; interacting)	Skidelsky and Skidelsky's basic goods needed for a good life
Life *Bodily health* *Bodily integrity* (ability to move freely from place to place; being secure against violent assault, having opportunities for sexual satisfaction and for choice in matters of reproduction) *Senses, imagination, and thought* (being able to use the senses, to imagine, think and reason, being informed and cultivated by an adequate education, freedom of expression with respect to both political and artistic speech and freedom of religious exercise) *Emotions* (to love, to grieve, to experience longing, gratitude and justified anger, supported by forms of human association that can be shown to be crucial in their development) *Practical reason* *Affiliation* (being able to live with and toward others, to recognise and show concern for other humans; empathy, protective institutions; being treated as a dignified being whose worth is equal to that of others; non-discrimination on the basis of race, sex, sexual orientation, ethnicity, caste, religion, national origin and species) *Other species* (being able to live with concern for and in relation to animals, plants and the world of nature) *Play* *Control over one's political environment* (being able to participate effectively in political choices that govern one's life; the right of political participation, protections of free speech and association) *Material* (being able to hold property and having property rights on an equal basis; the right to seek employment on an equal basis with others; being able to work as a human, exercising practical reason)	*Subsistence* (physical and mental health; food, shelter, work; feed, clothe, rest/sleep, work; living environment, social setting) *Protection* (care, adaptability, autonomy; social security, health systems, work; cooperate, plan, take care of, help; living space, social environment, dwelling) *Affection* (respect, sense of humour, generosity, sensuality; friendships, family, relationships with nature; share, take care of, make love, express emotions; privacy, intimate spaces of togetherness) *Understanding* (critical capacity, curiosity, intuition; literature, teachers, policies, educational and communication policies; analyse, study, meditate, investigate; schools, families, universities, communities) *Participation* (receptiveness, dedication, sense of humour, adaptability; responsibilities, duties, work, rights, privileges; cooperate, dissent, express opinions; associations, parties, churches, neighbourhoods) *Leisure/idleness* (imagination, curiosity, tranquillity, spontaneity; games, parties, peace of mind, clubs, spectacles; day-dream, play, remember, relax, have fun; landscapes, intimate spaces, places to be alone, free time) *Creation* (imagination, boldness, inventiveness, curiosity; autonomy, determination; skills, work, abilities, method, techniques; invent, build, design, work, compose, interpret; spaces for expression, workshops, audiences, cultural groups) *Identity* (sense of belonging, self-esteem, consistency; symbols, language, religions, work, customs, values, norms, habits, historical memory; get to know oneself, grow, commit oneself, recognise oneself; places one belongs to, everyday settings, maturation stages) *Freedom* (autonomy, passion, self-esteem, open-mindedness, tolerance; equal rights; dissent, choose, run risks, develop awareness, be different from, disobey; temporal/spatial plasticity (anywhere))	*Health* (for a reasonable span of life) *Security* (being undisturbed by crime, war, revolution, major social or economic upheaval) *Respect* (recognition and having your views taken account of) *Personality* (autonomy, practical reason, individuality, spirit, living according to tastes and ideals) *Living in harmony with nature* (in contrast to alienation from nature, which comes from consumer culture) *Friendship* *Leisure* (what is done for its own sake rather than as a means to something else)

us as human beings and is being brought to our attention by emerging research in the fields of neuroscience, epidemiology and psychology. For example, research shows that people are happy because of good family relationships, good health, good friends, falling in love and having a child they want.[25] Analysis of self-reported wellbeing shows that people who are active in their communities report higher wellbeing;[26] and people who see their social relations to be good quality have higher levels of life satisfaction.[27] Robert Manchin from Gallup Europe reports that the 'relation between level of trust and subjective wellbeing is strong and measurable'.[28] Neuroscience tells us that cooperative behaviour activates the reward areas of the brain, which suggests that human beings are 'hard-wired' to enjoy helping others, cooperating and being kind: doing so brings a warm glow.[29] In fact, life expectancy; voice; government accountability; climate and natural capital are more important than GDP per capita in predicting mean levels of life satisfaction in 79 countries.[30]

To all of this we can add a slew of scholarship about psychological needs. For example, American-Israeli sociologist Aaron Antonovsky suggests that a 'sense of coherence' is crucial for good health, particularly pointing to the relationship between health and stress.[31] A sense of coherence encompasses comprehensibility (the extent to which events in one's life can be understood and predicted); manageability (having necessary skills and resources to manage and control one's life); and – the most important according to Antonovsky – meaning (feeling that there is a clear meaning and purpose to life). Epidemiologist Michael Marmot's work confirms this, explaining that factors that impact on health include control, predictability, degree of support, threat to status and presence of outlets and access to coping mechanisms.[32] Sociologist Emile Durkheim suggested that people enjoy higher wellbeing when their needs are proportionate to their wants and when they have means to satisfy those wants.[33] Scholars such as Rawls, Sen and Nussbaum all agree that autonomy is one of life's basic goods.[34] We could also consider the work of Deci and Ryan (2000), whose empirical analysis has focused on motivation and goals that lead to high wellbeing. They also highlight autonomy and add in competence and relatedness as the three basic psychological needs.[35]

In many ways, this great crowd of witnesses is only shouting what we already know. All the major religions teach moderation and warn against an obsession with money: 'do not exult in wealth' says the Qu'ran, while the Bible describes the love of money as 'a root of all kinds of evil'.[36] History is full of sages who taught and demonstrated contentment. Aristotle taught moderation in possessions and wealth, as 'any excessive amount of such things must either cause its possessor some injury, or at any rate, bring him no benefit'.[37] We could consider Epicurus, the desert fathers, Thoreau, William Morris or more recent figures such as Gandhi, who saw Western consumers as 'enslaved' by money and possessions.[38]

Then we have the testimony of many rich people themselves, the supposed paragons of capitalist success, who insist that their wealth is not what they find satisfying in life. On the one hand, we have newly minted billionaire Markus Persson, the developer of the computer game Minecraft, lamenting on Twitter that he is 'able to do whatever I want, and I've never felt more isolated'.[39] On the other hand we have Warren Buffett, explaining his decision to give away 99% of his wealth: 'the asset I most value, aside from health, is interesting, diverse, and long-standing friends'.[40]

The reflections of the richest people like Persson and Buffett are not far from the innate wisdom of the general population. A fascinating reminder of this comes from Bronnie Ware, a palliative nurse in Australia. Ware has documented some of the common regrets that her patients express in their last days:[41]

1. I wish I'd had the courage to live a life true to myself, not the life others expected of me.
2. I wish I hadn't worked so hard (which Ware reports was expressed by 'every male patient').
3. I wish I'd had the courage to express my feelings.
4. I wish I had stayed in touch with my friends.
5. I wish that I had let myself be happier.

These sorts of stories echo the findings of various surveys that ask people to describe the good life, to identify what makes them happy or to paint a picture of what matters most to them. For example, the UK's Office for National Statistics (ONS) carried out an extensive consultation into Britain's wellbeing and established that the three most important factors were self-reported health, employment status and relationship status.[42] The My World Survey (conducted to inform the SDGs) placed 'a good education'; 'better health care'; 'an honest and responsive government'; and 'access to clean water and sanitation' as top global priorities in terms of what matters to people and their families, wherever they are in the world.[43]

Of course, when people don't have enough, then more is required. But the *more* is not an end in itself. Neuroscience, religion, development scholars and communities themselves all point to the end goal of human flourishing. Amartya Sen's understanding of development is instructive here. 'Development,' wrote Sen, 'is the process of expanding human freedoms'.[44] It is about enabling life choices, which means that ending the 'unfreedom' of material poverty is just the start. Under this definition, broadening people's freedom to choose the lives they value should be the goal of development. The benefit of *this* sort of development is that it could continue long after material needs were satisfied, independent of GDP. It allows us to ask a broader, and ultimately political, question – what holds people back from living the lives they want? What are the unfreedoms of current ways of life and this period of time? With basic needs met, what can society do next?

In Britain, for instance, ill health is something that holds many back. Under a wider definition of development, improving health outcomes would be a measure of progress that could continue with or without economic growth, especially given the link between health on the one hand, and distribution of economic resources (including the quality of jobs) on the other. As we have seen, many feel that they don't have time for the things they enjoy. They are materially rich, but time poor – yet more time would improve relationships, ease stress and make room for activities that benefit wellbeing. In the current economic model, only the material side is recognised, leading to ever-increasing consumption without dealing with the unfreedom of wasted or restricted time. Giving people more time rather than consumption might result in lower GDP and therefore cannot be countenanced in our growth-obsessed rubric, even though many experience lack of time as a type of poverty. Opening up new possibilities for development beyond growth, shifting from quantitative to qualitative development along these lines is what Arrival and making ourselves at home is all about.

To sum up, the evidence tells us that people are not happiest when they are consuming, but when spending time socialising and engaged in meaningful activity. Not when working longer hours to make more money, but when they are in nature, learning and undertaking fulfilling activities. Making ourselves at home means clearing away the pseudo-satisfiers and the obstacles – including, vitally, that of material poverty – to these activities. This view counters the view of humans as inherently selfish or greedy, seeking simply more and more.

It also suggests that people have an innate appreciation for the notion of making ourselves at home. Back in the 19th century John Stuart Mill knew this: 'the best state for human nature is that in which, while no one is poor, no one desires to be richer, nor has any reason to fear being thrust back by the efforts of others to push themselves forward'.[45] Giving ourselves permission to acknowledge the achievement of Arrival and designing our economies in a way that aligns with fundamental human needs could be very positive, beneficial and nurturing. It can also avoid the collateral damage created by an economy designed for growth. The following section considers some of the changes that this would entail.

Getting it right first time around: preventing uneconomic growth and failure demand

> *The quick fix addresses the symptoms before the root cause. It puts short-term relief before long-term cure. It makes no provision for unwelcome side effects.* –*Carl Honoré*[46]

An economy that has Arrived and is focused on making itself at home will be one that enables people to build good, healthy lives: a wellbeing economy. It will not harm people and the environment, and so will avoid having to deliver expensive downstream intervention to fix the damage caused by the current economic model. A regime of late, last-minute, downstream intervention that seeks to cure and heal is an approach to progress and development that demands more resources, more effort, more political agreement and more patience than is really needed. It is an inefficient approach to delivering good lives sustainably. And it is bumpier, has more distractions and diversions and flimsy political bridges to cross than the route that economies could be taking. At its simplest, this 'long way' to realisation of the goal of good lives on a sustainable planet entails three protracted and often fraught steps.

- First, get the economy to grow bigger, but don't fret too much about the damage to people or the environment that this does.
- Second, sequester a chunk out of this economy via taxes (warning: this is a strategy that is vulnerable to fleeting and flippant political will. It depends on the consent of those being taxed, a consent that is often undermined by the current levels of inequality that separate communities from each other and that undermine solidarity across society).
- Third, channel some of this money into helping people and the planet to cope with step number 1.

As seen above, the damage of step 1 is multifaceted. The response (step 3) to the damage that step 1 causes is evident in, for example, tax credits for those in jobs that do not pay enough to live on; interventionist medical and psychological treatment for those alienated and stressed by the precariousness of this economy; welfare payments for those cast aside by companies that downsize in their quest for short-term shareholder value; flood defences and shelters for those whose homes are flooded as climate chaos worsens; and carbon capture and storage. In other words, it is failure demand and defensive expenditure. Of course, the step 3 measures are vital in the short term, but they are clearly attempts to repair and redress, rather than to prevent harm in the first place. This is redistribution as a sticking plaster.

These are the sorts of problems that vexed Japanese farmer Masanobu Fukuoka, and he developed a whole philosophy out of the idea that societies spend too much of their energy fixing problems that they have brought on themselves. 'When the corrective actions appear to be successful,' he wrote, we 'come to view these measures as splendid accomplishments'.[47] A similar point was made by J.K. Galbraith when he stated: 'One cannot defend production as satisfying wants if that production creates the wants'.[48] It also speaks, on an individual level, to the notion of the 'consolation goods' that Serge Latouche warns of, as we explored earlier.

This is where we are today. As the examples we have shared demonstrate, a considerable proportion of current spending (whether by individuals or collectively via the state) is necessary because of environmental harm, inequality and failure to enable people to flourish. This is spending brought on by collective failure. Growth built on such foundations is, as seen above, 'uneconomic'.

The notion of society's taking action – usually, but not always, via the state – and spending money to address problems brought on by the economic model seems to resemble Karl Polanyi's observation that there is a 'Double Movement': the inevitable reaction of society to the deleterious impact of the excessive spread of market economy. Polanyi explains that as the consequences of unrestrained markets become obvious, there are two potential outcomes (like an overstretched elastic band, as sociologist Fred Block described it in his introduction to Polanyi's book *The Great Transformation*[49]). Scenario one is that it snaps, and there is social disintegration. Scenario two is that it reverts to its previous position: laissez faire is wrangled back under control through protective labour, civic, social and political movements and legislation on public health, factory conditions, social insurance, public utilities, municipal services and trade union rights.

These are all important measures to humanise the current system, but wouldn't it be better not to over-extend the elastic band in the first place? Surely it is possible to design institutions, policies and practices so that more of them function according to principles of proactive prevention rather than panicked rescue? That is what making ourselves at home entails.

Focusing on prevention requires a shift to upstream investment and early action to tackle underlying root causes, rather than singularly – and hence continuously – dealing with the consequences and mitigating damage wrought by inability (or unwillingness) to recognise that the economy has Arrived, and the inability to make ourselves at home.

Through the changes outlined in this book, and many more besides, being at home means protecting people, keeping them safe, meeting their needs, ensuring their security (of income, of identity and of body) and recognising the whole ecosystem in which people live their lives and maintain health. With positive feedback loops and co-benefits, virtuous circles will be set in motion. More egalitarian societies are better for all their members: delivering better health and higher life expectancy; fewer drug addictions; less violence; lower teenage pregnancies; higher wellbeing for children; lower obesity; less mental illness; and fewer people in prison.[50] Prevention will reduce poverty, unemployment, illness, illiteracy and homelessness.[51] In doing so, it reduces the need for costly state services, highly paid 'downstream professionals' and the politically fraught and inefficient process of redistribution. Encouraging this focus on prevention requires long-term horizons, long-term planning and long-term budgeting. Tackling root causes is complex and difficult to measure – and hard to singularly attribute. It therefore faces a political bias against necessary shifting of investment towards upstream change.

Box 6.2: Planning for the long term

> *What kind of ancestor did my own ancestors want me to be? What kind of ancestor do I want to be? What kind of ancestor do I want my children to be?—Lowitja Institute International Indigenous Health and Wellbeing Conference Statement 2016*[52]

Short electoral cycles make it difficult for authorities to plan for long-term change, preferring instead to focus on quick wins and short-term targets that will prop up their case for re-election (for example, less than 5% of England and Wales's £110 billion annual health budget is spent on public health and health promotion[53]). Here we can learn from the US state of Oregon. Under the leadership of then governor John Kitzhaber, the state introduced a 10-year budget cycle in 2011. It was designed to meet long-term goals, including fiscal savings. It covers six policy areas (economy and jobs, education, healthy environment, healthy people, public safety and improving government), developed in consultation with Oregonians. Delivery agencies are jointly responsible for implementing programmes under the 10-year budget. These flow from a 10-Year Plan that maps those initiatives that take more than two years to implement and materialise. There are new incentives for policy makers and managers of programmes that encourage them to look to and act for the long term.[54]

This kind of long-term planning is unusual, and it is worth considering other projects with extended time frames, as they can help to remind us of the wider perspective. NASA space missions are a case in point. It takes decades to research and engineer a space probe, and potentially decades more for it to reach its destination. Scientists have to work to target dates well into the future, and then be very patient in waiting for data. Voyager 1 launched in 1977, and NASA had to wait until 2013 for it to send back the first images taken from outside the solar system.[55]

While the space age was associated with national competition, today's most ambitious scientific projects rely on cooperation between states. The International Space Station, the Large Hadron Collider at CERN, or the experimental fusion reactor at ITER all rely on long-term investment. If they were funded by individual governments, they would be subject to funding reversals and political whim. Multiple stakeholders and international treaties can ensure that politicians don't get impatient and pull the plug.

Sometimes projects run a lot longer than decades. At the time of writing the English city of Newcastle-upon-Tyne is debating handing its parks over to a citizens' trust on a 125-year lease.[56] Antoni Gaudi's famous Sagrada Familia in Barcelona has been under construction for 135 years and has another decade to go. The Royal Society for the Protection of Birds has a 200-year regeneration plan for the Abernethy forest. A church in Halberstadt, Germany is hosting an organ piece by John Cage that runs for 634 years. The Arctic World Archive aims to store information for 1,000 years. The Long Now Foundation is building a clock that will tick for 10,000 years, as a symbolic call for longer-term thinking. And finally, Finland's Onkalo repository takes the top of the list – it is designed to lock away spent nuclear fuel for at least 100,000 years.

Dealing with long-running and complex problems such as climate change needs this kind of approach, beginning projects now that may not bear fruit for many years. Such thinking does not come easily in a world of election cycles, cost-benefit analysis and quarterly reports, but it is vital. Jonas Salk, who developed the polio vaccine and set in train the decades-long fight to eradicate the disease, put it this way: 'our greatest responsibility is to be good ancestors'.[57]

It could be argued that much philanthropy – the spending of great sums of money, sometimes earned at the expense of people's health and the environment – is similarly about downstream mitigation. Peter Buffett (youngest son of Warren) has famously, if controversially, written that 'inside any important philanthropy meeting, you witness heads of state meeting with investment managers and corporate leaders. All are searching for answers with their right hand to problems that others in the room have created with their left'.[58] The logic of prevention would contradict the 'rescue principle' that defines such philanthropy.[59] So, making ourselves at home is about initiating virtuous cycles in which interventions ultimately, if not immediately, pay for themselves. As such, the state and society aren't constantly cleaning up after themselves or trying to put individual lives, communities and the planet back together: and hence wouldn't demand growth to pay for it. This is a direct counter to uneconomic growth. Instead, Raskin et al suggest that the economy and society can benefit from various 'dividends': a green dividend from cost savings and eco-efficiency; a peace dividend from reduction in military expenditure; a human-capital dividend from the creativity and contribution of those currently consigned to poverty; a technological dividend from new opportunities from innovation; and a solidarity dividend from reduced security and policy costs.[60] The dividends – savings – will help to dismantle the structural dependence on growth.

What about decoupling?

Economic growth and carbon emissions are inconveniently linked. As the World Bank puts it, 'economic growth causes environmental degradation – or has for much of the past 250 years'.[61] If growth is to continue while carbon emissions decline, they must be 'decoupled'. That is, the link between the two must be severed, so that economic growth no longer leads inevitably to higher emissions and materials use. Decoupling is the solution proposed by those who apparently recognise the environmental harms of growth to date, but are intent on hanging on to growth. The OECD, for example, has made it a major focus of the work of its Environment Directorate. But holding out for decoupling only side-steps the mounting evidence of diminishing marginal returns to growth in terms of social progress, and even as 'uneconomic growth' and 'failure demand' abound, it ignores the dubious evidence about the potential of decoupling itself.

Decoupling occurs as economies become more efficient, generating more income per unit of resource used. Cleaner energy, for example, is a key aspect of efforts to separate the historically close relationship between economic growth and carbon emissions. Energy-saving measures also contribute, and the shift from heavy industry to services further improves the carbon efficiency of a particular economy.

It is thus possible, in theory, to decouple emissions from economic growth, and there are a handful of measures that can make a big difference, such as phasing out coal or a decline in heavy industry. As a long-term strategy, however, it is easier said than done.

First, we must ensure that decoupling is absolute, and not relative. This is important. If the economy is getting 2% more efficient every year, but is also growing at 4% a year, then we aren't making any positive difference to the atmosphere. There has been a relative improvement, but any efficiency savings have been eaten by a growing economy and the overall situation is actually getting worse. Resource efficiencies need to increase at least *as fast* as the growth of economic output for true absolute decoupling to occur. It's only then that any real difference is made to the health of the planet. Unfortunately, as professor of ecological economics Tim Jackson observes, evidence 'for declining resource intensities (relative decoupling) is relatively easy to identify ... Evidence for overall reductions in resource throughput (absolute decoupling) is much harder to find'.[62]

Second, efficiency gains can easily be lost through the rebound effect[63] – just spending the gains on additional consumption. These dynamics are complex and difficult to model, but it has been estimated that oil and electricity efficiencies are subject to a rebound effect of 5–25%.[64] Research has found that the improvements in the energy efficiency of lighting have been overwhelmed by additional lighting use, spurred perhaps by the lower cost of lighting.[65] In other words, a certain amount of efficiency gains are likely to be clawed back by increased consumption – fitting energy-saving light bulbs and then abandoning good habits and leaving lights on in empty rooms. The same logic applies with materials. New designs or technologies that use materials more efficiently may not necessarily lead to 'dematerialisation' overall.[66] A new lightweight method for packaging fresh fruit might encourage supermarkets to sell more fruit pre-packaged rather than loose, thereby erasing any savings in materials. Fortunately it is rare for efficiency measures to backfire entirely and end up being completely counter-productive, but any plan for decoupling needs to take account of how gains can be eroded.

Third, if a country has decoupled by transitioning to a services economy, with industrial operations simply moved overseas, then nothing has changed at the global level. Claims that we are starting to see signs of decoupling are often found to ignore offshore emissions, which mean that countries are simply outsourcing their GHG pollution and other environmental impacts. Instead of linking material footprint to countries where a product is consumed, most decoupling studies attribute it to the producing country.[67]

For example, 'offshored emissions' appear to negate all the cuts that the UK has made since 1990, which were largely an artefact of switching from coal to gas and the decline of manufacturing industry.[68] Analysis by Wiedmann et al shows that as wealth grows, 'countries tend to reduce their domestic portion of materials extraction through international trade'.[69] This means that resource-intensive processes are being externalised rather than reduced. Across the group of mature economies in the study* their conclusion was that 'no decoupling has taken place over the past two decades'.

Moreover, aviation emissions are also frequently missing from decoupling calculations.*, [70] As a result, not only are decoupling studies misallocating impact, they often do not paint a full picture. While relative decoupling in some areas may be happening in terms of some types of impact, decoupling from overall material consumption remains elusive.[71]

Finally, the speed of decoupling matters. Some countries have shown that it is possible to grow the economy while reducing emissions, but reductions have not been fast enough to remain within the carbon budget.** As Tim Jackson has shown, the rates of decarbonisation required to prevent dangerous climate change have never been achieved outside of a recession.[72] This is supported by the findings of Wiedmann et al, whose assessment of the material flows of 186 countries over time revealed that 'achievements in decoupling in advanced economies are smaller than reported or even nonexistent'.[73] In summary, as one study has concluded, it is 'misleading to develop growth-oriented policy around the expectation that decoupling is possible'.[74]

* EU-27, the OECD, the US, Japan and the United Kingdom.

* A 2015 report for the European Parliament's Directorate General for Internal Policies found that in both aviation and maritime transport the associated emissions are mostly international (79% for aviation), which means 'they are not counted towards domestic emissions by a specific country'.

** Carbon budgets are scientifically determined amounts of GHG emissions that can be released in a specified period of time to keep global warming, and thus climate change, within a certain range.

SEVEN

What we might find in making ourselves at home

We are in need of a single, powerful concept to rival growth as a development paradigm. —Henk Molenaar[1]

As far as individuals are concerned, success in our definition of making ourselves at home is to orient ourselves around what is most worthwhile, and having permission and capacity to be oneself rather than what the current economic system compels and demands. On a wider level, making ourselves at home is a narrative of a new purpose for the economy and institutions. Pope Francis comes somewhere near this with his 2015 encyclical, which implores humanity to 'care for our common home'.[2] Other religious leaders have a similar vision. Even some economists already embrace this notion. Kate Raworth points out that lots of work has gone into studying how growth can 'take off', but that every plane needs to eventually land and that part of the metaphor is missing. 'What would it mean to prepare high-income economies for landing so that they could touch down safely and become thriving, growth-agnostic economies when the time was right?'[3] At both the individual and system-wide levels there are concrete objectives we could aim for, policies that could get us there and real-world examples. In the next chapter we will explore a diverse range of specific projects that demonstrate the principles we advocate. But first, let's look at some broader themes, movements and ideas that show what embracing Arrival and making ourselves at home might entail.

Sharing and predistribution

> *If you are fortunate, build a longer table, not a higher fence.* —*Anon*[4]

At the heart of our vision is a shift in economic priorities, away from the supremacy of growth and towards an economy that delivers sustainable, shared prosperity. The most common defence of economic growth as a policy goal is that we need growth to lift people out of poverty. That is true in many situations when the design and distribution of growth is right, but in industrial economies in particular, inequalities complicate matters.[5] Per capita income may be high, but there are still deprived regions and sections of society left behind, a reality masked by the simplistic method of averaging income across the population. Since capital accrues fastest for those who already have the most capital in play, there's only so much that growth can do. Left to its own devices, it will make the rich richer much faster than it will make the poor less poor.[6] There's no call for absolute equality, of course; there will always be natural talent and initiative, and rewards for hard work. But, as we have already discussed, an economy that leaves individuals and communities behind entirely is inhumane and socially unsustainable. There is a need for balance, where excellence and hard work are rewarded, but where the gap between rich and poor does not stretch so wide that it tears society apart.

It is also worth noting that a more equal distribution of resources is an enabler of other ideas presented here. For example, if people feel secure in their livelihoods, they are more likely to be more receptive to other changes. Similarly, a more equal distribution is a first priority, since other ideas risk being unfair if things stay as they currently stand. (Shorter working weeks could penalise those currently earning insufficient wages, for example, or pricing goods to reflect true costs would have a harmful effect on those with less purchasing power.)

Ultimately inequality is a matter of politics. It stems from the structure of the economy, patterns of growth, the nature and impact of technological development and power imbalances that shape access to resources and reallocation of them. These are products of institutions and political decisions that can be changed.[7]

The usual default solution (beloved of social democrats around the world) is in great part to respond to unequal market outcomes by redistribution, using income taxes, and in some cases wealth and capital taxes, to redress the balance. Inheritance taxes, for example, work to prevent inequalities being passed on across generations. Higher earners contribute more in taxes (in absolute terms if not always in relative terms). This common pot is then parcelled out across the income spectrum through the 'virtual income' of government services, or via direct fiscal transfers such as welfare payments and child benefits. This does work and is vitally important. Countries with better redistributive policies and higher levels of government spending have lower inequality.[8] Countries with the lowest levels of child poverty, for example, invest considerably more in a welfare state that supports all families.[9] The 'virtual income' from health and education provision has reduced inequality by between 10% and 20% in Latin American countries such as Argentina, Bolivia, Brazil, Mexico and Uruguay,[10] and by an average of 20% in OECD countries.[11] Through such redistribution we can stave off the worst of the social problems that arise from unequal societies and a widening gap between rich and poor. During the years of Britain's 1997–2010 Labour government, for instance, it is estimated that poverty levels would have been 6% higher and child poverty 13% higher if transfers of extra income support had not been provided.[12] In a nice linguistic parallel to our notion of making ourselves at home, the Swedish welfare state (famous for the relatively equal society that it helps to deliver) is often referred to as 'Folkhemmet': people's home.

Of course, redistribution matters for poverty reduction too: redistribution can play as strong or even stronger a role than growth in increasing the income of people in poverty.[13] Economists Chris Hoy and Andy Sumner have calculated that three-quarters of global poverty (at \$2 a day, and potentially even using the \$5 a day measure) could be eliminated by redistribution of existing resources.[14] They point to funding cash transfers via new taxation and shifting public spending away from fossil fuel subsidies and 'surplus' military spending. Their findings highlight the extent to which the majority of poor countries can dramatically reduce poverty using their own resources, even without economic growth.

Such analysis heads off the claim that the best way to reduce poverty is to 'grow the pie'. Instead, the need is to share it better, not least in the light of science around planetary boundaries, which place very real resource constraints on collective pie making – the oven is only so big, after all! The hope for poverty reduction via redistribution is fortunate when one considers David Woodward's findings that even the most optimistic assumptions (including pro-poor policies) for eradicating $1.25 a day poverty via growth would 'take at least 100 years'. And the confines of our finite planet mean that it might be impossible anyway: 'global carbon constraints raise serious doubts about the viability of this course'.[15]

However, redistribution is not only unreliable and vulnerable to political resistance; it does not address the root causes of skewed distribution. It treats the symptoms of unequally shared income, but not the cause of this inequality. It's like catching the drips from a leaky tub and pouring the water back in, rather than fixing the hole. Big and bureaucratic state machinery becomes almost unavoidable in the effort to enforce and collect taxes and to assess eligibility and deliver services. Taxation is politically fraught and a delicate balancing act. For example, citing the much-criticised but enduringly popular Laffer Curve, opponents of taxation argue that high taxation can disincentivise work and encourage avoidance and capital flight, resulting in lower revenue.[16] And of course, exposés such as those of the Panama and Paradise Papers* reveal the lengths to which people go in order to avoid paying tax. Redistribution can also be divisive, with misperceptions splitting society into perceived givers and takers, contributors and beneficiaries (despite the reality that most redistribution happens over people's life course, rather than being a simple transfer from richer to poorer groups[17]). The trouble comes when the system is seen to be exploited, when

* The Panama Papers and Paradise Papers were investigative journalism campaigns in 2016 and 2018 respectively, revealing the activities of tax havens.

those in power appear uncaring or when budgets are squeezed. The social safety nets that we should all be able to rely on and take pride in suddenly become a source of – and hence victim to – tension and resentment, barriers and 'othering'. Divisive dualistic categories such as 'strivers and skivers' or 'lifters and leaners' pitch people against each other and erode trust and compassion.

Redistribution is essential for redressing existing inequalities, but ultimately, it would be better for everyone if the economy did not create so much inequality in the first place. Jacob Hacker has called this solution 'predistribution', looking at 'measures to reshape the market so that it distributes its rewards more broadly in the first place'.[18] Predistribution entails, inter alia, a more equal share of capital ownership and fairer allocation of other endowments that generate financial returns (such as education or land ownership). This again is a political choice – proactively shaping the market so that outcomes are more equal, requiring less state intervention down the track. There are multiple ways to do this, from inclusive forms of business (including democratising the ownership of firms) and creating a stakeholder economy; from better jobs and higher minimum wages to a 'participants' income'* or even Universal Basic Assets (which, rather than a minimum entitlement to income, focuses on fairer entitlements to assets such as housing, healthcare, education and digital assets[19]). We shall come to some of these in more detail later.

Many of these ideas 'simply' require the political will to implement them – for example, legislating for labour rights or using the tax system to incentivise certain business models. When the political will is there, we can see the scope to deploy taxes to discourage ultra-high earnings: for instance, in 2016 the US city of Portland, Oregon, agreed to levy a tax on CEOs who earn 100 times more than their staff.** Portland proposes to use the revenue, estimated to be $3.5 million a year, to pay for services

* The 'participants' income' is derived from the notion of a 'citizen's income', but avoids two potential pitfalls: definitions of citizenship, and the purported moral hazard of 'something for nothing'.

** It will be levied via licence fees, with an additional 10% on the baseline 2.2% business licence tax, but companies whose pay ratios are over 250:1 will pay an extra 25%.

for homeless people.[20] This tax is enabled by the adoption, during the last few months of the Obama administration, of a federal regulation mandating publicly held corporations to report annual pay ratios.[21] Israel has taken a similar step and pegged CEOs' salaries to those of their lowest-paid workers: for those firms that pay their CEOs more than 44 times what they pay their lowest employee, there are punitive taxes. Turning away from taxes, the town of Preston in the UK is a hopeful example of proactive use of local authority expenditure to procure from local firms and support local employment.

The burden of taxation could be shifted away from income altogether and refocused on luxury products, wealth and unearned income and use of the natural commons (such as pollution or land use; see below for further discussion of the commons). Land value taxation could restrain rent-seeking* and curb long-term inter-generational inequalities. As will be discussed shortly, more people having a share in their workplaces would mean that wealth created by the private sector was automatically shared more widely. John Stuart Mill seems to have envisaged such equalisation, writing of a society in which there are 'no enormous fortunes, except what were earned and accumulated during a single lifetime'.[22]

As societies recognise that they have Arrived and making ourselves at home becomes the economy's goal and purpose, we would expect lower inequality and a more inclusive economy. So a country that has Arrived and has put its energy into making itself at home will no longer need to redistribute income to such a great degree, because its citizens will have a stake in the country's wealth. At the heart of it would be a move from an economy that aims for growth to a wellbeing economy that aims for sustainable, shared prosperity – a profound shift. This economic system would reward more fairly in the first place: the market would be able to do more of the heavy lifting, rather than relying on so much redistributive intervention by

* Rent-seeking occurs when business interests seek to profit by controlling something that people need, rather than producing something new. That might include land hoarding, access to finance, or it could be licensing or copyright rules that grant special privileges.

the state. Although redistribution will remain important for the foreseeable future, can we imagine an economy so inclusive that redistribution is obsolete?

Sharing better as part of making ourselves at home has a very literal dimension, too. We know that around the world resources and power within households are too often profoundly skewed – with women and girls receiving less, but often carrying out more work (particularly unpaid care work). Unequal division of labour at home, coupled with work in the formal sector, has been described as a 'double shift'. This means that simply rearranging paid work and even improving its quality is not sufficient to eradicate gender subordination. Sharing better within the home, in the literal sense, is an urgent aspect of making ourselves at home in the metaphorical sense. As feminists often observe: 'the personal is political'.

Shared work, better work

> *Common sense tells us that life is better when it is balanced, with time to look after ourselves and our loved ones, and to experience life in the round, as well as to strive and achieve.*
> *—Anna Thomas, Campaign for a Shorter Working Week*[23]

Alongside space holidays and kitchen robots, one of the key elements of the future that people once imagined is more leisure time. We used to expect progress to deliver more time as well as more stuff. A *Time* magazine article from 1966 foresaw a society in which only 10% of people would be working and the others would be engaged in the 'wholesome degeneracy' of endless free time. As more and more tasks became automated, work would be more or less optional, hours would be short and retirement would come early.[24] Or so it was hoped.

This hasn't happened, and that aspect of progress has almost vanished from the popular imagination. Many seem to have made their peace with long hours, the inevitability of alarm clocks and the commute to work. But plenty of others are giving more of their time to employers than they'd like, and they long to have more time at their disposal. Unpaid overtime is commonplace: according to the TUC, the British economy benefits from £31.2 billion in free work* from over 5 million British workers.[25] The Modern Families Study found that almost three-quarters of parents catch up on work at home in the evenings and at weekends (41% doing so often or all the time) and two-thirds cannot leave work on time every day.[26] This is not the desired state of affairs: a study of 15 countries shows that 41% of people would prefer to spend less time at work (and earn less), as compared to 10% who wanted to spend more time at work and earn more.[27]

In the broader definition of poverty that Arrival and making ourselves at home allows (see page 84 above), lack of time is a key 'unfreedom' that we could be addressing. More time away from work is a way to share the economic progress achieved thus far that does not entail increased income and consumption. For those looking for ways to raise wellbeing without raising consumption or income, more free time is a promising prospect.

But, alongside long work hours for some (often out of necessity, due to low pay), for others, unemployment is a major cause of misery and social dislocation, on a par with bereavement or separation in its impact on people's wellbeing. Yet others find themselves caught in a cycle between low pay and no pay, and often need to work multiple jobs to make ends meet.

What's more, the current economic model relies on a huge amount of unpaid work, disproportionately done by women and usually in the areas of housekeeping, child rearing and care. Britain's ONS has been calculating the value of this work for several years. In 2014 it was worth £38,162 per household – nationally, over £1 trillion, equivalent to 56% of GDP. In other words, over half of all work in Britain's economy goes unpaid.[28] This percentage is growing, and it may increase further with the rising care needs of an ageing population. Being unvalued by definition, unpaid care work is hard to quantify, but one estimate put the contribution of carers in the UK at £119 billion a year.[29] Globally, women do 2.5 times more

* The TUC highlights this with Work Your Proper Hours Day. It is held on 'the day when the average person who does unpaid overtime finishes the unpaid days they do every day, and starts earning for themselves'. In 2018 it fell on February 23rd.

unpaid work than men, but that can rise to 10 times more in lower-income countries where the women tend to carry out household tasks such as fetching water or gathering firewood.[30] If this work had to be paid for, it would add $12 trillion to the global economy, according to the McKinsey Global Institute.[31]

So, societies find themselves in a bizarre situation where some have too much work, some not enough and much of the work done in the economy is not only undervalued but also unrewarded in the financial sense. This is a tangle that cannot be resolved by the usual growth-orientated economic decision making, since unpaid work does not contribute to GDP and is therefore invisible in GDP terms; and also because GDP is neutral towards the quality and distribution of work.

With the qualitative lens that 'making ourselves at home' enables, we may be able to address some of these blind spots. Making ourselves at home requires new mechanisms to ensure secure and sufficient livelihoods. In addition to a fairer allocation of capital and other endowments mentioned in the previous section, recasting the nature and distribution of work, positioning it as a social good for those who can work rather than an obligation that is dependent on the whim of distant employers, is key to an economy that makes itself at home. Work would be distributed better across the labour force (not least so that those without enough work have more) and unpaid labour would be properly valued (for example, via a 'participants' income'). Making ourselves at home ensures that work is rewarded, whether or not it takes place in the context of formal employment.

A rebalancing of work along these lines could reduce the misery of unemployment and trim long working hours at the same time. Labour could be wrestled back from commodification and dignity would be restored to work. A sense of control over time would return, while allowing more time for relationships and the things that people value most. Reduced time at work would free up time so that people could build and sustain social networks and take part in their communities. It would release the time and mental energy to live more creatively and deliberately, enabling people to break free of the 'treadmill' of everyday life. After all, nature tells us that no ecosystem can be 100% productive all of the time: we all need fallow time.

This would have wellbeing benefits, because while income is positional (as seen above), free time is not; if society reduced working hours, this could generate higher wellbeing.[32] Ecuador's *National Plan for Good Living* includes the call to 'work less so we all work; let's consume less so we all consume ... let us not only question income distribution, but the form of production and the products consumed'.[33]

If greater quality of life, more vibrant communities and better gender equality were not enough, there might also be environmental benefits from sharing work better: longer working hours are associated with a higher national ecological footprint.* In fact, reduced working hours has been found to be more important than the shift from manufacturing to services in terms of reducing the environmental degradation of an economy.[34] This is because shorter working weeks can encourage and enable slower and more sustainable ways of living, releasing time for people to adopt greener lifestyles. More time can enable lower resource use and slower, less resource-intensive activities.[35] With an extra hour in the day freed up by shorter working hours, more might cycle to work, for example, or hang the washing on a line rather than run the dryer. This would be good news for climate change: studies have found that a shorter working week leads to lower GHG emissions. One study estimated that if working hours were reduced by 0.5% a year over the rest of the 21st century, one quarter to a half of global warming would be eliminated.[36] That may be optimistic, but Schor (with her colleagues Knight and Rosa) show that between 1970 and 2007 those high-income OECD countries which 'reduced their hours of work also reduced pollution and ecological degradation'. This was attributable to a combination of reduced consumption outright and a shift in what sort of consumption was undertaken.[37] Hope for similar progress in future thus depends on how we shift consumption from things to low-impact experiences – as discussed below.

* Controlling for income, GDP, productivity and other variables.

In this vein, in a service-based economy with a new emphasis on making ourselves at home, carte blanche pursuit of labour productivity makes little sense. Nobody wants unnecessary or meaningless work, so clearly efficiency and productivity are good things. But when economic value is the only thing that matters, productivity can be taken too far, and the 'human value' of work is lost. Maximising labour productivity can undermine service provision, degrade the worker, lead to job losses and be captured by the already-wealthy. In those circumstances, where productivity *is* appropriate, what if we turned down the opportunity of using productivity improvements to produce more? What if we used them instead to produce better-quality products, to increase quality of life via leisure and to share the available work more fairly? Making ourselves at home in this way might entail building the economy on its 'foundational' components instead of those sectors celebrated for their 'growth potential'. The 'foundational economy', according to one description, is 'very large, mostly unglamorous, rather heterogeneous, and distributed across the country. It is an economy that meets every day needs by providing taken-for-granted services and goods such as care, telecommunications or food'.[38] In the UK this sector employs 40% of the workforce (in both private and public organisations) in socially useful jobs that underpin economies and societies but that are also functions that do not necessarily lend themselves to being measured through the lens of productivity in a narrow sense.

From an environmental perspective, pursuit of *resource* productivity would also be a more sensible goal, given that it would reduce environmental impact per unit of output and so makes finite resources go further.

Perhaps the question to ask is this: what would society look like if we valued the business of taking care of everyday life more than the apparently more alluring business of making money? If greater productivity didn't always have to mean more output, it would enable a reallocation of the efficiency gains offered by some technologies, increase motivation to shorten the working week and enable more people to remain in employment. This would value purposeful work as a good thing in itself, rather than simply as a means to increase incomes and expenditure, and as a cost that employers should seek to minimise. The sort of work that is conducive to the task of making ourselves at home would be cultivated – via a new materialism (see below) that requires higher labour input.[39] Imagine, for instance, how the relatively labour-intensive craft, care and repair economy, supported by a high-technology base, could offer resource-light, income-earning activities in roles that enhance that scope to make ourselves at home: entertainers, for example, or preventative health workers, artisan manufacturers and organic farmers.

Warnings abound of jobs being made obsolete by technological change, with more optimistic analysis suggesting that new jobs created will offset those lost (see discussion below). Neither scenario is inevitable – it depends on decisions made by society, politicians and businesses. Making ourselves at home will involve harnessing technology to deliver high-quality goods and services with fewer of the earth's resources. In some cases that will involve less labour too, and will thus require new ways of sharing wealth and work.[40] Making ourselves at home would embrace the possibility that technological advances make some jobs obsolete: the dirty, the painful and the relentlessly monotonous.

Enabling a move away from life being marketised ad nauseam and labour commodified, and towards a scenario in which work is meaningful but not all-encompassing, chimes with the work of feminist economists. They suggest a move away from an economics focusing 'simply on the market economy with growth and accumulation as its primary goals' and towards one centred on the 'provisioning of human needs and human well being'.[41] This vision embraces the call from feminist socialist Hilary Wainwright: 'equality, we want better than that'. After all, what is equality worth in an exploitative system? So Wainwright goes further and demands new structures of society and the economy, including changes in not just the distribution of work, but also the nature of work.[42]

Let us turn to the nature of work itself – an area often neglected and passed over as a 'black box' inside enterprises, beyond the reach of much external understanding or influence. Pursuit of alternative fulfilment (discussed below) as part of making ourselves at home opens up heightened expectations of work. We need to do better at creating work that delivers fulfilment through non-material value – 'work as participation' as Tim Jackson imagines it.[43] People who say that their work is meaningful and serves some social or communal good report better psychological adjustment, greater wellbeing, greater job satisfaction and tend to practise more active citizenship. Experts such as Steger suggest that meaningful work encompasses dimensions such as skill variety, the opportunity to complete an entire task, pride, engagement, sense of calling, challenge and good pay.[44] Meaningful work will deliver a sense of authenticity, self-efficacy, self-esteem, purpose and belonging. Offering the capacity to plan and balance work with other family and community responsibilities is a crucial component of job quality.[45] Many improvements can be attained by some imaginative reorganisation of tasks, job descriptions, decision making, hierarchies, team design and lines of autonomy.

Of course, there will always be jobs that people do not enjoy, so it is important that they be sufficiently rewarded in other ways. Think of the example of hospital cleaners. The work includes antisocial hours, unpleasant tasks and the risk of infection, with little more than the minimum wage to take home. Unsurprisingly, job satisfaction is low and turnover is high. But take hospital cleaners away, and health services would cease to function. Conscientious and committed cleaners are vital in preventing hospital-acquired infections or the dreaded 'superbugs'. One study estimated that if we add up the direct and indirect services a cleaner provides, their work creates £10 of social value for every £1 they are paid.[46] That's a rough estimate of something that's hard to measure, but it's clear that the pay scale for hospital cleaners doesn't reflect the importance of the work. There's no real way to make this kind of work enjoyable, but we can make sure it's fairly paid – not least because if it were paid better, cleaners could work part time and have a richer life outside of work. In addition, there is scope to ensure that people have a say in working practices, so that they can take pride in what they do, and rotate tasks to deliver balance, skill variety and professional development. Workers could be given a stake in the company they work for and a share in any profits. And supporting re-training and life-long learning helps to ensure that nobody needs to feel trapped in an undesirable job.

When work is endured, this often reflects the way it is organised. Making ourselves at home would demand greater attention to how work is designed to be more meaningful. Historically, one avenue for improving work and conditions has been collective bargaining and unions. These remain vital in many working situations, although the rise of outsourcing and contracting has made it much harder for workers to organise as they did before. However, unions are often most important when workers and owners are seen to be in opposition to each other, where they have competing agendas – management wants to reduce labour costs to improve profits, while workers want higher wages and better conditions and benefits. In an economy that is working towards inclusion and cooperation, this tension is less relevant. If workers have a stake as employee-owners (discussed below), there is no 'us and them'. Just as a post-Arrival economy would eventually move beyond redistribution, so the old divide of workers versus managers would gradually close.

Other forms of work can also be more meaningful. For example, recent research has found that working for a not-for-profit organisation brings with it satisfaction, enjoyment of daily activities and feeling useful (a benefit that the researchers went so far as to monetise and estimate that it equates to the equivalent of £22,000 per year[47]). And, as we shall explore later, not-for-profit organisations may be more mainstream in the future, which could deliver more rewarding work. More people working in organisations in which they have a stake and a sense of ownership might go some way to addressing those depressing statistics on employee engagement. As discussed earlier, a sense of purpose, and of being part of something larger than yourself, are important elements of wellbeing and are key goals of an economy making itself at home.

The joys and sorrows of automation

It's all very well talking about good jobs, but, if we listen to the technologists, there's an inbound wave of automation that is about to revolutionise the idea of work altogether. For some, this is a huge advantage, unleashing a boom in creativity and entrepreneurship. Others foresee mass job losses and potential crisis.

There are historical eras that we can learn from when it comes to technological change. The mechanisation of agriculture made millions of jobs obsolete on farms, but in the process opened up all kinds of new opportunities. It was massively disruptive for the generations that lived through it, but today's manufacturing and services jobs would be impossible without mechanised farming freeing up labour. While new technologies do destroy jobs, they can also create jobs on the other side of the turmoil. There are a couple of reasons why it may not work out quite so neatly this time, but first, what can we expect from a new wave of automation?

Digitisation has already changed the way we communicate, entertain ourselves, socialise and much else besides. As digital technology continues to develop it will come to threaten a growing number of tasks that currently make up a lot of people's jobs. Factory robots made workers on many production lines obsolete, and this time it seems to be the turn of many office workers. Accounts, clerical and legal work, journalism or design, all of these can be done by computers – or rather, the basic and routine bits of those jobs, the work that usually occupies new recruits and younger staff members. There won't be any robot judges in court any time soon, but experts predict far fewer legal secretaries.[48] A computer can't devise and write a weekend supplement feature article, but Associated Press, Forbes and others already automate market updates and corporate reporting.[49] This creates a few well-paid jobs running the computers and developing the algorithms that automate these processes, but removes opportunities at the entry level. Someone is spared an unrewarding and repetitive task, and that's a good thing. But those who were depending on that sort of work as a stepping-stone into a law firm or a journalism career are going to have to find another route.

The most obvious outcome of job losses is unemployment, a labour glut or what Ryan Avent more charitably describes as 'a wealth of humans'.[50] When there is oversupply (and no mitigating policies), prices fall. The new wave of automation will lower the economic value of a lot of human labour, and reduce wages. A knock-on effect of people earning less is that they are likely to spend less, which will lower demand – and falling demand is kryptonite to a growth-dependent economy.

As we have learned from the earliest years of industry, the bulk of financial benefits of automation go to the owners of the machines (usually capitalist investors). Machines will be more productive, the wage bill will be lower, they won't unionise and demand better conditions and they don't need lunch breaks. Take the car-sharing app Uber, for example. Its success is based on a network of car owners operating as taxi drivers. Established taxi firms are less happy about it, and unions and the drivers themselves complain of exploitation. But in matching customers with a nearby driver, Uber has enabled tens of thousands of people to earn a little on the side or, for those fortunate enough to earn a sufficient income via driving for Uber, possibly even to create a job for themselves. However, Uber is also now investing in driverless cars. If it gets its way, a fleet of Uber-operated autonomous vehicles could eventually replace that network of freelancers (and, some argue, public transport systems too, leaving city travellers reliant on Uber). Drivers' earnings will evaporate, any semblance of jobs as drivers will disappear and the tranche of income that once went to drivers will *all* come home to Uber and its investors instead.[51] The rest of us might get cheaper taxi fares, and appreciate the fewer cars on the roads and lower carbon emissions.[52] But the clear winners and losers from the expansion of Uber's presence provide an illustration of how 'technological progress does not automatically benefit everyone in society equally', as Brynjolfsson and McAfee warn.[53] Some types of automation could exacerbate inequality and economic exclusion, and eventually lead to stagnation.

To prevent that, social innovation is just as necessary as technological innovation. First, society needs to help individuals whose livelihoods have been disrupted by technological changes to retrain and move into new opportunities (supporting the person as opposed to protecting the position, if you like).

Second, social innovation can help to determine and decide which technologies are pursued and adopted and which are deemed antithetical to making ourselves at home. The world of medicine gives us a potential model: in England, the National

Institute for Health and Clinical Care Excellence (NICE) is a proactive mechanism by which new developments in medicine are assessed for their societal benefit prior to their adoption by the public health system. The NICE process sees a group of independent academics take evidence and views from patients' groups, from healthcare professionals and from manufacturers regarding the medicine (or medical technology) in question. After considering the arguments, costs and likely benefits, this group submits a report regarding the clinical and cost-effectiveness of the technology to NICE for its approval. Another model is the global group of experts in technology, law, social science, business and government that has drawn up guidelines to ensure that technology design complies with five criteria to be 'Ethically Aligned'. These criteria are protecting human rights; prioritising and employing established metrics for measuring wellbeing; ensuring that the designers and operators of new technologies are accountable; making processes transparent; and minimising the risks of misuse.[54] Both approaches show how new developments can be scrutinised in advance, and we do not need to be hostages to 'progress'.

Progressive taxation is another option: it can be used to capture some of the benefits of automation and redistribute them, perhaps through a participant's income. Better still, we should look at how to give more people a stake in the companies generating the wealth, so that nobody is left behind in the first place.

As Ryan Avent writes: 'the worst inequities of industrial history were never a necessary accompaniment to the march towards greater prosperity'.[55] There is no need to repeat the mistakes of the past. If society is on the cusp of another technological leap forward, let's make sure that our common successes are better shared this time.

Fulfilment beyond consumption

> *A cultural revolution ... would challenge the advertisers' monopoly on the depiction of prosperity and the good life. It would make the stuff that is now seriously messing up the planet – more cars, more planes, more roads, more throwaway*

> *commodities – look ugly because of the energy it squanders and the environmental damage.—Kate Soper*[56]

In order for people to be able to relax in a post-Arrival world, consumer economies need to find ways to slow the rush towards more consumption, while still meeting citizens' needs and aspirations. Fortunately, a survey of six major economies found that nearly two-thirds of people would agree, believing that as a society we need to consume a lot less in order to improve the environment for future generations.[57] There is an apparent recognition that economies need to move beyond consumerism, and look instead at how to make ourselves at home. In 2014 the advertising company Havas surveyed over 10,000 people across 29 countries. It found that 70% worried that over-consumption was threatening the planet and harming societies, with half saying that they could happily live without most of the possessions they currently have.[58] Futurist James Wallman sums up the possibilities in his hopes for 'happier, healthier people, leading more sustainable lives on a less damaged planet'.[59] The sequence in which Wallman identifies cause and effect is a hint of a useful confluence: a life designed around relationships, experiences and participation will almost invariably be one of less consumption. Hence sustainability emerges here as a side-effect of pro-social activities.

Embracing a more holistic conception of a good life allows one to find a more comfortable and more sustainable spot on the 'fulfilment curve', as depicted by Dominguez and Robin's 1992 graph (see Figure 4) – a spot that is also gentler on the planet. Once that 'sweet spot' is attained, any further wealth brings only marginal benefits and serves merely as a 'way of keeping score' – but the tally is unrelated to fundamental needs. Fulfilment would be better achieved not through consumption, but through supporting one's community, sustaining relationships and experiencing life.

Being part of a community is good for mental health and general wellbeing.[60] The feeling that one belongs and is appreciated gives people security and confidence (and here we see another dimension to the idea of making ourselves at home). There is a range of evidence for this – not least recent findings that the risk that children will experience mental health problems can be curtailed by participation in collective activities.[61]

Figure 4: Fulfilment curve 2. Beyond luxury, further fulfilment lies in participation, rather than more consumption.

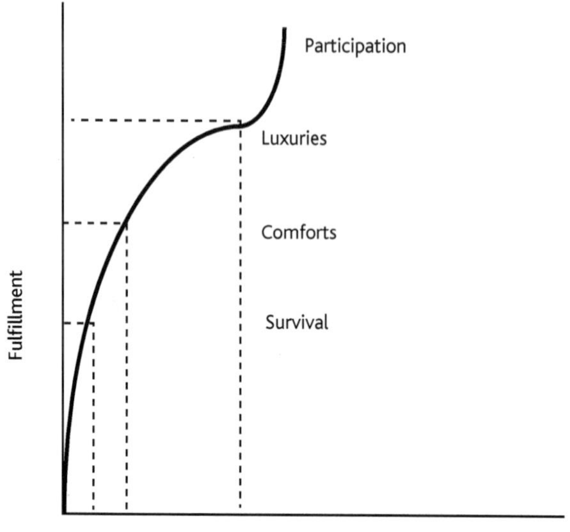

Source: Financial Integrity, reproduced with permission

Thinking about it more literally, home is the place where people can kick off those work shoes and put their feet up. Constructed images can be dropped and people can be themselves. There are elements of this in the more inclusive, more supportive society that we imagine on the other side of Arrival – an economy where we can be at home, where identity is secure and people belong and are valued for themselves and not for their financial contribution.

Back in the 19th century John Stuart Mill was already picturing what this would look like, describing his vision (which hinged on greater levels of equality) in which people enjoyed 'sufficient leisure, both physical and mental, from mechanical details, to cultivate freely the graces of life'.[62] Activities and experiences – the 'graces of life' as Mill wrote, bring better rewards than the short-lived and disappointing 'sugar highs' of passive consumption.[63] Focusing on experiences is also more rewarding: *doing* rather than owning, and engaging in collective activities rather than the often solitary and fruitless consumption. For example, arts or sport can feed the soul and allow self-expression, and often take place in a social context. Being active, giving, supporting others and being social all lead to increases in life satisfaction and life expectancy, and it seems that people recognise this. For example, 80% of British people say that sharing makes them happier.[64] Moreover, being in a place that is special to you activates areas of the brain linked to positive responses – more so than even sentimental objects such as a wedding ring.[65] Such places bring feelings of belonging and self-identity.

If making ourselves at home facilitates a move from materialism to 'experientialism', people may come to pursue conspicuous consumption of experiences rather than things. Traditionally it has been easier to display status by consumption, but a nascent shift to experientialism, evident in some places, would suggest that leisure could become a significant form of status display – telling the world what we do and get up to, rather than showing each other what we own. Social media is now making that possible. Think of shared photos of craft projects or home baking, a sunset to appreciate or a barbecue with friends – all activities inherent in making ourselves at home, and many of them free. Obviously the idea of status display can be problematic, breeding anxiety, envy or feelings of inadequacy that consumerism is able to prey upon. Nevertheless, it is a very human instinct, and some forms of status display are healthier than others. As Wallman argues, if we swapped a consumerism based on possessions for a consumerism based on experiences, that would still be an improvement. There are exceptions such as travel, but generally speaking, experiences are less resource intensive.[66] Experiences become memories rather than possessions and clutter, and they are more likely to involve others. Since experiences can be shared in ways that possessions can't, experientialism does not tend towards individualism in the same way that acquisitive consumption does. In particular, while income is positional (and hence breeds status-seeking pursuit of more income), leisure time is not – people are not anxious if others gain more leisure at the same time as them.[67] Moreover, such community-based activities, development of authentic relationships and experiences that enhance people's connection to the natural world not only reduce the environmental impact of consumerism, but can counter individualism and isolation, and have proven health benefits.[68]

Dematerialisation in pursuit of fulfilment would not only see an increased consumption of services, but would likely be associated with an improvement in the quality and appreciation of the things that are consumed.[69] Hence they would last longer and be shared more often, with a consequent benefit in terms of reduced resource use. The circular economy (discussed below) also offers opportunities for everyday people to participate in the making, repair and repurposing of products – with social and potential employment benefits. A little ironically then, breaking free of consumerism means caring more, not less, about the things we own. Fast consumerism encourages disposability: it needs things to be consumed, used up and thrown away, rather than owned and cared for, and mended. On the other hand, 'repair connects people and devices, creating bonds that transcend consumption', says the Self Repair Manifesto, put together by enthusiasts on iFixit.com.[70] For these repairers, you never really own something if you cannot care for it and fix it if it breaks – it remains a disposable item. If people value and appreciate what they own, they are more likely to look after it. Previous generations would have known how to do this, and community groups like the Restart Project are encouraging those skills again.[71] They run repair drop-ins in cafes and public places where people can bring broken things and learn how to fix them themselves with a little expert help. Across the UK, similar facilities are being set up. Edinburgh Remakery is one such project. It runs a shop selling refurbished goods, and trains people in repair.[72] This social enterprise teaches skills to repair computers and furniture, but also builds a community: in 2016 its 10 employees, 20 volunteers and freelance tutors taught repair skills to over 1,000 people.[73]

This is, in many ways, a very active consumerism in which greater emphasis is placed on reuse, recycling and repurposing.[74] Many people want products that last longer – one study found that listing the expected lifetime of a product, alongside other sales information, made people much more likely to buy it.[75] Making ourselves at home in the world would mean a move from possessions to experiences, but it would also mean surrounding ourselves with things that we value and cherish and are prepared to care for – a deeper materialism, if you will.

Stewardship of the commons

> *Commoning means being aware that plenty of the resources we need to make a living, don't belong to individuals, [and] need to be shared with other people. And that need to share resources requires skills: of sharing; of knowing how to do it; of managing shared resources. So commoning is about taking responsibility for common stewardship of resources, processes, spaces and the time we have available together.* —*Silke Helfrich*[76]

As societies that have Arrived shift towards making themselves at home in the world, they will need to learn to protect and cherish the world better. To qualify as truly sustainable, our vision of a society that has Arrived *and* made itself at home would need to fulfil Herman Daly's three criteria for sustainable development:[77]

1. Exploit renewable resources no faster than they can be regenerated.
2. Deplete non-renewable resources no faster than alternatives can be developed.
3. Emit wastes no faster than they can be assimilated by ecosystems.

When renovating a house and making it a home, people might take the opportunity to modernise it and add efficiency measures that increase comfort and save energy, water and money. Similarly, Arrival and making ourselves at home with the economic wealth we collectively have means harnessing innovation and creativity to provide better stewardship of the earth's resources and waste-sinks than is evident to date. Fortunately, there are examples from which to take direction.

There is an established precedent for the shared ownership approach in Alaska and Norway and in the 80 or so other countries or states that have sovereign wealth funds. Believing the state's minerals to be the property of all, Alaska established the Alaska Permanent Fund in 1976. The fund pays out an annual dividend to every citizen as their share of the collective wealth. In 2015 this was $2,072.[78] Rather than pay a dividend, Norway has opted to save surplus revenue from its oil and gas for the future. Oil reserves are a single-use resource, so putting the income into a fund spreads that wealth across the generations, putting it to long-term use. Norway's sovereign wealth fund grows by $1 billion a week, and by 2014 had accumulated enough to make everyone in the country a krone millionaire (albeit on paper).[79]

If this can be done with fossil fuels, it ought to be possible to do it with other strategic resources held in common. Doing so could prove to be a useful tool in tackling climate change. For example, the atmosphere would be declared to be the common property of all, whether nationally or internationally, and companies or individuals would be charged for emitting GHG and other pollutants. Those polluting the most would pay the most. These funds could then be distributed as a dividend, saved or used to fund decarbonisation. This would end the market-failure aspect of climate change, where CO2 is an externality (Lord Stern described climate change as 'the greatest market failure the world has seen'[80]). Creating a common fund would give everyone a stake in our common wealth. Mineral extraction, logging and fishing rights and aquifer withdrawals could be dealt with in a similar way, with the revenues distributed through government spending or, to better demonstrate common ownership, via a dividend payment direct to citizens. Authorities would need to be alert to the perverse incentives that might be created (such as encouraging further exploitation in order to pay a higher dividend), but this could be managed through quotas, resource-use caps and so on.

The US state of Vermont has perhaps come closest to this. In 2010 the Senate proposed a Common Asset Trust that would declare the state's atmosphere, aquifers and various other natural resources to be the common property of all citizens. Vermont's resources would be held in trust for present and future generations, and managed for their benefit. Entities using those assets would need to pay for the privilege, with the funds becoming available for public welfare and payments to citizens. While the idea is radical in comparison to most current policy and practice, the proposing senators pointed out that it is not a new idea: in ancient Rome, citizens could be confident that the air, running water, the sea and the seashore were 'by natural law common to all'.[81]

If every citizen were receiving a dividend from the collective wealth, those payments would support people on lower incomes without depending on the mechanisms of taxation and redistribution. This would mesh with the concept of a basic income, and reward unpaid work and improve gender inequalities. Moving from growing the economy to widening participation in this way is what making ourselves at home is all about.

Speaking of participation, the first (and only) woman to win a Nobel prize for economics, Elinor Ostrom (2009), was in fact a political scientist. Her work* on collective management of common pool resources showed how the commons could be managed for the benefit of the community, by the community. Ostrom's research put a dent into one of the bastions of neoclassical economics, the tragedy of the commons.** Instead, she found that 'under the right circumstances, people are willing to accept additional efforts and costs. It all depends on trust in the fact that others will also act'.[82] Ostrom distilled eight criteria for cooperation, including group identity and knowledge of the rights and obligations of group membership; evenly distributed effort and reward; shared decision making and rule setting; monitoring of cooperation; and fair and rapid resolution of conflicts.[83]

* Her fieldwork, conducted together with her husband, Vincent, included visits to communal landholders in Ethiopia, rubber tappers in the Amazon and fishers in the Philippines.

** 'The tragedy of the commons' was a paper by Garrett Hardin, published in 1968. He argued that since everyone would act in their own interests, over-exploitation was inevitable and common ownership was always doomed to failure.

The commons approach helps to steward natural resources for the good of humanity, but there is a growing recognition that we may need to go further than that in protecting the natural world. In Ecuador a new constitution has incorporated 'a commitment to the rights of nature', and a national strategy explicitly 'sets aside the restricted visions of development exclusively based on economic growth' in favour of a more holistic vision of 'good living'.[84] Bolivia has gone further still, drawing up a Bill of Rights for the 'Madre Tierra' (Mother Earth). These include the right to life, diversity, clean air and water, and the right for natural cycles to proceed without human interruption. How they will be applied remains to be seen, but the idea that humanity has no inherent rights over the earth is a deeply counter-cultural proposal in international politics.[85] New Zealand has also bestowed rights on nature – giving a river a version of legal personhood. At the request of local Maori communities, the Whanganui River now has a legal right to its own integrity. Two appointed river guardians will speak for its rights and interests.[86] Around the same time as New Zealand was acting, the Uttarakhand High Court in India declared that the Ganga and Yamuna rivers are 'living human entities'.[87] Further, in 2016 the International Criminal Court changed its prioritisation of the sorts of cases that the Court will pursue and prosecute, and it will now consider illegal exploitation of natural resources, cases of environmental destruction and 'land grabbing'. In other words, people can be prosecuted for destroying the environment in which we live and on which we depend.[88]

An ecologically sensitive approach would ask more of agricultural practices. History has plenty of examples of civilisations that exhausted the soil, leading to food crises and then political collapse – the Sumerian city states, the Mayans, the fall of Rome.[89] We should farm as if we wish to stay. That means practising agricultural techniques that protect the soil from erosion, using water wisely and reducing the impact of farming on biodiversity. Some of the relevant techniques are ancient or traditional, such as agroecology, crop rotation, using cover crops or strip farming. Others are sophisticated and rely on new technology, such as precision farming.* With a growing global population and declining soil fertility, all of these tools and more besides will have to be deployed.

John Stuart Mill reminded us to cultivate the earth's gifts in a more sustainable way, writing that there is little

> satisfaction in contemplating the world with nothing left ... every flowery waste or natural pasture ploughed up, all quadrupeds or birds which are not domesticated for man's use exterminated as his rivals for food, every hedgerow or superfluous tree rooted out, and scarcely a place left where a wild shrub or flower could grow without being eradicated as a weed in the name of improved agriculture.[90]

A circular and collaborative economy

> *Within a circular economy, from the outset, you design the economy to be regenerative.* —*Ellen MacArthur*[91]

Along with preserving nature for future generations – and for itself – making ourselves at home implies better use of existing resources. Rather than increasing extraction from the natural world, more efficient use of resources already in circulation would reduce the pressure on natural systems, and halt the encroachment of extractive industries. This would reduce the need for more and more materials extracted from the natural world: what is already dug up and cut down would be reused. All energy would be renewable.** As globalisation and rising consumption have pushed up demand for metals in particular, increased competition for resources has triggered the beginnings of a fundamental shift: a move from a linear model of production to a circular economy.

* Precision farming is an advanced farm management technique that uses satellite imagery and ground-based sensors to optimise water and fertiliser use.

** Numerous studies have shown this to be possible. For a recent example see: Jacobsen et al (2017).

According to the linear business model, it is generally considered cheaper (under current prices) to discard rather than recycle or reuse.[92] Materials are collected, made into products, worn out and thrown away. This was always inefficient, driving resource depletion on the one side and accumulating mountains of waste on the other. The rising consumption of a growing global population means that it's now expensive too, and it doesn't take much to see that things could be different and that there are major business opportunities in intercepting and redirecting waste. One fifth of all waste electronics is reusable or easily repairable, for example.[93] Some materials can be recovered, and a growing number of companies are developing ways to take back products at the end of their useful life. There is already a transition underway from the take-make-waste linear business model to 'lease the resource, make the product, recover the resource and then remake it'.[94] By maintaining control of goods at the end of their life, companies can retrieve materials and reuse them, keeping costs down. Leasing also encourages repair and regular servicing, prolonging the life of equipment and incentivising modular and sustainable design.

This new approach to materials has created all kinds of opportunities for niche businesses. A company called Portal Power deconstructs rather than demolishes buildings, recycling the steel. Rubies in the Rubble buys up unsold market produce that would otherwise be thrown away and makes jams and chutneys. Freitag creates colourful courier bags from retired truck tarpaulins and old car seat belts. Not everything can be reused or recycled. For some forms of waste, such as packaging, the focus of circular-economy interventions has been to make them biodegradable. This turns them into a feedstock for nature, or at least makes them benign if they accidentally end up in the wild.

Finding treasure in the trash is one aspect of the circular economy, but in the longer term much waste can be designed out entirely. Approximately 80% of a product's environmental impact is 'locked in' at design stage, with the long-term legacy of a product becoming apparent only later, once it's too late.[95] Manufacturers need to shift how they design and make products, using principles of responsible research and development to account for the whole life cycle of a product beforehand.[96]

London's Agency of Design demonstrated this with a project showing three basic ways to make a sustainable product: it can be made as durable as possible; it can be built in a modular fashion so that it can easily be repaired; or it can be designed to be dismantled at the end of its life and either recycled or composted.[97] More and more products that meet these criteria are reaching the market as the waste of planned obsolescence becomes uneconomic in a world of expensive materials. Of course this trend would be accelerated if charges for the use of the commons, and especially for polluting it, were introduced and if firms had to account for their environmental impact.

In a circular economy, all waste becomes a feedstock for something else, making zero waste a realistic possibility – as reflected in policies like Scotland's Zero Waste Plan.[98] There are major financial opportunities here too. A report from the World Economic Forum, the Ellen MacArthur Foundation and McKinsey Circularity suggests that implementing the circular economy in manufacturing offers potential cost savings of US$630 billion a year for the EU.[99] Globally, the savings in materials alone could add up to US$700 billion a year, a recurring gain equivalent to just over 1% of global GDP.[100]

Alongside the new approach to materials in a circular economy, there are new collaborative approaches to doing business and alternative modes of 'selling' – even a move away from how ownership is understood. For example, in the past a music fan would have collected records or CDs, and a film fan would have shelves of videos or DVDs. Today, people with the resources to do so can buy *access* to music through online subscription services, or watch a film through one of dozens of on-demand streaming services. Consumers do not 'own' these cultural products, but pay to access them. While admittedly the servers needed to provide these services are energy hungry, the move towards digital services can play a part in reducing resource needs. It also presents a compelling example of the growing acceptance that people do not need to own something in order to enjoy it. Quite the opposite. Streaming services offer instant access to a vast catalogue of music and film that no one individual could ever hope to afford if they had to buy them all.

Within this rise of new modes of delivery, other companies are experimenting with leasing. If a company retains ownership throughout, it can maintain control over the full life cycle of the product, including maintenance and recovery for remanufacturing. Buyers are no longer 'consumers' of a product, but 'users', paying for a service rather than owning the thing itself. For example, Philips now provides light ('lux') as a service to Schiphol Airport and others, rather than selling light bulbs.[101] Car clubs have proved more convenient than car ownership in some urban areas. This model can be used for power tools, farming equipment, household appliances, kids' toys or office furniture and carpets, all helping to reduce the need for new materials. It's also good for customers, as they get access to a higher-quality product than they would be able to afford if buying it outright for themselves.

This kind of sharing is a mechanism to 'sweat' under-utilised assets, and as resource constraints become more acute it can be expected that the leasing of equipment will grow. One of the leading thinkers in this field, Michel Bauwens of the Peer 2 Peer Foundation, calls for an economy guided by the principle of 'If it is light, share globally, if it is heavy, share locally'.[102] The contrasting examples of music and power tools illustrate what Bauwens has in mind.

Many of the new business approaches enable ordinary people to participate. They may let out a spare room on AirBnB, for example, or let others park on their driveway for a small fee. In particular, trends suggest that some people are shedding ownership ambitions in favour of renting access or 'fractional ownership' (this is often referred to as the 'sharing economy'). In many instances this will be genuinely collaborative – for example, a number of families sharing a car or working together on a shared garden. For some people shared ownership has proved to be a useful way to earn money from their spare resources. Others deem it more pernicious, creating the potential for exploitation and vulnerability – and tax evasion as authorities scramble to bring these new models into the tax system. Criticism of some online sharing platforms is growing, under the pejorative term 'platform capitalism'.[103] These new approaches can also harm existing businesses, and represent encroachment of the market into new spheres of life. So, there's a need to be alert to potential negative effects, and to do what we can to encourage fair and sustainable business. This is what we examine next.

New business practices

> *For the first time in modern history we have the structures, capabilities and impetus to evolve to [a not-for-profit] world, in which the best energies and drivers of good business are harnessed for our collective flourishing.—Donnie Maclurcan and Jennifer Hinton*[104]

A grown-up economy would see a wider purpose for business, one that encompasses more objectives than simply short-term profit for shareholders. Puvan Selvanathan, of the UN Global Compact, issued a blunt indictment of the potential for social and environmental goals to be pursued concurrently with pursuit of profit when he resigned from the UN Working Group on Business and Human Rights. His resignation letter stated: 'The loudest calls within a company for higher goals are distant echoes if even a whisper for profit exists'.[105] The critiques of corporate social responsibility (CSR) as too-often meddling around the edges of a business's behaviour are well documented, and there is a growing, if quieter, concern about the incompatibilities between the demands of investors and those of communities.[106] Allen White from the Tellus Institute similarly warns about the focus on short-term profits:

> Transience breeds carelessness towards future generations and drives the tendency to seek short-term gains at the expense of long-term stewardship of physical and human resources ...[107]

There have been efforts to more closely align the role of business and investment with that of social need or environmental necessity – from CSR activities to impact investing. But are they enough?

The fact that investors and communities are generally separate entities speaks volumes: rarely are so-called impact investors *part* of the community they purportedly seek to benefit. This means that, despite often very sincere intentions to 'give something back' or 'do well while doing good', for every dollar that is returned to an investor, that is $1 that is not going to a community or to a worker or to a supplier. It instead adds to the wealth of those who are fortunate enough to have enough to invest, their often laudable intentions notwithstanding. Injections of external investment have a role in spreading risk and funding larger expenditures, so we would not want to rule it out completely. But ideally, narrowing the separation between the owners of financial capital in a firm and other stakeholders would increase circular financial flows and reduce extractive ones. Imagine if the investors were the workers themselves or members of the wider community, or even suppliers. Business models such as employee ownership, community cooperatives and financing via community shares present potential vehicles to reconcile a firm's need for injections of financial capital at certain junctures with the economic vitality of its stakeholders.

In an economy making itself at home, businesses would pursue a social purpose, with profitability serving as the *means* to that end, rather than the other way around. Far from demonisng profit and commercial viability, profit making and commercial activities become a vital vehicle rather than the destination. Such repurposing can be positioned as a reclaiming of corporations as creations of public law, rather than remote entities over which society seems to have little control. Tim Jackson captures it nicely with his call for investment to be about commitment, rather than opportunity, and the notion of enterprise as service.[108]

In 2012 financial commentator John Kay carried out a review of short-termism in business for the UK government. He concluded that stock markets encourage short-termist behaviour, since shareholders of companies are not sufficiently engaged in the direction of the companies that they own shares in.[109] We can see how this has worsened in recent years: by '2008 in all the main OECD stock exchanges the average holding period was less than a year and in the case of the USA had fallen from 5 years in the 1980s to around 5 months by 2011'.[110] Providing stock options as remuneration, fees per transaction and other incentive structures encourages churn (on the UK's stock exchange, hedge funds and high-frequency traders accounted for 72% of market turnover in 2012[111]) and drives a short-term focus in the stock market, undermining attention to long-term considerations.[112]

The primacy of shareholder profit is a mantra that legitimises all kinds of corner-cutting on environmental or social welfare along the way (not least because such concerns are beyond the limited cost-benefit imagination of many corporate decision makers). The need for shareholder profits is also a major impetus for expansion – companies need to grow if they are going to compete in these terms. And yet, delivering shareholder value became the overriding priority of many corporations not so much because of legal mandates, but because of mindsets and internal incentives that flow from the nature of the economic model.[113]

Fortunately, there are signs of resistance. As CEO of Unilever, Paul Polman stopped issuing full reports every quarter: 'We needed to remove the temptation to work only toward the next set of numbers,' he explains. The logic being that 'in the longer term, the company's true performance would be reflected in the share price anyway' and that longer-term shareholders would gravitate to the company.[114] Unilever's expectation that shareholders with a longer-term outlook would come to dominate their share base illustrates the way that ownership of firms needs to reflect wider time frames. This could happen via different classifications of shares, with committed shareholders receiving favour in dividends or bonus shares and greater voting rights. Google and Facebook, for example, have two-tier voting rights to allow their respective founders to retain control of the company when it listed and to avoid the negative effects of shareholder pressure on research and development and on long-term planning.[115] Polman's observation suggests that incentive and reporting structures can and must be altered. Alongside reducing quarterly reporting, ending the practice of providing stock options as remuneration (which creates incentives for managers to maximise short-term shareholder value) would help to shift priorities.[116] Other compensation mechanisms, promotion criteria and directives also need to align employee incentives with the longer-term goals of the company. Those in turn need to be aligned with social and sustainable goals if an economy is to be configured for making itself at home. This means ensuring that the firm's objectives and internal architecture are aligned with those of society so that more people can benefit. This is more than meekly assuming 'what is good for GM is good for America', but saying that companies can be designed in diverse ways that prioritise what is good for people and planet. With that in mind, making the stock market work better for long-term flourishing is the tip of the iceberg. There are other alternative business practices that could be much more transformative.

In recent decades an array of pro-social business forms have emerged: cooperatives and worker-owned companies; neighbourhood corporations; new ways of banking and investing; regional and decentralised energy; benefit corporations; community interest companies; and social enterprises. Together they constitute what political economist Gar Alperovitz calls a 'pluralist commonwealth'.[117]

In particular, broadening the ownership of assets – democratising wealth and widening the economic franchise – has multiple benefits. Cooperatives, for example, measure performance not by profit but by the benefits that flow to members.[118] They are distinguished from other modes of business by, inter alia, an internationally accepted framework of values and principles.[119] Their beneficial impact can be seen in developed and developing countries, where cooperatives create more equality and social cohesion and have been proactive in addressing crises of climate change, biodiversity loss and the need for transition to a green economy.[120] Worker- or employee-owned firms generate positive externalities in the form of happier, healthier employees and surrounding communities.[121] A major shift towards more inclusive business models would improve both accountability to communities and environmental performance. Employee ownership has been found to combine high levels of economic performance with progressive forms of accountability and governance.[122] Such decision-making mechanisms can improve work satisfaction and wellbeing, with more people feeling in control of their work – after all, it is the workers who employ the capital, rather than vice versa. Importantly, more people holding a financial stake could reduce inequality. Jones and

Kalmi found greater inequality where there are lower numbers of cooperatively owned workplaces (but they do recognise that inequality itself might undermine the formation of cooperatives in the first place, due to lower levels of trust, concentration of capital and so on).[123]

This range of benefits to the wider community has been borne out by David Erdal's research in northern Italy. He investigated the circumstances and quality of life in a town hosting a high proportion of cooperative businesses and compared this to a nearby town with considerably fewer cooperatives. He found that in the town without cooperatives people were more alienated from institutions and education was delivered in an 'authoritative manner'. In contrast, in the cooperative town, education was valued as a lifelong process and institutions were seen as being 'on our side'. People had others to call on in times of trouble, larger social networks and a pro-social attitude (for example, giving blood at more than twice the rate of the non-cooperative town, and a higher proportion of people voting in elections).[124] Erdal also reports that people in the cooperative town lived longer, with fewer incidences of cardiovascular disease evident amongst men. He asked the UK retailer John Lewis, also a cooperative, about life expectancy, and its actuaries reported that John Lewis retirees live longer than retirees from non-employee-owned competitors. Erdal found similar emerging evidence from Mondragon in Spain (although this could be due to lower unemployment in the region).[125] Other research supports the benefits that Bologna and other 'cooperative towns' in the Emilia Romana area of Italy enjoy: compared to other parts of Italy, Bologna reportedly has the highest female participation in the labour force, some of the greatest wealth and high wages, and high levels of political activism.[126] Inevitably, cooperatives rely on a sense of community, but they clearly are part of engendering this solidarity and compassion. Done well, we can envisage another virtuous circle.

Profitability is not the same thing as commercial viability, and it is entirely possible to run a major enterprise without making profit the central concern. Such business models can keep costs down in ways that shareholder companies cannot, because no surpluses are required for profit taking. Mutual finance institutions and credit unions are able to lend at better rates than commercial banks, for example, and community energy projects are free to deliver energy at cost price, without a premium for profit. When the last of the coal mines in Wales were being closed in the 1990s, the management and 238 miners at Tower Colliery used their redundancy pay to buy the mine and keep it open. With a focus on providing employment rather than solely turning a profit, the mine was able to remain in production until its coal seams were exhausted in 2008.[127] The carbon cost of the project is nothing to celebrate, but the project demonstrates how removing the profit imperative can in some cases make an activity financially viable in ways that it would not be if a surplus had to be generated for distribution to outsiders. Such business models with broader missions may thus be able to maintain production on the margins where a profit-orientated company could not, hence maintaining jobs and provision of the good or service (for example, a general store in a remote village).

Cooperatives and the like also tend to benefit from the ingenuity and energy of engaged workers.[128] For example, as workers glean innovations, observations and insights in the course of their work, they are then able to communicate them via participatory engagement mechanisms.[129] Altman's research, for example, found that the cooperative mentality, loyalty, sense of solidarity and trust – combined with the fact that they benefit directly from the firms' success – imbues members with an incentive to work harder and smarter and thus reduces the agency problems faced by hierarchical firms.[130] In addition, as Zamagni explains, creativity and tacit knowledge is generated when employees feel involved in their firm.[131] David Erdal, who transferred his family owned business to the employees, observed something similar. He notes that when the

> employees understood that their environment was changing from a top-down hierarchy, in which they were mere servants, to a shared enterprise in which they were full partners, they changed overnight from being hostile, suspicious and repressed to being energetic, positive and ready to take initiative.[132]

This surely contributes to cooperatives showing considerable resilience to economic crisis.[133] The Employee Ownership Index (measured since 1992) tracks listed companies with at least three per cent of employee ownership (an admittedly modest democratisation of ownership) and finds that the index out-performed the Financial Times Stock Exchange Index in 10 of the 13 years to 2015, with an average margin of 13.9% each year.[134]

Governments can take measures to encourage employee ownership or cooperatives and other pro-social business models, especially to create a level playing field, or even preferential procurement and proactive business advice services. For example, in Oakland in the US, the local council has passed an ordinance to promote worker cooperatives. A dedicated help centre provides resources and information for 'individuals seeking to launch new worker cooperatives or convert conventional businesses to worker ownership'.[135] Soon after, places such as Berkeley, New York and Austin followed suit. Such proactive support is not confined to US localities: Scotland has a rich programme of support for cooperatives,[136] and in countries such as India and Italy the promotion of cooperatives is mandated by the constitution. Ultimately, however, alternative businesses still have to operate within the markets and succeed or fail on their own merits. Firms structured along these lines are not necessarily uncompetitive in a 'horizontal' sense of one firm vis-à-vis another. Firms will still vie with each other on the basis of value and quality to attract custom. But there will be less harmful 'vertical' competition, where corporations compete against their suppliers or employees, or even relevant governments.[137]

That makes cooperatives relatively uncontroversial, and yet they may still prove to be transformative. As Maclurcan and Hinton argue, not-for-profit businesses have an inherent competitive advantage in not having to distribute profits and being able to offer lower prices.[138] Back in 1853 John Stuart Mill seemingly predicted the role of pro-social businesses in making ourselves at home:

> The form of association, however, which if mankind continues to improve, must be expected

> to predominate, is not that which can exist between a capitalist as chief, and the work-people without a voice in management, but the association of the labourers themselves on terms of equality, collectively owning the capital with which they carry on their operations, and working under managers elected and removable by themselves.[139]

The unfolding narrative of Arrival and making ourselves at home would include greater participation of people in the businesses that matter to them and serve them, as opposed to businesses being governed by pursuit of a narrow growth agenda. Some of this would make us financially better off, making us richer in the conventional sense. Some of it would build qualitative development, a society enjoying a richer sense of participation, cohesion and meaning.

Participatory democracy

> *Politics is the art of living together.* —*Anon*[140]

To create the inclusive society that comes with making ourselves at home, decision-making processes that reflect long-term collective interest need to be developed. That's not something that will emerge overnight. It will require processes and structures that can cultivate participation, and that encourage thoughtful and magnanimous deliberation. That kind of decision making is easier from a position of security and confidence. There are many examples, including some very recent ones, of people making political decisions out of fear or anxiety.

Current democratic thought points to two broad conceptions of the democratic process – representative, on the one hand, and direct and participatory, on the other.[141] In the former, individuals are elected to represent the interests of many citizens, and in the latter citizens are more immediately involved in decisions about public affairs. Representative democracy adds together citizen preferences in the selection of representatives. The mechanisms to do this vary, but political equality is proclaimed in the sense that all eligible citizens are given votes with equal weight. It is purportedly accountable because politicians will advocate for those policies that people desire and hence vote for.*[142]

Representation is necessary in modern times because no individual can ever be present when all those decisions that affect their lives are taken. It remains a crucial component of a wider democratic system, but it has several shortcomings. For example, most citizens are only occasional participants in democracy – called upon periodically to elect a representative, but otherwise unconsulted. That creates a relatively passive and disengaged citizenry.[143] If all that is required of us is to tick a box once every five years, it's little wonder that only 13% of Britons feel that they 'have some influence over decision-making nationally'.[144] Another problem is that many global processes are beyond the responsive and management capacity of representative democracy.[145]

These inadequacies seem to be reflected in the association of formal 'politics' with insincerity and manipulation.[146] When politicians are no longer trusted and change seems impossible within the usual structures of government, citizens may look outside of the political elite and find hope in so-called 'anti-establishment' candidates. In recent years the world has seen how these sentiments have fuelled support for populist leaders. Yet, whether they are activists from the Left such as Syriza in Greece, an insurgent candidate from the Right such as Donald Trump, or differentiated by religion like Egypt's short-lived Freedom and Justice Party, the actual business of government often proves harder than citizens might expect. There are established power networks, external pressures, budgetary constraints and profound inertia to overcome. The entrenched objectives of growth and international economic competitiveness often take precedence over the demands and needs of some citizens, as government alternatives are curtailed by the perceived risk of repelling investors.[147]

* Interestingly, representative government used to be referred to as a republic, with the word 'democracy' reserved specifically for direct government by the people. America's founding fathers, for example, were very clear that they were founding a republic, not a democracy.

Thus, government action often does not reflect the values or wishes of wider society, let alone those of minorities. Skewed influence over political processes reinforces social and economic inequalities and deepens political inequality, and vice versa. For example, Korten complains that the influence of 'corporate money' in the political process has rendered democracy meaningless and a 'charade'.[148] Many wouldn't go that far, but poverty, homelessness, increasing inequality and social discontent illustrate that current configurations of democracy do not address the interests of certain groups. Women's priorities, for example, may be overlooked in a toxic cocktail of patriarchy and capitalism. Minority voices are under-represented. In an ageing population, the young may be regularly out-voted by the 'silver power' of older generations.[149] The frustrations of the resulting democratic deficit are manifesting in sometimes terrifying ways.

Fortunately, new modes of political participation are arising to supplement, if not replace, formal mechanisms of politics.[150] None of them is perfect. There is the risk that deliberative and participatory processes will replicate existing societal inequalities and barriers to engagement, such as competing pressures for people's time, rendering the processes themselves unrepresentative. Attention therefore needs to be paid to these risks, and action taken to mitigate them and care taken to ensure that women's voices are heard in all political, social and personal spaces – including the home. Nevertheless, active citizenship and a vibrant and responsive democracy are exactly the kind of qualitative progress that comes with making ourselves at home.

One element of a richer governance ecosystem for making ourselves at home would be deliberative decision making: a process through which preferences are formed and changed via communication and sharing of information respectfully.* It uses public reasoning to reach informed and considered positions, and involves people encountering differing perspectives and having to explain their opinions and views in ways that make sense to others.[151]

* The quality of the process matters, and key criteria for authentic deliberation include transparency and openness of debate; inclusivity and accessibility of the process; clear communication and provision of information.

As always, locus matters. In 1987 the sociologist Daniel Bell warned that the 'nation-state is becoming too small for the big problems of life, and too big for the small problems of life'[152] – and it is often dwarfed by the might of large multinational companies. An implication is that sites of potential democratisation should vary according to the decision in question. Making ourselves at home thus encompasses diversity, decentralisation and subsidiarity, and the plethora of nodes of power that Elinor Ostrom would refer to as 'polycentric governance'.

A promising example is participatory budgeting (PB). Pioneered in the Brazilian city of Porto Alegre in 1989, this is a bottom-up process through which community members collectively decide how tax money is deployed. Invariably, community members identify a set of priorities and individuals and experts then shape them into proposals that are then voted on by the community.[153] In Porto Alegre this involved 20% of the city's annual budget; in other localities it still pertains in much smaller proportions. As with any policy, PB is no silver bullet and runs the same risks of capture and exclusion as other democratic processes, but evidence from around the world shows that 'participatory budgeting produces more equitable public spending, better quality of life for individuals, increased satisfaction, and greater government transparency'.[154]

Globally: convergence, climate justice and leap-frogging

> *[W]e have better things to do than to follow that same Europe … so long as we are not obsessed by the desire to catch up … But let us be clear: what matters is to stop talking about output, and intensification … No, we do not want to catch up with anyone.* —*Frantz Fanon*[155]

Planetary boundaries and the constraints of a very real carbon budget point to a stark reality: if poor countries are going to have room – in an ecological and hence literal sense – to develop in a finite environmental space, the richest consumers (be they individuals, institutions or entire economies) need to make room by cutting their ecological footprint.[156] The current pursuit of further growth for its own sake for wealthy nations threatens to reduce the amount of ecological space available to low-income countries. Citing slavery, colonialism, unfair terms of trade, debt repayment, tax dodging, the impact of climate change and so on, Jason Hickel has set out in stark detail the devastating journey that the global North took to get to its current economic size.[157]

And it is those very places where so much harm was wrought (and others like them) where good quality growth is now most needed to help people escape poverty. In terms of the threshold we pointed to earlier, even countries officially designated as having 'medium human development' have a GDP per capita of just $5,875. That's far from a point at which more wealth will bring decreasing returns to wellbeing. With an average of $2,830 per capita, low-income countries are further away again.[158] The current system locks in inequality: calls to 'grow the pie' as a solution to poverty ignore the reality that the oven is only so big. A conversation about better sharing of the pie is more necessary than ever, within and between countries.

Under the current development model, it is assumed that all countries will continue to grow, rich and poor alike. Less-developed countries grow faster, so there is a degree of 'catching up' or convergence, as seen in the emerging middle classes of China. The trouble with this view is that current 'Western' levels and types of quantitative consumption cannot be universalised without destroying the environment on which we depend. High-consuming countries such as the US or the UK use more materials and natural resources than can be sourced within their own borders, and rely on the surplus of others to maintain their levels of consumption.[159] With a few notable exceptions such as Russia and Canada, which have huge land masses, most developed countries are 'ecological debtors' that need the biocapacity of others, either in imports or in land leasing.[160]

Just as it is impossible for every country to run a trade surplus, it is impossible for every country to consume more than it can produce within its own borders. Somewhere else has to be able to take up the slack. Developed countries have been able to tap developing countries for raw materials for decades, centuries even. But as those countries develop and their own consumption begins to rise, they will need more of their own resources for domestic use. The most high-profile example of this is the number of countries that are using more of their own oil rather than exporting it, including Iran and Venezuela. Jonathan Porritt warns that

> the poor [sic] are not going to escape from poverty by a process of 'catch-up development' ... Today's rich nations got rich primarily because of the easy availability of fossil fuels and because of 'empty' continents into which they could expand and commandeer plentiful raw materials. This 'bonfire of resources' simply cannot be repeated.[161]

Two things need to happen, then, if development is to continue equitably, and if everyone is to get to a point where they can make themselves at home.

- First, the world's industrialised economies need to recognise that they have Arrived and reduce their emissions and material footprints, through technological change and via the cultural and systemic shift that we have been describing. This ecological resizing would free up resources for others in a 'contraction and convergence' dynamic.
- Second, developing countries need to 'leap-frog' the energy and resource-intensive journeys of the global North. Instead, so-called developing countries need to create renewable and circular economy systems first time around, cutting to the chase and taking an easier, cleaner path to arriving at a safe and prosperous 'home'.

The first of these means that as industrialised countries Arrive they will shift their priorities accordingly: we would expect a move away from systems geared to GDP and profit making, and towards something more akin to the steady-state economy. This would be a state where material throughput would have levelled off and energy use would be renewable. There are some bright minds modelling this scenario, including professors Peter Victor and Tim Jackson. Their *Green Economy Macro-Model and Accounts* – short name GEMMA – models how a society not pursuing economic growth will operate. It takes into account economic and financial stability, employment and social outcomes in a context of environmental and resource limits. This builds on Victor's model of a low-growth economy Canada from 2005 to 2035,[162] which revealed that the following adjustments are key, many of which echo Herman Daly's criteria for a steady-state economy:

- new measures of progress and success for the country and for individuals – especially better measures of success than growth in GDP;
- stabilising consumption, including controls on advertising;
- fewer status goods and more public goods (shared provision rather than individual ownership);
- zero net investment and a shift to green infrastructure and public goods;
- limiting material and energy flows;
- pricing carbon via ecological fiscal reform (including taxing the carbon content of energy) and shifting taxes from labour to those who damage the environment;
- harvesting renewable resources at a pace less than the regeneration rate and depleting non-renewables at a pace less than the creation of renewable substitutes;
- ensuring that waste emissions do not exceed assimilative capacity;
- stabilising government spending;
- balanced trade;
- stabilising population – and so stabilising and retraining the labour force;
- reducing work time and increasing leisure time;
- slower technological change, with an emphasis on preventive technology and social and ecological benefit;
- more jobs in human services (which have less scope for productivity than jobs that make things);
- reducing poverty via redistribution and in-kind support (social wage), including a strengthened social safety net and guaranteed basic income so that people are less reliant on income from employment;

- localising and strengthening local economies;
- ensuring that education is for life, not just for work.

In Victor's model, with these changes in place and a steady state, unemployment fell to 4% after a few decades; poverty fell and most people's living standards rose; and GHG emissions decreased to below Kyoto levels.* Compared to the current set-up, Victor's model demonstrates that economic growth is not needed to deliver social and environmental objectives, and that wellbeing can be realised via public goods and via services rather than commodities. It would not be a static and unchanging state of being, but development would move from growth to improvement. There would still be innovation, entrepreneurship and ambition. It's also important to note that it is *material* throughput that levels off and reaches equilibrium – GDP growth may or may not continue (see Box 6.1). The point is that GDP as the ultimate goal would be eclipsed by the higher priority of improving quality of life. In other words, a society making itself at home.

While this new approach emerges in the world's mature economies, the second element of transition would occur in parallel: so-called developing nations would identify alternative paths to development, learning from and avoiding the destructive developmental path taken by the global North. Countries that have not yet Arrived can choose to build sustainable economies right now, otherwise they will face the same costly, difficult and disruptive policy reversals and retrofit in the future that the rich world now needs to adopt. One obvious example of this is transport infrastructure, which can be low carbon and publicly oriented as soon as possible, rather than having to unpick and dismantle the petrol-centred transport systems of GDP-rich countries.

The process of Arrival in the global context also means support for developing countries to 'leap-frog' over extractive paths that, as demonstrated above, have proved to be so harmful on so many levels. Generous transfer of technology and finance

* The Kyoto Protocol was an international agreement that set climate change emissions targets for developed countries.

from GDP-rich countries to those that have not yet Arrived is a key part of this. Calls for such transfers are not just pragmatic – there are also moral arguments around historical emissions and the funding of future climate adaptation. The notion of 'climate justice' is an important aspect of making ourselves at home – ensuring that individually and collectively everyone has the ability to prepare for, respond to and recover from climate change impacts and that those who have done the most damage bear a proportionate burden.

The process of leap-frogging need not be confined to conversations and policies about low-carbon transitions. Instead, leap-frogging will be based on learning from the cautionary tale of GDP-rich countries' development journey, and opting for a gentler path. Some of this will involve the translation and amplification of certain ideas and concepts emerging from countries and communities seeking to make themselves at home, wherever they are in the world and in Arrival terms. It will involve creating an economy centred on pro-social business models such as cooperatives, community interest companies and social enterprises rather than one where extractive, shareholder-orientated businesses dominate. Another example would be designing a tax system that taxes social and environmental 'bads' and focuses on wealth and assets, rather than income taxes. And of course, the opportunities abound to avoid the carbon-heavy mode of development by, for example, skipping straight to renewable, decentralised energy systems rather than retrofitting the fossil-fuel-heavy generators, and to design products and buildings so that they benefit from nature's intrinsic design principles rather than running counter to them. Circular economies can be built first time around. Private motoring and urban sprawl could be skipped in favour of walkable cities and rapid-transit systems.

Crucially though, leap-frogging is not just about importing the supposed wisdom of the newly enlightened global North: many aspects of making ourselves at home are already in existence in the global South. We mention just a few of these in the next chapter – not least by way of highlighting that the GDP-rich world has much to learn from apparently 'less developed' countries. More broadly, many of the key components of an economy that makes itself at home are already key components of economies in so-called developing countries – they are just ignored or downplayed by GDP. What Karel Williams terms the 'foundational economy', for example, makes up an important part of the livelihoods of people in the global South. As do localised economies, the practice of being 'prosumers',[163] the importance of the care economy and the value of ecosystem services.[164] Where resources are scarce, they are more valuable, and many low-income countries reuse and recycle on a scale that richer countries cannot match. Repair skills have not been lost, and there are often established communities of craftspeople. Prioritising these areas for the benefit they bestow on communities, rather than seeking them to add to the GDP ledger, would enable countries to flourish and hasten the process of creating an economy that makes itself at home.

EIGHT

Arrival and making ourselves at home in the real world

We may now be well into the prehistory … [of] longer-term changes much greater than many have contemplated.—*Gar Alperovitz*[1]

As the previous chapter has shown, shifting the purpose of the economy to making ourselves at home entails a wide variety of social, economic and political changes. Arrival and making ourselves at home are not new or unique ideas so much as a fresh articulation of something that many others have foreseen and hoped for. There are dimensions to explore across economics, politics and culture. We seek to offer an honest appraisal of where we find ourselves in the 21st century and what development might mean from here on. As we saw with Keynes and his hopes for his generation's grandchildren, today's generation in GDP-rich countries are the inheritors of progress.

Fortunately, we do not need to dream up theoretical examples of what life after Arrival might mean: we are surrounded by real-world examples – from all corners of the globe.[2] On their own, these do not represent systemic transformation – indeed, many remain isolated examples in economies still straining for more GDP growth. We share them here as a selection of initiatives that offer proof of the possibility of a different approach – and proof that development can be more than a linear process of following religiously in the footsteps of GDP-rich countries. We see them as confirmation of Cohen's observation that new forms and practices 'will emerge out of prevailing forms in a halting and partial manner'.[3] It is these new ways of living and working that we shall explore next, beginning with a global tour of more holistic concepts of 'development'. In Chapter Ten we explore how they can be connected and amplified to yield wider systemic change.

Development as creating the conditions of wellbeing

The world is not short of inspiration for ways of living, working and organising that put aside the goal of more and embrace community and nature instead. From South Africa we could draw on the notion of *ubuntu* ('I am because you are'), a useful counter to the West's individualism; or *gotong-royong* in Indonesia, a deeply held spirit of mutual aid and consensus. There are many others, some traditional, some emerging. They represent the breadth of language, globally, that we have for articulating different visions of the good society. As we look at moving from quantitative to qualitative development, we find that there are deep cultural roots to draw on, all around the world.

Take *Nuka*, for example, a word used by Native Alaskans that means a vast living system. It informs social structures based on reconnecting people with the entirety of their community: prioritising physical, mental, emotional and spiritual wellness. It has inspired healthcare practice based on restoring people's connection to the living systems that support human lives and recognising that health is a product of quality relationships. For example, Alaska's Southcentral Foundation in Anchorage used Nuka to design its approach to caring for patients and the broader community that it serves. In fact, as part of the Nuka approach, the word 'patient' is not used at all – they are 'customer-owners' of the healthcare trust, and treated as equals. The focus is on shared responsibility for health, with people empowered to make decisions about their own health rather than being told what to do by experts. The community is directly involved in the running of the organisation, rather than delegating this role to local government.[4]

Another example is *Buen Vivir*. Buen Vivir – 'living well' – arises from recognition that the individual is always and inherently part of the community. For the indigenous and Andean peoples in South America, Buen Vivir 'expresses a sense of satisfaction in achieving the ideal of the community ... through the equilibrium between the living forces of Nature and the commonwealth of the community'. It carries a strong sense that 'wellbeing is enjoyed collectively'.[5] According to Buen Vivir, wellbeing is not tied to material or individual fulfilment; instead it includes the collective and spiritual dimension as well as an ecological dimension.[6] Crucially, Buen Vivir is an implicit challenge to the classical view of development as perpetual economic growth – a linear and anthropocentric process.[7] The implication of embracing a notion like Buen Vivir for development is that

> development becomes a qualitative process that must consider the community's enjoyment of material goods and subjective, spiritual and intellectual realisation ... The accumulation of wealth and industrialisation are no longer the aims of a desirable future, but are means for attaining the harmonious co-existence between communities, and between communities with nature.[8]

Some countries are taking steps to apply Buen Vivir to their understanding of the purpose of the economy and the role of government. In Bolivia the 2006 National Development Plan highlights the need for Vivir Bien. President Evo Morales contrasted the notion of 'vivir bien' with the more competitive, more acquisitive 'vivir mejor'. The terms lose something in translation from Spanish, but his contrast between 'living well' and 'living better' is still powerful:

> Indigenous people propose to the world the idea of 'living well'. Capitalism is based on 'living better'. The differences are clear: living better is at the expense of the other, exploiting the other. It plunders natural resources, violates nature, and privatises basic services. Instead, living well is living in solidarity, equality, harmony. It is complementary and reciprocal.[9]

Similarly, Ecuador's 2009 Constitution refers frequently to the importance of 'vivir bien' and contains provisions to ensure the people's 'rights' to 'living well'. For example, in Article 3 the text talks of the duty of the state to eliminate poverty and promote sustainable development and the equitable redistribution of resources and wealth in order to enable people to obtain a good way of living.[10] It also enshrines the rights of nature, making Ecuador the first country in the world to do so. This arguably goes beyond Bolivia's statement of principles.[11] In 2013 Freddy Ehlers, a former television star and tourism minister, was named Ecuador's State Secretary of 'buen vivir' and brought in a range of policies from labelling foods based on their health values to meditation classes for school children. Ecuador's current National Plan recognises that development must be broader than growth alone. What must be measured, therefore, is not GDP but the living standards of people, through indicators related to the satisfaction of their human needs.[12]

There is also a recognition of what feminist economists have been telling us for decades. Ecuador's *National Plan for Good Living 2009–2013* describes Good Living as paying attention to the care economy and aiming for

> productive processes which are compatible with the reproductive processes. A development model based on Good Living must pursue a fairer social caring regime, in which caring active ties are better valued, distributed, and expressly directed at eradicating the sexual division of labour, for a more equitable provision and reception of care.[13]

There are inevitably contradictions and gaps in its implementation thus far, but an economy based on these priorities would be doing a great job of making itself at home.

Other examples abound: E.F. Schumacher (the economist and statistician who wrote the 1973 book *Small Is Beautiful: A Study of Economics as if People Mattered*) famously called his overall approach 'Buddhist Economics', and the same principles that he espoused can be seen in Thailand's concept of the Sufficiency Economy. Championed by King Rama IX, this philosophy prizes moderation, resilience and wise living – 'a Thai version of sustainable development' as the Thai sustainability professor Sirimas Hengrasmee describes it.[14]

Two candidates for Arrival

Perhaps the country best positioned to embrace Arrival is Japan. Much has been made of the fact that its GDP stopped growing in the mid-nineties. To mainstream economists this was a lamentable failure, but it ably demonstrates the redundancy of growth in an advanced economy. Despite years of low economic growth, Japan scores highly on almost every measure of progress that one could mention. Analysis of its performance against the SDGs shows that Japan is a leader in sustainable consumption and production patterns (Goal 12) and the Japanese have least cause to fear homicide in all of the OECD countries. It is famously first in healthy life expectancy.[15] The UN's Human Development Index places Japan 20th out of 165 countries surveyed.[16] David Pilling, who spent many years in Japan as the Asia correspondent for the *Financial Times*, captures how obsolete GDP becomes in such a context. 'Our habit of seeing everything through the prism of economic growth is distorting our view of what is important', he writes in his book *The Growth Delusion*. 'Japan's supposed misery – as measured by nominal GDP – really didn't feel like misery at all'.[17]

Prime Minister Shinzo Abe came to power with promises of a return to growth, but other voices in Japan recognise the privileged position that the country finds itself in. 'People in Japan are beginning to wonder whether those "two lost decades" really were "lost" after all,' writes Norihiro Kato: 'Perhaps those years were simply the prelude to a new post-growth era'.[18] For Kato, the end of growth is positive. Japan can show us what it looks like to 'outgrow growth' and reach economic 'maturity'.[19] Economist Noriko Hama echoes this language of growing up, and sees the transition as aspirational. She writes:

> It could be all about affluence, maturity, refinement, and leisureliness. It could be all about being grown up. A grown up economy that is the envy of the rest

> of the world. That could be Japan's position in today's scheme of things.[20]

However, Japan seems reluctant to embrace the probability that it has sufficient material and wealth, that it has Arrived. Instead of making itself at home, it goes on searching for more, at great cost. Indications abound that the fruits of Japan's growth are being lost in the pursuit of yet more: work–life balance is infamously lacking,[21] despite high youth unemployment and possible scope for redistributing available work. Wages have been falling for millennials, and many expect to be worse off than their parents, so there is real work to do on inter-generational justice.[22] Japan has yet to share resources and power sufficiently, as is evident in relatively high rates of rural poverty and poor performance on gender equality and the empowerment of women and girls.[23] These are not the problems of a country that does not have enough. They are the problems of a country that is struggling to share its wealth across generations, regions and minorities.

Yet Japan does seem well placed to embrace its low growth, and would find itself more comfortable and at home if it did. As Dolan reports, common causes of stress in Japan relate to income, personal finances, work and study, as opposed to health, relationships or caring for family members. Dolan points to the strong negative correlation between the amount of personal time people have and their level of stress and suggests that 'less time spent generating GDP would improve the quality of life'.[24] Perhaps Japan bears out Latouche's observation that 'just as there is nothing worse than a work-based society in which there is no work, there is nothing worse than a growth-based society in which growth does not materialise'.[25]

One reason to be cautious about Japan as an example is that it still has a very high rate of consumption. If Arrival were taken to mean a levelling-off of growth at Japan's material footprint, the earth's resources would be exhausted long before poverty was eliminated. But there's no reason to believe that every country needs to reach that level of consumption. It's possible to deliver high welfare with much lower consumption. For evidence of that, we can look to Costa Rica.

Costa Rica is one of the best 'over-performers' on the Social Progress Index, in that it delivers social progress better than other economies that have greater levels of GDP per capita. It was also in the headlines in 2016 after scoring highest in the Happy Planet Index, for the third time in a row. By combining wellbeing, life expectancy and inequality measures with ecological footprint data, the Happy Planet Index aims to identify countries that deliver the best quality of life with the lowest impact on the earth.[26] Costa Rica does this best, delivering longer life expectancy and higher wellbeing than the US, but with just one third of the ecological footprint. The latter is kept low by 99% renewable energy, and the country is a notable example of successful reforestation. Costa Rica is one of the few countries to have a made a commitment to carbon neutrality, a promise that has survived changes in government and enjoys broad support.

Costa Rica has distinctive social policies alongside environmental ones. It is in the globally unique position of having no armed forces, having disbanded them in 1948 and redirected funding to education and healthcare instead. Its national healthcare system offers the same quality of care as the US, but at a fraction of the price. Some 40,000 American health tourists visit every year for surgery or dental work.[27] Costa Rica is committed to open government, and Freedom House gives the country its highest score for political freedom and civil rights.[28] In presidential elections in early 2018, Costa Rica continued the tradition of The Children's Vote. While this is only symbolic, children are given their own ballot papers and encouraged to vote alongside their parents, involving them in debate and the democratic process from an early age.[29]

Costa Rica has its problems too, and it would be wrong to portray it as an ideal state. Like most governments, it is committed to economic growth, and its environmental impact may rise in future. The point of the two examples of Costa Rica and Japan is to show what is possible. Japan demonstrates the redundancy of growth in a mature economy and proves that it is possible to run a world-leading economy for over two decades without substantial growth. In Costa Rica we see an example of high wellbeing with low resource and energy consumption.

Taking the two examples together, the idea of Arrival does not seem so far fetched.

Stakeholder decision making

Around the world there are examples of innovative, inclusive and deliberative decision-making projects and processes. Here we mention just a few of them – not because they are perfect, but because they show what can be realised.

It is estimated that there are over 3,000 participatory budgeting (PB) programmes around the world.[30] At the smaller end of the scale is Luton Borough Council's 'Your Say Your Way' scheme, which disperses £133,000 in small grants for community projects (among them are a community gardening project that Jeremy has been involved in).[31] At the larger end of the array of PB projects, Paris dispersed €100 million in 2016. In the same year Portugal launched Orçamento Participativo Portugal – making it the first county to initiate the PB process across an entire nation, with people voting at ATM machines.

In the UK, Udecide is a PB programme in Newcastle-upon-Tyne, allocating sums of money ranging from $15,000 to £2.5 million. It has been running since 2006 and has been developing in breadth and sophistication each year.[32] In an interview in 2014, programme manager Ali Lamb said that 'the benefits that we always cite in Newcastle are about increasing confidence and trust between public service providers and citizens ... much better working relationships emerge between service providers and citizens; there is more trust and accountability'.[33] Decisions are often voted on after pitches from various projects, including short films on DVDs so that people can consider the options at their leisure. A bus visits various communities so that people can vote where they live. Initiatives funded via Udecide include environmental projects, activities for disabled children, community artworks and educational trips.[34]

New York City began an initiative in 2011, thought to be the largest PB project in the US. Four council members enabled residents of their respective wards to determine how an element of their capital discretionary fund would be spent. They have since been joined in this by another 24 council members, and the budget shared out according to PB comes to more than $30 million of public money.[35] The process encompasses neighbourhood assemblies where community members learn about PB, discuss their area's needs, brainstorm project ideas and select budget delegates. Meetings then turn the initial ideas into proposals, supported by council members, staff and other experts. Project expos and a community vote complete the sequence and allocate the funds. The process is careful and deliberative, involving a year-long series of public meetings to ensure that people have time and resources to take considered decisions. Projects have included park revitalisation, library improvements, sports fields, urban greening, school air conditioning, security fittings and a school music studio. An assessment of the demographics of those participating found that nearly 60% identified as people of colour and one in five used a ballot in a language other than English.[36]

As well as budgeting, some cities are experimenting with Participatory Municipal Planning, where residents can help to design public spaces, street layouts or redevelopments. Aspects of urban planning are a science that cannot be delegated to lay people, but neither should it left to the professionals to dictate the geography of a space that they don't have to live in. 'Since citizens are in the neighbourhood every day, they can provide observations and knowledge that are different from the experts, thereby enriching the analysis,' says the Montreal Urban Ecology Centre, which runs planning projects in Quebec, Canada.[37]

The more transformative the development, the more important it is to involve local people and include them in planning. Some of the most pioneering work on this front has been undertaken in slum communities. After all, as East African architect Michael Majale points out, a slum may be informal and illegal, but it's still a functioning urban development that has been built and organised by its residents.[38] Participatory urban planning holds that residents' insights should be incorporated as local infrastructure is either upgraded or delivered for the first time. For example, the town of Kitale in western Kenya used participatory planning to bring water and sanitation to slum areas. A community inventory was produced to map any local institutions, including businesses and churches, and to work towards formal land rights. Women's groups and young people were consulted, and priorities were set through 'design clinics'.[39] Kitale's inclusive approach shows how good development is not just about delivering services or infrastructure, but about empowering people and building participation.

Social auditing is another avenue for citizen involvement in decision making, serving to keep public bodies transparent and accountable to the people they serve. The idea is perhaps best understood by comparing it to a financial audit. With the latter, accounting professionals assess a company's or organisation's financial performance and profitability. The most important thing is that the numbers add up and everything is above board. Matters such as purpose or effectiveness, or social or environmental impact (both positive and negative) are outside the scope of the financial audit and are not considered. A social audit brings such issues back into the frame and aims to hold an organisation accountable to its mission as well as its finances. And it is participatory, with intended beneficiaries taking part in the measurement and appraisal.

Nepal has adopted this approach in its education system, and schools hold a social audit every year with the local community. This is overseen by representatives from the council, the staff of the school and the parent-teacher association. Two parents and two students (one male and one female) are elected to contribute. Together they assess the school on a number of different measures, from attendance and student achievement to staff training, the quality of the school's library or the condition of its toilets. This is drawn up in a report and presented to the community, giving local residents a sense of ownership over their children's education.[40] After proving successful in education, social auditing is now being applied in healthcare in Nepal.[41]

Seeking similar goals of accountability and transparency, the Open Government Partnership was launched in 2011. It is an international platform for people in various countries who want to make their governments more open and responsive to citizens. Over 75 countries participate, with government working with civil society to pursue open government reforms. Countries are allowed to join if they endorse an Open Government Declaration, plus implement an action plan that has been developed through public consultation. They must also commit to independent reporting on how they are progressing in delivering their action plans.[42]

One of the most ambitious initiatives in collective decision making we have come across has come from Iceland. The country was turned upside down by the 2008 financial crisis, and the overreach of its offshore banking industry brought down both the economy and the government. As part of rebuilding the nation, Parliament chose to write a new constitution in an open and unifying process. Nine hundred and fifty people were chosen by lottery to contribute, with a broad range of ideas being slowly honed into a new draft. It included many familiar rights and freedoms, but also some more unusual ones: access to government documents, a commons approach to natural resources or the right to call referenda both nationally and locally. There were new protections for animals and the environment, and for access to them: 'all shall by law be accorded the right to a healthy environment, fresh water, unpolluted air and unspoiled nature'.[43] Bold though this collaborative approach was, it faltered at the final stages. The whole process was not binding and depended on Parliament to vote it through. That has not been done, and that failure has led to a renewed round of political turmoil. The anarchist Pirate Party pledged to implement the people's constitution, and won 10 of the 63 seats in the 2016 parliamentary elections. At the time of writing, the story of the world's first crowd-sourced constitution is not yet over.[44]

On a smaller scale, but no less radical, is what happened in the small English town of Frome in 2011. Feeling that their town was held back by party-political squabbling, a group ran as a coalition of independent candidates with no manifesto or stated policies beyond a short commitment to working together for the good of the town. They won 10 of the 17 seats, and set about opening up meetings to the public and working towards consensus-based decision making. They called their do-it-yourself approach 'flatpack democracy',[45] and under their leadership Frome council has gone on to demonstrate a more open, more informal and shared way of working.[46]

These participative approaches to decision making would give more people a say in their local areas, in the services they use and (as will be discussed shortly) in their workplaces. They would give people the sense of agency, purpose and belonging that are so important to wellbeing. At a time when a lot of politics seems to be becoming more extreme and faith in political processes is low, they could also prove important in reinvigorating the idea of democracy. Making ourselves at home means having faith in what people, with time and space to deliberate, discuss, learn and enquire, can create together.

Good work

One of the principles of making ourselves at home that we have investigated is a healthier relationship with work. We can look to the Netherlands for a demonstration of making ourselves at home in the area of employment. Here, working less is the norm – the Dutch work 1,430 hours a year, as compared to annual US hours of 1,783 and 1,676 hours in the UK.[47] Almost half of Dutch employees work part time,[48] and most part-time workers have no wish to increase their hours. Workers in the Netherlands have strong rights to reduce working hours and take career breaks, with incentives to do so, underpinned by the 1982 Wassenaar Agreement in which Dutch trade unions promised to limit demands for higher pay in exchange for policies encouraging people to work less. Although it has since been curtailed, the country pioneered a Life Course Savings Scheme: a government-backed plan that allowed people to save towards career breaks of up to three years.[49]

There are other lessons to draw on: during the recession in the early 2010s governments in many OECD countries (but not the UK) supported temporary programmes to subsidise short-time working, making it easier to adjust hours so as to preserve jobs.[50] In fact, 25 of the 33 OECD countries used shorter working time to avoid redundancies during the economic downturn.[51]

Other scenarios in existence include closing public buildings on one day a week, a policy that has been implemented in the Philippines and the Gambia.[52] In 2015 the Chinese government recommended that firms should operate a 4.5 day week as part of a plan to encourage more domestic tourism and leisure spending.[53] Other strategies include supporting early retirement;

increasing vacation time (by collective agreement, Dutch and German workers have 30 days a year); facilitating more part-time or school-time working; job sharing; sabbaticals and career breaks; and longer parental leave. Maximum working weeks are also part of the story – for example, the EU's Working Time Directive of 48 hours.

A healthier work–life balance doesn't just depend on government intervention. Plenty of companies are experimenting with new approaches to managing staff, giving them greater flexibility and autonomy and reaping the rewards in increased loyalty and rising productivity. Under the leadership of Ricardo Semler, Brazil's Semco has been gradually extending its democratic experiments since the 1980s. Employees are in charge of their own quotas and work time, and vote on major decisions. Most radically of all, they can set their own salaries.[54] Other pioneers include Valve, a video games company that operates with no management. Staff are completely in charge of their own work, forming teams and initiating projects. Their model was studied by economist Yanis Varoufakis (later famous for his brief stint as Greek finance minister under Syriza), who wrote:

> The idea here is that, through this ever-evolving process, people's capacities, talents and ideas are given the best chance possible to develop and produce synergies that promote the Common Good. It is as if an invisible hand guides Valve's individual members to decisions that both unleash each person's potential and serve the company's collective interest (which does not necessarily coincide with profit maximisation).[55]

The largest firm to experiment with this kind of radical leadership is Haier, the giant Chinese appliance manufacturer. CEO Zhang Ruimin restructured the company from a traditional top-down hierarchy to an ecology of self-managing teams. Any employee can generate an idea, form a team around it and share in any profits it creates. The theory is to foster a culture of entrepreneurialism within the company and operate as a network of small businesses. 'Entrepreneurialism means our employees need to look for opportunities on their own. If they find one, they can self-organise and get self-motivated. In this kind of organisation, there is no leader,' says Zhang. 'Our people are given the power to make their own decisions, hire their own people, and distribute their own profits'.[56] Using this model, Haier has grown to become the world's largest supplier of white goods by market share.[57]

While these are radical examples, there are many more low-key ways to empower employees and increase work satisfaction, from job sharing and task rotation to flexible hours and working from home. Renegotiation of power between employees and employers, together with the growing number of people choosing to work part time or for themselves, would be a big shift towards better work. It would also be a good example of Sen's 'development as freedom', discussed in Chapter Six.

Pro-social business models

As outlined above, making ourselves at home requires new business models. Cooperatives are one form of business that serves the goal of making ourselves at home. There are plenty of examples to build on, perhaps because the cooperative model predates the corporate one by many years, with its roots in places like Robert Owen's New Lanark in the south of Scotland, but also because cooperation and mutuality is part of what makes us human. As with other examples presented here, they are not perfect, nor will they on their own deliver wholescale change, but Alperovitz considers these forms of ownership as important:

> Not only in their own form, but also in that they begin to offer handholds on a new longer-term vision ... to challenge the dominant hegemonic ideology and to build a democratised economic basis for a new vision and new system.[58]

Box 8.1: Employee-owned companies

Altman's collated research in 2014 showed that about half the world's agricultural produce was marketed by cooperatives; there were 120 million credit union members across 87 countries; and healthcare cooperatives served over 100 million people across 50 countries.[59] In the US, some 130 million citizens – 40% of the population – are members of some form of cooperative, albeit mostly consumer- and producer-owned cooperatives rather than cooperative workplaces.[60]

Besides the often-cited Mondragon in Spain, the following are some other exemplary firms that we can learn from.

- One of Britain's leading retailers is John Lewis, which operates department stores and over 200 supermarkets (under the Waitrose name). It is owned by its staff, all of whom are profit-sharing partners in the business. This arrangement dates back to 1920, when founder John Spedan Lewis drew up a co-ownership constitution for his London-based drapery store.
- When lens-maker Carl Zeiss died in 1888, his business partner Ernst Abbe made a radical gift in his memory: he gave his shares in the company to its staff. The optics company Zeiss has been owned by a foundation ever since, with profits partly going towards research and partly shared by employees.[61]
- Arup is an engineering firm that has overseen building projects across the globe, including iconic buildings such as the Sydney Opera House, London's Barbican and Beijing's 'Bird's Nest' stadium. It is owned by a trust and profits are shared between current and former employees. It has grown to over 90 offices around the world since its founding almost 100 years ago by philosopher and engineer Ove Arup. Arup (the business) is not growth orientated and is instead led by values including social usefulness, being a humane organisation and ensuring the 'reasonable prosperity' of its members. It is at the forefront of engineering for the circular economy and its remuneration structures reward collaboration rather than competition.
- Green City Wholefoods[62] is a workers' cooperative in Scotland's biggest city, Glasgow. It has been selling food wholesale since 1978 to better coordinate transport between existing cooperatives in the city. All of its 35 workers are able to become members and thus participate in

the cooperative's decision making. Members are organised into teams to take responsibility for their own areas (sales, warehouse, buying and so on), and involving others when necessary. The annual general meeting elects a management team to make day-to-day decisions, but its meetings are open and financial and recruitment decisions involve all members. Green City has a policy of local recruitment and using local suppliers.[63]

- Fedecovera Guatemala is a federation of more than 43 Mayan cooperatives supporting coffee, tea, cocoa and cardamom farmers. It was created in the mid-1970s and describes its values as: acting for 'the human wellbeing'; protecting and improving the environment and biodiversity; customers as a partner; and integrity, fairness and independence. It concertedly promotes women's entrepreneurship and women's leadership within the cooperative movement.[64]

Sharing (and decentralising) the benefits of economic activity can be seen in the growth of energy cooperatives and community-owned energy companies, including micro-generation owned by individual households. In the US cooperatives and municipal utilities account for over a quarter of total electricity production. Across Germany, 44 new municipal companies (Stadtwerke) have been established and over 100 energy concessions have been returned to public hands since 2007.[65] Denmark, with its strong tradition of more decentralised forms of public and collective ownership, features a range of collectively owned institutions, from state-owned energy producers to local wind cooperatives.[66]

Community- and worker-owned businesses are just the start – there is a growing array of 'pro-social' business models, or what Harvard economist Heerad Sabeti terms the 'fourth sector',[67] such is its significance. For example, in the US the growing Benefit Corporation movement began as a formal extension to the purpose of incorporation (beyond creating shareholder value), towards an entity that generates impact or benefits for society as a whole. Taking on 'B Corp' status requires the company to consider all stakeholders, not just shareholders, when making decisions and to deliver social and environmental commitments. These are written into governing documents, and directors and company officers can be sued for failure to pursue their social purpose.[68] In 2010 Maryland became the first US state to pass a Benefit Corporation Bill, giving B Corps legal status. Similar laws have now been passed in over 34 states, with more considering such legislation.[69] Among them is Delaware, home to 1 million businesses, including 50% of the US publicly traded companies and 64% of the Fortune 500. Hundreds of companies have signed up to the certification scheme. The legislative framework for Benefit Corporations varies across the world. Some countries, such as Britain, are able to give them legal status already. In other places new legislation has been required, with Puerto Rico and Italy leading the way in 2016 and plans moving forward in several other countries.

In the UK, Community Interest Companies (CICs, a legal form introduced as part of the Companies Act 2004) are attributed with helping to reignite interest in cooperatives and mutual ownership. A CIC is a business with primarily social or environmental objectives and a legal obligation to invest surpluses for the good of the enterprise rather for the benefit of shareholders or owners. Social enterprises are a growing group of businesses using enterprise to deliver social goals. One example is iShack, which has installed solar home energy systems for over 1,200 households in informal settlements in South Africa. iShack is a social business and does not extract profits.[70] Not only does it provide clean, cheap and reliable energy, but it also creates jobs for residents who receive training in installation and maintenance.

Beyond cooperatives, CICs, B Corps and social enterprises, there are businesses that seem to be pushing the envelope of even the most innovative organisational forms. One example is Premium Cola in Germany, a small beverage company based in Hamburg. It has no actual boss (despite being in operation for over 14 years) and members choose how much of their time they are going to work for the company. Decision making is based on the principle of consensual democracy – business decisions, finances and investments are discussed and voted on via an online forum. Everybody in the company earns the same €18 per hour, with top-ups for those employees with children or additional needs. Employees are paid even if illness or life challenges such as divorce or family crises prevent them from working. Premium

Cola has intentionally moderate growth, intended to avoid stress for employees and to prevent rapidly changing the Premium Cola culture by adding too many new people too quickly. Its focus is on relationships and a shared appreciation for its product, rather than growth and profit, which means that it sometimes makes decisions that might seem to be the antithesis of normal business behaviour. For example, it does not undertake any marketing. It keeps transport emissions low by limiting distribution to German and Austrian regions within a 600km radius of their operations. A share of profits is directed to carbon-offsetting and it uses and reuses glass bottles rather than bottling in plastic. Premium Cola allows its recipes and expertise to be accessed by anyone wanting to replicate its model. In fact, the founder, Uwe Lübberman, says that its alternative business ideology is a more important product than the Premium Cola itself.[71] As he says, 'we have to get back to a culture or society where we have an amount of income and things that is enough'.

Turning to the world of fashion, we can also find deliberate choices to make business an agent of wider benefit. Eileen Fisher is a major US-based clothing brand, designing and producing high-quality women's clothing. It was founded in 1984 and now employs approximately 1,200 people directly, with a supply chain including around 10,000 people. It is well on its way to converting to 100% organic cotton and is scrutinising its rayon suppliers to ensure that the material is not coming from deforestation of rainforests. The company is both an ESOP (employee owned) and a Certified B Corporation. It is committing to a scorecard process reporting financial, environmental and social profits and losses and has both a sustainability design team and a social consciousness department. Founder Eileen Fisher, while in a business meeting, noted one of her employees commenting that the company needed to 'feed the monster' of growth.[72] Fisher said that the comment scared her. As the company grew she noticed increasing stress levels among her employees. So the company deliberately slowed down. It had been in a pattern of opening two or three new stores a year, but in 2016 it decided to pause. Instead, it reorganised its business model and sustainability measures: in lieu of new retail outlets, the company has opened a recycling centre designed to recycle and up-cycle old Eileen Fisher clothing. Another strategy for slowing business down a bit is reducing the number of styles. For its 2015 Fall collection, the company reduced the number of fabrics, yarns and styles it produced by 33%. The company is trying to define 'good growth' and move forward in a way that does not create a mess for the environment, its own employees and its supply chain communities.

Natura is an organic cosmetics company that works with communities in rural Brazil and in some of the low-income parts of Brazil's cities.[73] It uses traditional knowledge to source raw materials sustainably and promotes the reusing, refilling and recycling of its packaging. Bonuses paid to workers are based on reduction of environmental impact. In 2012 it became the first publicly traded company to gain B Corp status. As we were writing, Natura acquired the Body Shop, purchasing it from L'Oréal – giving rise to hope that the Body Shop's environmental and ethical credentials will be revived.[74]

Beyond individual companies, there's a movement building in Europe (and more recently entering the US) called the Economy for the Common Good (ECG). It constitutes an example of how pioneering work can build towards regime change (something that we discuss further below). Its ambition is not just surviving in the current economic system, but flourishing in a new system that it will be part of creating. The ECG was an initiative of a dozen companies in Austria and is now supported by over 2,000 companies and over 100 local chapters. Miranda de Azán is the first Spanish town to become an official ECG city and the state of South Tyrol in Italy officially supports the ECG and gives preferential treatment to any business that completes the Common Good Balance Sheet. Five cities in South Tyrol have now completed the Common Good Balance Sheet themselves. The concept emerged in a book by Christian Felber published in 2010 (first printed in German, and since printed in French, Italian, Spanish, Polish, Finnish, Serbian, and Catalan, and finally in English in 2015). Christian Felber is quoted in the *Financial Times* as explaining that ECG companies 'know the essential role of profit. Profit is like the blood, without it, an organism is dead within a short period of time. But blood is not the meaning of life. And no one needs more than seven litres of blood'.

Instead the mission is 'a holistic, alternative economic model which envisions a free market economy, in which the common good is the ultimate goal of economic activity'.[75] The ECG has three goals: first, to end the contradiction between the values held by many business interests (such as profit maximisation), on the one hand, and the values held by society in general, on the other hand. Second, to ensure that the values and goals laid down in most Western constitutions are implemented in business practice. And third, that economic success is no longer measured simply via profits and growth, but according to a company's contribution to the common good (such as improving human rights, social justice and environmental protection).[76] Common Good businesses adhere to a 'Good Balance Sheet' comprising 17 indicators. For example, do the products and services satisfy human needs? How humane are the working conditions? How environmentally friendly are the production processes? How ethical is the sales and purchasing policy? How are profits distributed? Do women receive equal pay for equal work? Are employees involved in core, strategic decision making?

Another trend worth noting is interest in 'flat organisations' (or so-called 'de-layered organisations'). The idea is to minimise or even eliminate managerial hierarchy in an organisation and has been promoted by Fredrik Laloux in his 2014 book *Reinventing Organisations*. This approach has been found to increase the sense of autonomy and self-realisation of staff. It is likely that there are limits to the size of a flat organisation, and of course it is possible that alternative power dynamics will arise (not all of which will be bad, of course). But there is something symbolic behind the flat organisational structure: a recognition that everyone is equal, that all people bring worthy skills and contributions and everyone is needed to make up the whole. This seems to chime with an economy that makes itself at home.

Islamic economics, while its potential remains untapped at the global level, has much to offer as a counter-balance to modern capitalism. 'Its goals are not primarily materialist,' write Ronnie Lessem and Alexander Shieffer. Instead, Islamic economics focuses on the twin ideas of 'falah' and 'hayat tayyibah' – holistic human wellbeing and a wholesome good life, respectively.[77] Aspects of it have been adopted, particularly in banking and finance. Institutions such as London's Al Rayan Bank operate on Islamic principles of ethical investment and profit sharing rather than payment of interest.[78] If banks and other institutions based on these principles can prove that they offer a better service to consumers, then Islamic finance could make a wider contribution.

The Christian tradition also has a different approach to banking. Archbishop Justin Welby calls for 'an economy that facilitates mutual flourishing and the common good', and he has led the Church of England to support and set up credit unions.[79] By focusing on serving their members rather than growing profits for shareholders, credit unions are able to offer much more generous terms to borrowers. An example is Reliance Bank, which is run on ethical principles by the Salvation Army.[80] The utility company Ebico was set up by Christians aiming to address fuel poverty.[81] By running on a not-for-profit basis, it is able to target its services towards customers that other utility companies would avoid, due to their perceived lack of profitability.

Other mission-minded companies are motivated by the environment and climate change. The banking sector has Triodos and the Ecology Building Society, the latter set up because mainstream banks were reluctant to give mortgages to self-builders constructing their own eco-homes.[82] The energy supplier Ecotricity was founded by environmentalist Dale Vince, with the primary purpose of expanding Britain's renewable energy capacity. It describes itself as a 'not-for-dividend' company, with all profits going to the cause. 'With no shareholders to answer to we're free to dedicate ourselves to the task of building new sources of green energy'.[83]

Finally, the internet has made it possible to create businesses that tap the power – and the pockets – of crowds, presenting an alternative to issuing of shares as a means to raise financial capital. Alongside social stock exchanges and community shares, is the emergence of peer-to-peer lending sites such as Zopa.com that offer loans that are funded by ordinary people. Investors can choose the interest rate at which they lend, and the risk is spread by drawing a small amount from many people to finance the loan. Where in the past one might have gone to a bank for a loan, with any interest payments returning to the bank and its (often wealthy) shareholders, a peer-to-peer loan is provided by fellow citizens and the profits are shared widely. Similarly, crowd-funding platforms such as Seedr, Kickstarter or CrowdCube allow ordinary people to participate in funding start-up businesses they are interested in – something previously the domain of venture capitalists.[84]

This same sense of participation is present in the arts world too, where people crowd-fund films, stage plays or art projects. Writers can find their readers in advance and fund their next book through the Unbound platform.[85] Other forms of diverse media include a comedian building up a following by recording a weekly podcast. An aspiring fashion commentator can make a living by uploading YouTube videos. A journalist might write a blog instead of working for a newspaper and a graphic artist might publish their comics as e-books and develop an audience for them on Instagram. Such practices are relevant to Arrival and making ourselves at home in several ways. First, they reduce the role of capital and big corporations in the arts, democratising creative endeavour and making it accessible to more people. This helps to create the more inclusive economy that we imagine, where people have a stake in the things that matter to them – whether that is something as important as banking or energy, or more trivial such as a hit music single. Second, co-producing the arts and relating more directly with artists creates community and a sense of belonging, which is good for wellbeing.

From conspicuous consumption to experientialism and conspicuous citizenship

As we've noted already, an increase in material prosperity after a certain point has its downsides, not least the threat of environmental harm. A more immediate (and prosaic) hazard for those with ample material prosperity is cluttered homes and the stress of having too many things to manage. That has triggered a nascent move towards simpler lifestyles. There have been several waves to this movement, from the voluntary simplicity experimenters in the 1970s to the minimalism advocates or 'tiny home' devotees of today. What unites these groups is a desire to clear away the distractions of possessions and live more fully with fewer things. While these have tended to be subcultures or alternative lifestyles, a more mainstream change may be underway along similar lines, not least as people seek satisfaction from experiences rather than materialism.

One of the places where there has been a visible shift from ownership to experience is in the music industry. Sales of CDs have nose-dived in the digital era, in a de-materialising of music listening that is in line with collaborative economy principles: a move towards 'fractional ownership'. Music is enjoyed as an experience, and often a collective one. That could be radio listeners tweeting their reactions to the first play of a new song or the internet buzz around a new album from an iconic artist. Live music continues to thrive, and the number of music festivals in Britain has expanded even as music sales fell. As one attendee told researchers: 'It's not just about the music. It's the feeling I get when I'm there, the feeling of being alive'.[86]

The music industry is still worth over £4 billion to the British economy,[87] but other aspects of experientialism are distinctly non-commercial. Park Run is a case in point. Beginning in 2004 with a handful of friends running together in the park, it is now an international network that brings people together every week for a 5-kilometre run: anyone is welcome to register and take part.* Although the times of each person's run are recorded so that participants can see how they're doing, it's not a race. Families can run together, there's no embarrassment about having to slow down and walk and people of any ability are welcome. There's no charge, and events are facilitated by volunteers. 'I'm surprised something so simple and obvious has become a runaway success,' says founder Paul Sinton-Hewitt. 'But it's free, it's community-owned and it speaks to the things people really want'.[88]

In a world where people have more time away from formal work, we could look forward to a revolution in volunteering and community participation – a foundation of making ourselves at home. There is already a trend toward regulators playing a proactive role in building citizenship and mobilising community

* At the time of writing over 1.5 million people had taken part in over 500 locations.

action. One of the most notable examples is New York City (NYC), where Michael Bloomberg made volunteering a priority during his 12 years as mayor. NYC Service launched in 2009, dedicated to sweeping away barriers to volunteering, bringing companies and non-governmental organisations (NGOs) together and encouraging ordinary citizens to step up and help out in their neighbourhoods.[89] Among the projects associated with this push is the NYC Go Pass. Previously, those who volunteered with multiple agencies would need to be screened by all of them, taking up charities' time and money. Go Pass does a background check, certifies the individual and issues them with a volunteering card and ID number.[90] Inspired by New York, an alliance of city mayors founded the Cities of Service scheme to encourage other authorities to put together civic action plans. Over 200 US cities have signed up, and in 2014 the programme opened to cities in Britain as well.[91]

Already there is emerging evidence that materialistic values are declining in the West, while they are rising in emerging economies: 71% of people in China say that they measure success by what they own, whereas this figure has fallen as low as 16% in Britain.[92] This suggests that materialism could be a phase of development rather than a permanent state. Indeed, history suggests that consumerism is something that has been deliberately fostered at key moments of development. For the US, that moment came in the 1950s, when the advertising industry actively encouraged a shift in values away from mending and saving, and towards credit and disposability. This was documented at the time by Vance Packard, in his book *The Waste Makers*. 'The people of the United States are in a sense becoming a nation on a tiger,' he wrote. 'They must learn to consume more and more or, they are warned, their magnificent economic machine may turn and devour them'.[93] China may find itself in a similar position today, purposefully championing consumerist values in an effort to nurture domestic markets.

In the West, though, there are some hints that erosion of materialism is gathering momentum – driven by demographic change, by post-materialist values among some or perhaps, in some cases, by necessity borne of the 2008 financial crisis and ensuing austerity. It may be because in these societies people are beginning to recognise that they are at an optimal point on the fulfilment curve (discussed above), a point after which more consumption can be counter-productive and participation becomes a more effective means to attain fulfilment. Senior citizens in particular tend to shift their spending away from consumption of things to more activity-based consumption of experiences.[94] These trends suggest that some individuals at least are reaching a point where they feel they 'have enough' and want to take more time out of paid employment so as to undertake their own production (such as cooking rather than buying ready meals). Perhaps trends also reflect that many are reaching a point where they feel that their identity is not contingent on display of 'stuff'. This is a key sign of feeling at home.

Box 8.2: Slowing down to make ourselves at home

Slow food began in Italy in 1986 as a protest movement against fast food. It was initially defensive, seeking to protect traditional food and farming from corporations and highly processed diets. Early projects like the Manifesto in Defence of Raw Milk Cheeses may not have wildly captured the imagination, but the movement has matured. It has grown into a wider role and now takes an active interest in biodiversity, sustainable fishing, food security and the rights of indigenous people. At the heart of the movement is the appreciation of good food, and the conviviality that is fostered by enjoying it together. Local Slow Food chapters are actually called 'convivia' (drawing on Ivan Illich's notion of conviviality). The movement is all about savouring rather than consumption, and exemplifies the values of quality over quantity, local specialities over industrial production and craft over commercialisation.[95]

Similar approaches to food can be seen in craft brewing, and the number of people baking at home has risen by a third in recent years in Britain.[96] More people are taking pride in producing these things for themselves and enjoying them with friends. It's possible that some new skills are spreading while others atrophy, and time will tell if these are passing fads. But in the past, many households would have brewed and baked out of necessity. These skills are being rediscovered, and food and drink once again prove their age-old power to bring people together.

As well as preparing and enjoying food, growing it also brings people together around shared skills and a common purpose. A 2012 survey found that nearly a third of British adults grow some of their own food.[97] It's a similar percentage among Americans, and 2 million households in the US participate in community gardening, a number that has tripled since 2008.[98] Gardening has been shown to reduce stress, promote mindfulness and improve overall health.[99] A 2015 study of community gardens in Glasgow pointed to health and wellbeing benefits, the constructive engagement of vulnerable people and, via the collective management spaces, an enrichment of participatory skills.[100] Growing food in school raises pupils' achievement in science and improves healthy eating choices.[101]

Gardening together can take on a radical edge when it is taken into the streets. Incredible Edible Todmorden began with volunteers in the English village growing food on grass verges and abandoned plots, looking for ways to reduce food miles and improve food security in their local area. It spawned the Incredible Edible network, which facilitates groups across Britain and around the world, building community and improving health and the environment through growing. Pam Warhurst, an economist by training and food activist by calling, explains that food offers a means to unify people of all ages, incomes and cultures so that they 'themselves find a new way of living, see spaces around them differently, think about the resources they use differently, interact differently'.[102]

A renewable and circular economy

The transition from fossil fuels to renewable sources of energy is a key priority for industrialised economies, but it's also a huge leap-frogging opportunity for so-called developing countries.

Examples of action by both companies and governments abound. We could look to Iceland, where its huge hydroelectric and geothermal resources have enabled it to be 100% renewable in electricity and 87% renewable in heat.[103] Denmark is on track to achieve its target of 100% renewable electricity and heat by

2035.[104] China has reportedly passed 'peak coal'.[105] Ethiopia has low-carbon electricity and is committed to expanding capacity through renewable energy.[106] The falling price of solar panels has opened up opportunities for self-standing solar infrastructure, solar roofs and walls – even solar roads, such as an experimental road surface in Normandy, France.[107] Sub-national governments are forging ahead – often despite, rather than because of, the national policy regime. For example, the Australian Capital Territory is on track for 100% renewable electricity as early as 2020.[108] The German city of Freiburg (often referred to as one of the birthplaces of the German environmental movement) is famous for its proactive use of renewables and green transport, low-energy buildings and waste reduction.[109]

In many instances, the roll-out of renewable energy generation is being harnessed to deliver 'co-benefits' such as employment. Tanzania, for example, has ambitions to capitalise on its transition to 100% renewable energy by simultaneously reducing poverty with quality local jobs.[110] Local generation is of particular relevance to an economy making itself at home – it offers autonomy, local control and local employment. For example, energy generated by homes and small businesses constitutes almost a third of Germany's energy.[111] There are also examples of renewable energy directly taking the place of livelihoods derived from fossil fuels – even driven by fossil-fuel workers themselves. In Canada, tradespeople who hitherto worked in the oil sands sector have established an organisation called 'Iron and Earth' that trains people in renewable energy. Not only is it supporting the shift to renewables, but it is led by its 450 worker-members.[112]

Caring for scarce environmental resources goes beyond the shift to renewable energy: the business community has taken strides towards a circular economy, with a growing number of companies applying its principles and incorporating them into their business models. At the top end of that scale are major international corporations such as French car manufacturer Renault. Materials account for 20% of the cost of production, so the company has been pioneering the use of recycled materials. A third of the materials in a new Renault car are recycled, with 90% of the car recyclable when the time comes to retire it.[113] Danish shipping company Maersk is applying a similar logic to ship building. Its latest container ships come with a deconstruction manual for future scrappers, indicating in detail the grades of steel and other materials used throughout.[114]

At the other end of the scale are the many small businesses that have formed around the idea of the circular economy. Some of these are very simple. Struck by the waste from India's thriving takeaway culture – throwing away 120 billion plastic utensils a year – entrepreneur Narayana Peesapaty invented an alternative and founded a company to promote it: Bakey's Edible Cutlery (made from flours blended with rice and wheat).[115] Edible spoons are a little piece of the puzzle for one of the circular economy's biggest challenges: plastic, particularly one-use packaging. Seventy-eight million tonnes of plastic packaging are produced every year, of which just 14% is recycled. As a non-biodegradable material, no plastic should end up in landfill, and yet 40% of it does.[116] Worse, almost a third escapes any sort of waste processing altogether and ends up in the natural environment.[117] This is a particular problem in middle-income countries that have access to processed foods and modern consumer goods, but where waste-recycling infrastructure remains inadequate.[118] Effective recycling infrastructure and investment in rubbish collection are vital, but developing better plastics is also an important way forward. There are multiple approaches, including new forms of bioplastics made from biomass or seaweed. One of the more unusual is to grow packaging to order. A company called Ecovative does this by seeding fungi spores on post-harvest waste, and growing the packaging to the required shape in a mould. Called 'Mycofoam', this sustainable replacement for Styrofoam padding is used by a variety of corporate companies, including Dell computers.[119] Other businesses are simply weaving circular economy principles into existing business practices, rather than developing entirely new products. One example is found on the island of Islay, off the north-west coast of Scotland, where the local community swimming pool is heated by waste heat from the next-door Bowmore whisky distillery.[120] Another example is in South Africa, at a school just outside Johannesburg where compost from the school kitchen goes to a biomass composter that generates heat for the classrooms.[121]

Reuse is fairly familiar: crates are reused, or glass milk or soft-drink bottles can be taken back for refilling (and often a small refund). Remanufacturing is less common: 54% of manufacturers are still unaware of it or have not considered it, but it is a promising approach.[122] Remanufacturing was defined by a UK All-Party Parliamentary Group as 'a series of manufacturing steps acting on an end-of-life part or product in order to return it to like-new or better performance, with warranty to match'.[123] It goes one better than reconditioning or refurbishment, and allows products to be returned to the same quality and condition as new (or in some cases better, if upgrades are included in the remanufacturing process). While it is applicable in lots of situations, certain industries and companies are well known for remanufacturing. Caterpillar remanufactures its engines, Kodak has reprocessed over 1.5 billion of its one-use cameras.[124] Volvo has been incorporating remanufacturing into its business model for over 50 years, and its sustainability reports explain why: 'Remanufacturing minimizes the need for raw materials. It also significantly reduces energy consumption and emissions. For example, a remanufactured engine saves up to 80% of the energy needed to build a new engine and dramatically cuts the emissions of nitrogen oxides and carbon dioxide'.[125]

There is a growing drive to take the experience of these pioneering companies and apply it more widely, bringing down materials costs, lowering environmental impact and creating new business opportunities. Some countries are already pursuing a circular economy as a matter of policy, including the Netherlands and China. In 2000, Japan introduced the Law for Promotion of Effective Utilisation of Resources, which promotes reduction of waste in the first place, reuse of parts and recycling of used components by treating materials as circular goods, focusing on products' entire life spans and mandating that manufacturers run disassembly plants and recover materials. The EU's 2013 Waste Framework Directive requires member states to develop waste-prevention programmes, and a 2015 plan builds on this to explicitly direct an EU pivot toward the circular economy.[126] Some European nations are going further than the EU's goals, with Spain passing a law to prevent reusable goods being disposed of in landfill.[127] France has introduced a legal definition of planned obsolescence, making it a criminal offence.[128] France is also working to curb food waste by banning supermarkets from throwing away edible food,[129] and in 2020 a law is set to come into effect that bans all plastic cups, cutlery and plates in France (unless they can be composted or made of biologically sourced materials).[130] Sweden halved the rate of value added tax (to 12%) on repair work to encourage more people to fix bicycles and appliances rather than replace them.[131] Sweden can also boast the world's first shopping centre devoted entirely to reused and up-cycled goods. The council-run mall operates on the site of a municipal recycling centre, with operatives intercepting items that are brought in for disposal and sending them on for refurbishment instead. Fifty jobs were created in small businesses fixing up and selling on furniture, toys, tools, computers and a variety of other goods.[132]

In 2013, Scotland became the first country to join the Ellen MacArthur Foundation's Circular Economy 100 Network, and a host of different initiatives are being introduced.[133] The Scottish Government's paper *Zero Waste – Safeguarding Scotland's Resources* recognises the economic imperative of using finite resources more effectively. Twenty actions are listed to help businesses use resources more efficiently, promote better design, improve producer responsibility, improve information on materials, and stimulate a culture of resource efficiency.[134] These include the Waste and Resources Action Programme (WRAP) and the Scottish Loan Fund for innovation in reprocessing and remanufacturing. Scotland's pioneering work was recognised in 2017 at the Circular Awards, held at the World Economic Forum.[135] Wales also has a stated ambition to be a zero-waste nation by 2050. The Welsh plan includes a commitment to put recyclate to use locally where possible, creating jobs and keeping recycling loops tight.[136]

All of these waste-saving innovations and the development of sophisticated and cost-effective recycling and remanufacturing networks provide countries with a 'stock' of materials that can be kept in circulation – a kind of materials 'Arrival'.[137] For advanced economies, this has been a learning process, with a wasteful linear economy now needing to be replaced by something more efficient.

For developing countries, there is a real opportunity to reach this plateau of materials earlier, by building a circular industry from the beginning and embracing processes and goods that require fewer resources, and hence the total amount of materials in circulation can be lower. This is another example of finding a gentler path to a place to make ourselves at home. Adopting circular principles in developing countries would benefit the environment and the climate, avoid future health problems, create job opportunities and protect young industries from volatile prices for raw materials. As we have already discussed, the wasteful lifestyle of Western consumerism cannot be universalised, but neither can developing countries be held back, nor their emerging middle classes denied the consumer goods that they are justified in aspiring to. Here, according to the development charity Tearfund, the circular economy offers an 'alternative growth model that reduces the tension between lifting people out of poverty and protecting the planet'.[138] The good news is that it brings with it the potential for jobs, especially local ones.[139]

Collaborative economy

An economy with lower energy and resource needs has to make better use of what is already available. New ways of sharing, leasing and cooperating are emerging, often facilitated by the ease of internet communications and social media. 'Sharing and collaboration are happening in ways and at a scale never before possible,' write Rachel Botsman and Roo Rogers, who coined the term 'collaborative consumption'.[140]

We have already seen some of the commercial aspects of collaborative consumption and how they contribute to a circular economy by sharing assets and reducing the need for new materials. Lots of other activities within the sharing economy are non-commercial. Couchsurfing.com connects back-packers with hosts who let them sleep on their couches for free, while, as part of the City of Sanctuary movement, Share Tawe in Swansea allows residents to offer a spare room to asylum seekers or the homeless.[141] Local networks such as Streetbank allow neighbours to share things, from borrowing a ladder to passing on a glut of rhubarb. Some of this works on the basis of in-kind transfers, such as the credits that readers can accumulate on Bookmooch.com and then trade in to request books from other members.[142] Other services are beyond monetary exchange entirely, carried out in the so-called 'gift economy' whereby goods and services are given without payment or reward (or expectation of it).

Sharing includes digital assets as well as physical objects or services. Every day millions of images, artworks, songs and articles are shared online under a Creative Commons licence. This allows anyone to reuse them, free of charge, as long as there is appropriate attribution. With over 1.2 billion works published online in 2016, that is a vast pool of content available for people to utilise and collaborate around.[143]

Some places have seen the benefits of the sharing economy and are actively nurturing it. In Seoul, for example, city authorities are seeking to position the South Korean capital as a model city for sharing. Efforts include expanding sharing infrastructure; incubating sharing start-ups via office space; providing consultation and subsidies for sharing activities; vetting and designating sharing enterprises; providing access to data and digital works; correcting obstructive statutes and facilitating communication; opening government parking lots and municipal buildings to the public during idle times; tool libraries; and connecting senior citizens with extra rooms with students who need a place to stay.[144] Seoul's goal in this is wide ranging (and entirely compatible with the notion of 'making ourselves at home'): to create jobs and increase income; addressing environmental issues by making the utmost use of physical resources, reducing unnecessary consumption and waste; and building trust between residents.[145] In Europe, Amsterdam aims to do something similar, and a network of 'sharing cities' are coordinating to develop programmes in London, Milan, Bordeaux and several other places.[146]

NINE

Are we nearly there yet?

Once we allow ourselves to be disobedient to the test of an accountant's profit, we have begun to change our civilization.
—J.M. Keynes[1]

The title of our book inevitably begs the question: 'When is an economy "grown up"? And how will we know if we've arrived?' Part of the answer lies in calculating sufficiency of material resources. Another part is found by looking at the point at which growth no longer brings about improvements in quality of life. And yet another will be revealed when uneconomic growth sets in. These are all, inevitably, extremely difficult to pin-point precisely. So we make no claim to be the final arbiters of where 'there' is and who and what countries are 'there' – this is a conversation for communities and society at large, informed by science.

But we do want to offer a hint of the sort of conversations that need to be had and the issues that need to be considered in order to come up with more definitive answers.

Let us turn to the three dimensions of material sufficiency, diminishing marginal returns and uneconomic growth. Energy access provides us with a useful benchmark for Arrival in terms of material sufficiency. According to the NGO Practical Action, 2 billion people still lack access to energy that is 'adequate, safe, reliable, and affordable'.[2] Where a country's energy infrastructure is inadequate, more growth is clearly necessary – and from looking at developed countries we can get a sense of where the 'enough' point lies. Sustainability expert Chris Goodall notes that electricity use peaked in advanced economies in the early years of the 21st century and has actually gone into decline in some places. He estimates that access to '3 kilowatts per person can provide a decent standard of living, wherever you are in the world'.[3] That's 25% less than we use today in Britain, so it gives a point to converge towards.

Metals offer another natural 'enough' point. Because they can be recycled, countries don't need continuing growth in the quantity of metals in the economy. 'While a country grows richer, metal production increases to drive up stocks, but then it stabilises at some threshold required to maintain stocks at some plateau,' says a study from UIT Cambridge.[4] We can see this already with steel, and in advanced economies the amount of steel in circulation tends to level off as stocks reach 10 tonnes per person. Given the carbon cost of steel production, and known reserves of iron ore, pursuing 10 tonnes of steel per person as a goal would be deleterious. But it gives us another way to understand Arrival: what is a country's stock of materials? Does it have enough to work with? If it has too little, it will need to grow. If it is using too much, it needs to invest more in recycling and adopting the circular economy.

Energy and steel both have demonstrable plateaus of consumption, but we should not necessarily take those plateaus to be the ideal. As poorer countries leap-frog to less wasteful, more circular patterns of industry, plateaus will be reached earlier, at lower levels of materials use. Natural resources, which are more literally 'consumed', do not operate in the same way and need to be handled differently. If we divide the world's biologically productive land by the total current world population, we each get a 'one earth share' of 1.7 hectares. Due to poverty, half the world's ecological footprints fall below that 1.7 hectare limit across much of Asia, South America and Africa. In these places, the challenge is to leap-frog to cleaner forms of development that will improve quality of life without increasing ecological footprints. Americans, on the other hand, are looking at an 80% cut in their ecological footprint to wrestle their consumption back within a sustainable and fair share.[5]

At this point, it's fair to begin thinking about who has Arrived. Which countries are well placed to embrace Arrival and start making themselves at home? Who has reached 'the full complement of riches' that Adam Smith foresaw?

Those are questions that can be answered in a number of different ways, and there are fascinating attempts to quantify a 'sufficiency line'. Bhutan, for example, engages with the notion of sufficiency – a Bhutanese person is deemed to be 'happy'* if they attain sufficiency in six or more of the nine Gross National Happiness domains.[6] Professor of Ethics of Institutions at Utrecht University, Ingrid Robeyns, is carrying out work to specify a 'riches line' – an objective point above which people's wealth is morally problematic.[7] For its part, the New Economics Foundation (NEF) has sought to map a 'plenty line' – defined as the income level after which additional income delivers 'minimal additional benefit to the individual concerned to offset the associated costs to everyone else'.[8] This varies for the countries that NEF considered, but in most cases it was found to sit below the average income in each country.[9] In the US, Daniel Kahneman and Angus Deaton found no increase in wellbeing when incomes rose beyond US$75,000.[10] When mapping the GPI, Kubiszewski et al noted that beyond a GDP per capita of around $7,000, GPI per capita does not tend to increase (a level of income which could be provided by redistributing the GDP of the world economy at the time to 9.6 billion people).[11]

These are useful baselines that will help to inform the conversation, but we would frame the objective of making ourselves at home differently: as an invitation. Beyond the point when a country has enough, the pressure is off. It can step away from the 'trampling, crushing, elbowing, and treading on each other's heels' that John Stuart Mill lamented, and embrace the 'art of living' that Keynes imagined.

So for the time being, we are reluctant to draw a line in the sand and dictate that as a country crosses it, it has moved from one state to another. Arrival and making ourselves at home is a transition, a process, and one that may take decades. Our

* Sufficiency thresholds were derived by drawing on international standards (such as the Millennium Development Goals, International Labour Organisation, Habitat), national standards; normative judgements; and participatory meetings.

intention here has been to introduce the concept of Arrival and the importance of creating an economy that is conducive to making ourselves at home, rather than geared up for growth.

Charting Arrival

There are many ways to assess the point of Arrival: for example, the point where diminishing marginal returns to GDP set in; where failure demand comes to dominate spending; or perhaps even when wealth is so great that examples of what the writer George Monbiot calls 'extreme civilisation' abound. A thorough study of those trends is a task for another day, but a handful of charts demonstrate the kind of 'enough' point that we envision.

The chart in Figure 5 plots rates of extreme poverty, hunger and maternal mortality against GDP per capita, for 160 countries. There are lots of different measures that could be included here. These three are representative of the kinds of progress one would hope for as countries develop, all of them urgent matters of survival. As the chart shows, all the gains come early in the development process. The number of people in extreme poverty falls, maternal survival improves dramatically, and food deficit declines as people move from incomes in the hundreds of dollars a year to thousands a year. This echoes the fulfilment curve discussed in earlier chapters, with survival needs met early on, before moving on to comforts (and then luxuries with higher income).

On a similar theme, Figure 6 tracks average life expectancy across income. Again, the majority of the gains come at the start, and beyond $25,000 there is no correlation between income and life expectancy. Obviously, as we have explored, there are many other things that people will aspire to, but on this one measure of progress there is a demonstrably 'enough' point after which the benefit of more GDP loses its lustre.

The negative aspects of progress are more complicated, not least given the expenditure on healing those negative aspects – failure demand and defensive expenditures – which mean some harm is ameliorated. Energy is one example: since there are many different ways to supply energy, there are richer countries with relatively low CO2, and lower-income countries that use a lot of coal and have higher carbon footprints. Nevertheless, it is notable that no countries with incomes below $5,000 a year have high CO2 per capita, and very few countries with incomes over $20,000 have a low carbon footprint (Figure 7).

Figure 5: Rewards to GDP: GDP per capita of 160 countries against food deficit, maternal mortality and extreme poverty

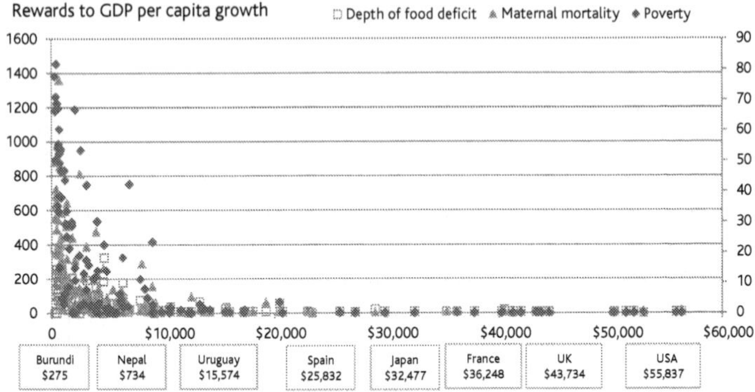

Source: Poverty data and GDP per capita from the World Bank (constant 2011); maternal mortality from the World Health Organization (2015); and food deficit from United Nations Food and Agriculture Organization (2016a).
Note: Left Y axis: maternal mortality (in deaths per 100,000 births); right Y axis: extreme poverty and malnutrition rates (%).

Figure 6: Life expectancy across income

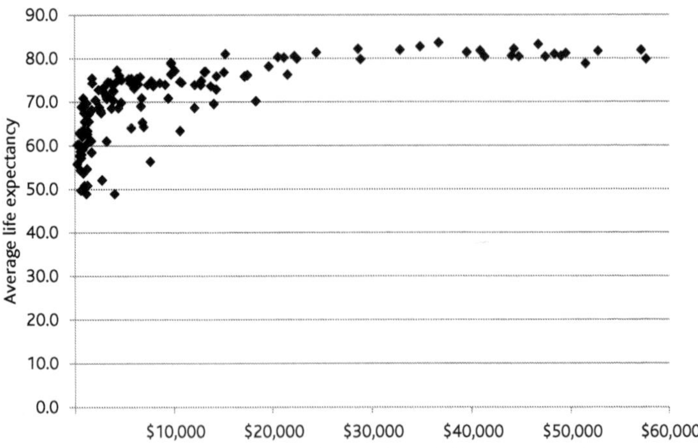

Source: Data derived from the Happy Planet Index, which uses UN Population Division (2012).

Figure 7: GDP per capita against CO2 emissions per person

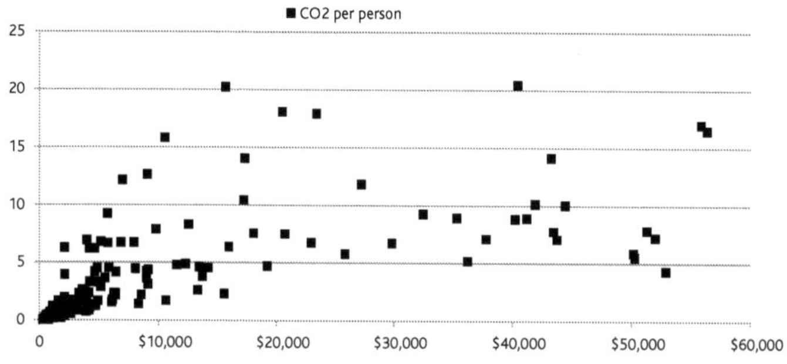

Source: GHG (in CO2 equivalent) from World Resources Institute, 2014 and GDP data from the World Bank.

If we expand footprint data from CO2 to the fuller perspective of ecological footprinting, the trend is more stark (Figure 8). While there are both good and bad outliers, there is no mistaking the fact that higher incomes tend to have a higher environmental cost.

To complement this sketch of the data, let us move from statistics to two specific examples.

Figure 8: GDP against ecological footprint

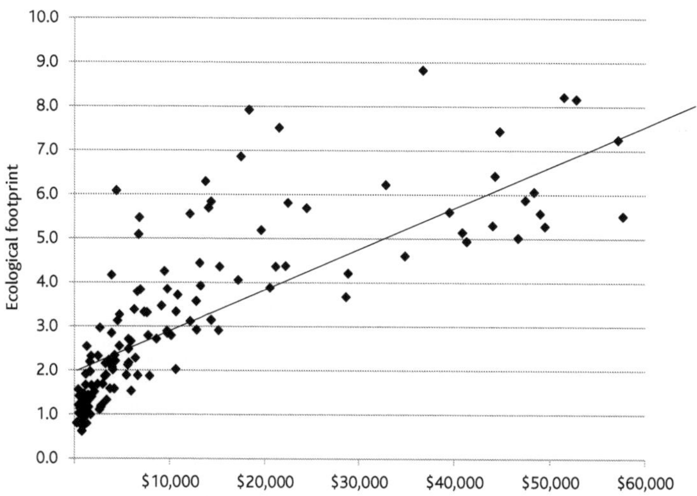

Source: Ecological footprint data from Global Footprint Network (2012) and GDP data from the World Bank.

Two contrasting countries

To look more closely at these general trends and how they inform Arrival, we can consider the contrasting circumstances of the two countries where we grew up. Jeremy was brought up in Madagascar. It was a poor country at the time and it still is – total GDP in 2016 was a fraction below US$10 billion. To put that in some kind of context, in 2016 Madagascar's total economy was worth about the same as Marks & Spencer, the British retail corporation (by market capitalisation).[12] Divide that by the population and you have an average income of just $401 a year.[13] Needless to say, this is disastrously short of any definition of 'enough'. Arrival is many decades away as Madagascar develops, raises incomes, lays down infrastructure, provides services and matures in its institutions. What's more, Madagascar has a very young population, with a median age of just 19 years.[14] As that younger generation comes of age, it will create huge demand for homes, energy, water, food and so on – all on top of the existing challenges.

Our other author, Katherine, grew up in Australia, which finds itself in a very different place. At almost $50,000 (USD) per capita, the average Australian takes less than three days to earn what a Malagasy person makes in a year.[15] Australia's median age is approaching 40, and the birth rate is below replacement rate. This suggests that it won't have a big rush of infrastructure to provide in the coming decades, and the challenge will be to age gracefully instead. As we would expect from a maturing economy, Australia's energy use peaked in 2008 and has been declining for several years.[16] Material consumption remains very high – the highest in the world, in fact – at 35 tonnes per capita per year. That's 10 tonnes more than the UK or Japan, so clearly Australia could scale back on its resource use and still have plenty to go around.[17]

Madagascar clearly needs growth. Mainstream voices in Australia also claim to 'need' more growth. But it is clear that economic growth is so much more important in the former than the latter. What would growth in Australia be for? Raising already high standards of living even higher? To lift the last few marginalised communities out of poverty? These are worthy goals, especially the latter, but not ones that necessarily need further growth: they are ambitions that could be met in other ways. Indeed, they *should* be met in other ways: Australians need to learn to make themselves at home. Australia's challenge is sharing, inclusion, participation, reducing inequality and improving lives. Growth may or may not deliver those outcomes, and imbalanced and unsustainable growth could even work against them, especially as Australia is so vulnerable to climate change. Boosting the material living standards of its people remains Madagascar's first priority. For Australia, it needs to turn its attention to making itself at home with the prosperity it has already earned and, in doing so, to leave ecological space for those, such as the Malagasy, who are behind it on the development ladder.

TEN

From individual initiatives to wider change: agitation, amplification and attention

> *[T]he art of system innovation therefore entails finding the right steps and measures at the right time, and also being prepared to deal with unexpected results.* —*Maja Gopel*[1]

A browse through your local bookshop or library will turn up a whole collection of books on how to make the world a better place. They are written by politicians, environmentalists, feminists, entrepreneurs and futurists, but what they often have in common is more detail on 'what' than on 'how'. Laudable visions and compelling pictures are all very well, but they inevitably prompt the question, posed by critics and allies alike, 'But *how* do we get there?'

In some respects, demands for a precise blueprint should be resisted. Describing a compelling alternative to business as usual is a vital step towards system change in its own right. The commonalities across different visions for a transformed society help to build solidarity and reach in an expanding 'new economy' movement.

Yet we do want to go a bit deeper here by offering some ideas for *how* societies – and within them politicians, civil society, businesses, communities and individuals – can bring about an economy that is better at making itself at home. This chapter won't set out a strategy or be a comprehensive guide to processes of change. Others have written more thoroughly on that than we have scope or expertise to do here, notably Maja Gopel's book

The Great Mindshift or Duncan Green's *How Change Happens*.[2] What we seek to do in this chapter is to share some insights that emerge from political science, behavioural change and systems thinking. We hope that these insights will reassure readers that with sufficient agitation, amplification and attention a shift to an economy that makes itself at home is not an idealistic dream, but a possible alternative to the current state of affairs.

Change will not happen spontaneously. The transformations that we have been describing, especially the repurposing of economic goals, amounts to a paradigm shift. This is a deep shift in which social practices and world-views need to change and current path dependencies that lock-in the current way of doing things need to be broken.[3] Moreover, transition needs to occur at all *levels* of activity and action. Geels and Schot's oft-cited Multiple Level Perspective of Transition Theory explains that system transitions occur via interactions between three levels of the system:[4] (a) the niche, or micro-level (where innovation happens at community, grassroots and individual enterprise level); (b) the regime or 'meso level' (the realm of dominant norms, practices, policies and rules); and (c) the landscape or macro level (markets, the built and natural environments and cultural and political beliefs). As explored in more depth below, change at the landscape level begins when we create opportunities for people to ask big questions and to challenge what is considered 'normal'. It requires proactively sharing and disseminating new ideas, and illustrating the merit of alternatives.[5]

Dissemination of change across these levels inevitably takes time. Systems scholars[6] tell us that transformation of this extent emerges after moving through several stages:

1. Pre-development: at this stage alternatives are made 'thinkable', new possibilities are demonstrated and new forums for discussion are created.
2. Take-off: the system absorbs these new ideas, there are an increased number of pioneering practices that demonstrate new ways of doing things. Some of these niche-level activities and practices will be scaled up. Coalitions form and develop. While such alternatives are more visible, they are not yet established as the norm.

3. Acceleration: new solutions will be able to challenge the mainstream – they will be acknowledged and become widespread so that tipping points are reached and a process of mutual reinforcement is instigated. Opposition from those who benefit from business as usual will become overtly hostile to the changes underway.
4. Stabilisation or relapse: either a configuration of the economy has become bedded in or a relapse has occurred, in which the previous state of affairs has reasserted itself.

For example, the transition from fossil fuels to renewable energy is in the acceleration phase, at least when it comes to electricity generation. All the key technologies have been demonstrated, and as renewable energy becomes more cost-effective it is rapidly approaching the point where it becomes the default choice. Renewable heat and electric cars, two other important aspects of the clean energy transition, remain in the take-off phase.

Of course it is not a simple sequential process: change can come about in surprising, unplanned ways. Crisis can provide a breakthrough, but more often it takes the slow propagation of ideas as people change the way they look at the world. This can be frustrating when there isn't time for patience. In this chapter we will look at three key approaches for accelerating transformation and reaching stabilisation sooner: drawing attention to a new narrative; agitation and advocating for policy change and structural reform; and amplifying and cultivating positive disruptors.

The great systems thinker Donella Meadows (herself drawing on philosopher Thomas Kuhn) recommends that people seeking to change paradigms should

> keep pointing at the anomalies and failures of the old paradigm, you keep speaking louder and with assurance from the new one, you insert people with the new paradigm in places of public visibility and power. You don't waste time with reactionaries; rather you work with active change agents and with the vast middle ground of people who are open minded.[7]

From Meadows' advice four tasks can be distilled:

- Highlight the failures of the current system.
- Paint a compelling picture of what a new economic model might look like.
- Work with people who have power in the current system, or who could gain it.
- Support people who are seeking and delivering change themselves, and those who are open minded, leaving those who are unlikely to change where they are.

Of course, naming the four as 'tasks' is misleadingly reassuring. It suggests that the processes of Arrival and then making ourselves at home is a simple matter of picking up the right tools and hammering a new world into shape. We don't suggest such a thing. We expect strong headwinds and stormy seas. After all, the current order was decades in the making and its architecture is now deeply pervasive, constituting a powerful resistance to change. Opposition comes in the form of path dependency; in the often unspoken preference for the status quo; in the proliferation of short-term decisions; in a narrow conception of costs and benefits; and even more actively in the resistance of powerful lobby groups. In his famous book, *The Structure of Scientific Revolutions*, Thomas Kuhn spells out how the old guard will lash out against new ideas in a futile attempt to defend their own, albeit discredited, theories.[8] There is the awkward reality that for some – those who benefit most from the current economic model – a shift to a fairer and more sustainable world will represent a form of loss, be it of pride, status, power or influence. Even those who stand to benefit and who embrace the change will still face unsettling disruption.

Dismantling the contours of the current economy – its class structures, its power hierarchies, its patriarchy, its apparent 'common sense' and intellectual scaffolding and its sense of the possibility for change – will be a complex, messy, contested process. Compromises will be necessary, unusual alliances will need to be forged, and world-views will be challenged. Often, creating connections across divides is easier when the process begins by recognising shared interests and concerns. Start with common ground, not the points of difference. During the later years of the Cold War, Sting sang about common humanity across ideological divides and his faith that the Russians also love their children.* This is an approach that the charity Common Cause uses – not least because it seeks to activate shared values that all humans hold within them, to differing degrees.[9] In other circumstances, a compelling and prudential reason can be presented (the 'business case for making ourselves at home'). If the odds seem stacked against real change, it is reassuring to remember that unanimity isn't necessary. Inching towards critical mass is enough.

The shift to another gear for the economy certainly requires widespread adjustment. This is better done consciously, as a deliberate process, rather than by drifting inadvertently into a post-growth scenario as growth fails. As we discussed earlier, a post-growth world doesn't emerge by simply shutting off growth. Think about how suddenly adopting a vegan diet would be dangerous for one's health without consciously bringing in new sources of protein, iron and so on. Hence the need for multi-level and consciously *systemic* change – otherwise isolated initiatives will remain vulnerable and rarefied, not delivering on their potential to be part of the shift to making ourselves at home. The example of a shift to a shorter working week illustrates the interdependence: it will need to be accompanied by moves to ensure a more equal distribution of resources so that those on low incomes do not experience a net deterioration in living standards. It will also need moves to reduce the pressure to consume – supporting people in satisfying fundamental human needs through leisure, relationships and participation alongside or instead of consumption.

Pioneers, regimes and change agents

Activist Rob Hopkins celebrates 'the power of just doing stuff' in his book of the same name, arguing that small but visible actions are a key starting point for local change makers. These small changes can then be knitted together into something larger,

* See the song 'Russians' from the album *The Dream of the Blue Turtles.*

through cultivating new ideas and supporting innovators through communities of practice.

So, pioneering efforts are important for the function they play in demonstrating the possible and the desirable.[10] The merits of pioneering initiatives (experiments or prototypes) have informed plenty of stirring mantras that seek to motivate those attempting to create tangible, if small-scale, alternatives. 'We make the road by walking,' said Paulo Freire and Myles Horton. Buckminster Fuller assures us that 'You never change things by fighting the existing reality. To change something, build a new model that makes the existing model obsolete'. A direct example of this is the Tesla car company, which set out to design an electric sports car that could 'beat a gasoline sports car like a Porsche or Ferrari in a head to head showdown'. Founder Elon Musk says that 'the overarching purpose of Tesla Motors is to help expedite the move from a mine-and-burn hydrocarbon economy towards a solar electric economy'.[11]

The examples in this book, and hundreds of others like them, provide evidence that the vision of making ourselves at home is, in fact, realisable. They might be described as 'prefiguring' the new system while the old one is still here. They are also sources of inspiration that enlarge people's sense of possibility. Small-scale initiatives serve as 'magnet projects' that demonstrate what is possible, provide learning and help people to 'experience the future'.[12] As replication happens, early adopters are likely to be joined by others. Eventually a critical mass (estimated to be about 10% of a given population[13]) might be attained and a tipping point reached and new norms created. At this stage, the scene is set for political actors to further drive change by introducing enabling policies.

It follows that the extent to which pioneers and small-scale examples of change inspire each other is dependent on *horizontal* interactions and trend setting. Everett Rogers' 'diffusion of innovations' theory suggests that new practices will be taken up by others when they are visible and widely communicated, easy to understand, offer an improvement on the current context, and if they fit with current values and beliefs.*[14] Accordingly, steps that can be taken to advance this process include: encouraging highly respected actors (both individuals and organisations) to join the practice; communicating its benefits to those more likely to take it up; facilitating peer-to-peer learning; and ensuring that early adopters receive positive feedback and benefits.

'Goldman Sachs doesn't care if you raise chickens' was how political scientist Jodi Dean dismissed the threat of such small-scale actions.[15] And certainly, the institutions of the global economy are not intimidated by one or two people raising hens. But imagine if more and more people started to keep chickens, and grow their own food, and find satisfaction and empowerment in community gardening. Goldman Sachs might just start to care: a new norm would be in the offing; markets would be disrupted; and powerful actors would find their source of influence undermined. Stranger things have happened – Gandhi undermined the British empire by encouraging people to spin their own cloth.

While Arrival and making ourselves at home undeniably requires a concerted political programme, it will also be bolstered by the growing number of initiatives that embody the ethos of making ourselves at home – eventually adding up to create a new normal (a 'numbers game', if you like). Together, a political programme and supporting initiatives will be mutually reinforcing. The more people who are enabled to take steps to change their own lives, work and communities, the more others will see that it is possible and worth doing. Of course, people's agency to undertake such changes is bounded – hence the crucial political project to shift structures, including physical ones. But, in many cases there will be steps that people, communities and businesses can take (see Chapter Eleven).

* Rogers suggests that individuals go through a five-step decision-making process to adopt the innovation: knowledge, persuasion, decision, implementation and confirmation.

Arise and amplify

Many businesses and community groups are already taking the sorts of decisions and adopting practices that we would associate with a post-Arrival recalibration of economic purpose. So are governments, from municipal and regional to national and supra-national groupings. But the transformational shift from quantitative to qualitative development won't happen simply by tallying up good examples of small changes, despite the many case studies and interesting ideas that we can gather together. The shift needs to be more deliberate: a process of political struggle based on a widely shared vision – otherwise these examples might continue to exist *despite* the system, instead of being nurtured by it.

Are there ways to join up these various examples into something more strategic and to get things moving towards scale – both in size and in number? How can they be woven together to add up to wider economic change?

The notion of virtuous circles can provide hope – done right, we can pull at one or two threads of the current system, as Meadows recommends, and it will start to unravel. A compelling example of a changed practice might enable and encourage others to adopt new behaviours. New behaviours will coalesce into new norms. New norms can in turn convince policy makers that the public mood has shifted and policy can advance without risk that the policy maker will be dismissed as too radical or out of touch (recognising, of course, that policy makers themselves have a role to play in changing norms).

Writ large, virtuous circles can be instigated via movements which spur political change. Multiple benefits can cascade from enabling policy changes. For example, delivering more job and income security will be part of creating circumstances in which people are free to look beyond short-term survival needs and pay attention to creating a flourishing life (see Table 1 on page 81). This enabling context is another virtuous circle to help foster the process of making ourselves at home. Action by civil society can circumvent the state as sole conduit of change (although it does use the state as a tool) – a practice described as 'civil regulation'.[16] Note that the interaction between levels is important: regime change opens up new possibilities and changes the rules of the game; experiments and prototypes illustrate in microcosm what needs to be done on a wider scale and what policy shifts are due.

Box 10.1: Moving miners: why Rio Tinto responded to Indigenous demands[17]

Australia in the late 1990s and early 2000s gives us a remarkable example of how power can be wielded by those who lack economic resources. Instead of passively accepting the development of mining on their land, certain Indigenous communities – often in some of the remotest parts of Australia – were able to force their demands into corporate decision making.

To do so, they wielded almost every tactic open to them: protesting at shareholder annual general meetings, forming unusual coalitions, galvanising the United Nations protected areas system, physically blockading access to mine sites themselves or using legal land title to prevent miners entering, mobilising public opinion and impacting on the financial interests of owners of the mine. These activities created circumstances in which it was in the best interests of the company to attend to community demands. Doing so was positioned as prudent strategy, due to immediate financial circumstances, or in the longer term on account of the company's reputation. At a mine in Queensland, negotiations led to agreement with local Indigenous communities. After a protracted campaign against a uranium mine in Australia's Northern Territory, Rio Tinto deferred to local community wishes regarding mine construction.

In both cases, the extent to which Rio Tinto recognised and responded to community expectations depended on certain company employees, especially senior management, who were sensitive to community demands and who saw the need to be responsive. The most long-lasting agreements were forged and relationships established when this enlightened self-interest coincided with key individuals within the company acting on their own personal belief that it was time for a new mode of engagement with Indigenous communities. Sometimes this personal drive was itself a recognition of the business case for developing positive relations with Indigenous communities, but in other circumstances it was a personal conviction that such ways of working were the right thing to do that underpinned personal advocacy.

Focusing on building alternatives is all very well, but Srnicek and Williams warn that 'pathways of progress must be cut and paved, not merely travelled along in some pre-ordained fashion: they are a matter of political achievement rather than divine or earthly providence'.[18] A recurring theme in systems literature is that single projects tend to remain isolated. Concerted energy is needed to amplify the messages of pioneers, getting them in front of policy makers and others. Without this awareness-raising effort they will not impinge on wider systems and will hardly shift the 'Overton Window' (discussed below). In other words, they might make a road by walking, as Paulo Freire and Myles Horton suggest, but if no one knows about the road, few others will walk it and it will soon become overgrown.

This is not easy: builders of new worlds must engage with political change, deal in the messy world of compromise, work with people who might be seeking the same ends but perhaps for different reasons and be satisfied with incrementalism. Gopel encourages us to focus on portfolios, recognising that no project on its own will change the system, but many small steps do add up.[19] She calls for a strategy of 'radical incrementalism': actions by a few actors who work according to a long-term vision – their work can be deemed 'radical' because of the ambitiousness of its goal.[20]

Policy change occurs due to the confluence of external events, policy learning, failure of current policies, and/or the formation and action of coalitions.[21] External events create the most obvious opportunities for change – a financial crisis, an election that brings a new political party to power or the signing of a new international agreement. These 'teachable moments' that show the impossibility of business as usual might not bring change in themselves, but they create moments of opportunity. The 'Multiple Streams Approach'[22] argues that decision making is highly contextual and that a confluence of three factors is key: recognition of a problem; compelling policy solutions not only on the table but which also conform to policy makers' values; and conducive circumstances (for example, public mood, pressure-group campaigns or new staff in an administration).* We can extract some implications for our Arrival agenda from these conclusions: identify and harness open policy windows when the political conditions are right; frame and present policy solutions as feasible and in a way that fits with policy-maker and public values; and hook policy solutions to 'recognised' problems.

To go beyond small-scale initiatives, change agents need to harness the imagination of actors in the current regime. Action in one place can nurture change as other political actors draw on policies tested and proved elsewhere. Modelling, copying and adaptation are important to spread feasible solutions between different actors, including between governments.[23] See, for instance, the intense level of interest in pilot schemes around the universal basic income in countries such as Namibia or Finland. A process of observational learning can help a political actor to see and reproduce the initiative: this can enable seemingly less powerful actors to encourage the adoption of new practices.

Often this process will be accelerated in times of crisis. Despite the need to seize opportunity when it arises, political change is more often a slow and challenging process – held back by a bias for the status quo,[24] or by the influence of narrow interest groups.[25] This is what the Arrival agenda is up against: complacent and even hostile elites in the dominant institutions (especially economic and political institutions).** But the power and influence of elites is not automatic – it depends in part on whether they form a cohesive group or consist of competing factions. This gives us a possible way to counter their influence: by finding mechanisms to fragment groups and undermine their cohesion. We can see this in the response to climate change, where business is fracturing into those who want to play a role in decarbonisation, those who will need to be compelled to act and those who still actively oppose climate action. A

* This is sometimes called 'garbage can decision making' because, like a bin, every decision will have a messy mix of inputs, depending on its context.

** C. Wright Mills groups the power elite into six types – notable families, celebrities, CEOs of the most important companies, the corporate rich, senior military officials and senior officials in the executive branch of government.

changing operating context and new business cases can propel self-interested entities towards new behaviours (as seen in the Rio Tinto example above). To trigger such shifts, change agents need to convey to relevant actors why it is in their interests: present a 'business case' for an economy that makes itself at home. The divestment movement exemplifies this. Not only is it tackling root causes of environmental damage, but it shows how a financial imperative – in the form of 'stranded assets'* – can drive large entities to move their investments out of fossil fuel companies.

It is worth paying attention to which particular vested interests (or 'blockers') need convincing: there is a balance to be struck. How many converts are really needed? We noted earlier that social scientists suggest that 10% of a given population can be enough to constitute a tipping point. Meadows would caution against wasting time on those who will never change. Instead the focus should be strategic and on those who might change and who are in positions to catalyse others' change. With divestment, campaigners chose to go after the funders rather than the oil companies. With extraction so central to their business models, the oil majors were never going to agree to leave fossil fuels in the ground for the sake of the climate. Campaign actions directly against them would only get so far. The focus on funders is a good example of strategically prioritising action around those who might actually change. Ideally, combining the business case (or self-interest) with a moral imperative will bring vigorous action from those who were once hostile to change.[26]

The strength of civil society is a factor in all sorts of change. For example, the trade union movement has been a crucial player in realising labour rights and workplace laws; civil society has driven many examples of regulatory change (from the Arms Trade Treaty to increased fair trade). Getting political buy-in is insufficient – as neatly put in President Roosevelt's (reported) response after a meeting with civil rights leaders: 'I agree with you, I want to do it, now make me do it'. To do this, power of

* Assets whose financial value cannot be realised due to, for example, government legislation that limits the extraction of fossil fuels or the market shift to renewables.

some sort needs to be wielded, and there are many theories of power, its nature, its use and its creation. For example, hard or coercive power as opposed to soft or persuasive power; and then there is visible and hidden power. Equally, there are various other forms of power: 'power within' (personal agency); 'power to' (the capacity to exert influence); 'power with' (collective strength); and 'power over' (the ability to get someone to do something they would not otherwise do).[27] The strength of civil society – and hence its capacity to 'make' policy makers take action – tends to reflect all these sorts of power. And it is shaped by factors such as the extent of unity among various social organisations, quality of leadership and coalitions, clear objectives and so on.[28]

The new normal

Underneath both practical and political change efforts there would need to be a substantial shift in mindset if an economy that makes itself at home is to ever emerge. People hold deep-rooted and semi-conscious cultural beliefs and dominant ideologies. Cultural beliefs may initially be promoted through state institutions, the media and opinion makers, but over time they come to be seen as simple, inherent basic 'truths'.[29] As Jean Charles de Sismondi observed over 200 years ago, our 'senses have become so accustomed to … that universal competition which degenerates into hostility between the wealthy class and the working class, that we cannot imagine anymore any other type of existence, even of those whose ruins lie about us'.[30] What people have become accustomed to influences how they think about themselves, how they behave and whether they think change is even possible or not. The future we create begins in the future we imagine. As the opening lines of the Dhammapada put it: 'We are what we think. All that we are arises with our thoughts. With our thoughts we make the world'.[31]

A new economic maturity would need to activate the generous, compassionate and cooperative aspects of human nature, while downplaying the competitive, selfish and materialistic. Psychologists Tim Kasser[32] and Shalom Schwartz[33] reveal that everyone holds, simultaneously, all of these values – but to varying degrees. Certain values can be activated and prioritised by contextual factors such as education, early childhood experiences and advertising.

The good news is that new narratives (such as Arrival and making ourselves at home, or the 'politics of belonging' that George Monbiot has described[34]), if given the right enabling conditions, have the potential to elevate cooperative and sustainable values over those that are more selfish and materialistic. In practical terms, mechanisms to change mindsets might encompass bottom-up participatory awareness raising (such as learning journeys); public and social marketing campaigns; harnessing the influence of opinion leaders; or utilising the education curricula. Essentially, efforts to challenge people's assumptions so that they critically assess their own cultural and social beliefs: gently, perhaps not even overtly, opening people's eyes to the absurdity of certain views and the extent to which their assumptions are outdated.

This may sound abstract, but what is considered 'normal' in society is constantly in flux. New habits and practices are always emerging or receding. Consider recycling. It's a normal part of household routine today in Britain, but in 2000 it was a minority pursuit and only 10% of household waste was recycled. By 2017 the country had been educated, nudged and patiently cajoled into recycling rates four times higher than that.[35] It is not a huge stretch to imagine that this new awareness around waste could be extended more broadly through the narrative of a circular economy, especially for young adults coming of age today who have always recycled and don't remember a pre-recycling age.

Making good choices

Individuals' behaviours are shaped by, are embedded in and themselves shape wider 'social practices'. Contrary to the idea of humans as 'rational economic actors', research shows that people's attitudes, beliefs, motivations and intentions are influenced by a range of often non-rational and socially determined forces.[36] Behavioural psychology, and the related field of behavioural economics, offers a number of insights into how people make decisions, including:

- the cognitive short cuts that people take to deal with complexity (so-called 'heuristics');[37]
- values, both intrinsic (such as moral, pro-social, environmental) and extrinsic (those linked to money, status, power and so on), that motivate people;[38]
- the role of emotions;[39]
- the influences on people both in the way information is presented to them[40] (to the extent they can be 'primed' to react in a certain way[41]) and the salience of an issue (for example, having direct experience of an issue or information that stands out, or seems particularly relevant);[42]
- an individual's capacity and preparedness to perform a given behaviour,[43] including how our cognitive abilities and self-control are impaired by emotional effort.[44]

Alongside these decision-making mechanisms, the wider social contexts in which we live and work also affect our behaviour. Shifting behaviours requires a mix of new norms, but also a conducive physical environment, infrastructure, often financial incentives and so on. For example, the Scottish Government, influenced by the work of Dale Southerton et al, uses a tool[45] that draws attention to a person's individual, social and material context in understanding and influencing behaviours.

Changing the 'choice architecture' that people face can encourage new habits: for example, making desirable behaviours cheaper and easier, and undesirable behaviours harder and more costly.[46] Picture the suite of changes that would undermine the fashion for sport-utility vehicles (SUVs). Interventions might include making such shows of wealth unimpressive, via education, communications, framing and advertising. Increasing taxes on petrol and insurance would make driving SUVs more expensive: financial (dis)incentives. Boosting the quality, accessibility and convenience of public transport and of walking and cycling would actively encourage the alternatives: changing the physical and contextual environment. Raising the recycling rate for plastic bottles is similar. It could be done by adding dedicated recycling bins in public places to make it easier; by bringing in a deposit scheme to make it worthwhile; and by highlighting the problem of ocean plastic to make it morally rewarding. The change in the social practice of recycling wouldn't have happened without the very physical reality of the dedicated wheelie bin.

The more a person has internalised prevailing cultural ideas, values and power dynamics, the less likely they are to act outside of these. Their sense of powerlessness might lead them to conclude that change is impossible, let alone that they might themselves be an agent of change.[47] Mindsets will also be shifted by evidence that change is possible and desirable. This is why it is so important to demonstrate what change looks like in practice, and to showcase what is being achieved already, however small. Good examples sustain personal agency – they make us believe that we can make a difference. Personal agency in turn shapes whether people attempt a given action, how much effort they expend and how long they will persist in dealing with stressful situations that undermine momentum.[48] Accordingly, possible mechanisms to encourage people to become change agents might include awareness raising and peer-to-peer and shared learning; showing that people are part of a wider collective effort; and demonstrating the success of efforts to date.

Without politics and without social movements pushing the political change in the direction of making ourselves at home, any pioneers (be they in projects or in politics) will remain the exception and at risk because they are running against the grain of the dominant system. As economist Robin Hahnel explains, unless there is a movement that can build towards reform of the policy regime in the direction of making ourselves at home, the examples that we have pointed to above will not add up to systemic transformation. Hahnel's conclusion is that a combination is necessary: 'reform movements' and campaigns alongside experiments that grow and proliferate. He believes that the deficiencies of either tactic on its own will be countered by the other.[49] The same could be said for many of the policies identified as key to making ourselves at home: not one will be sufficient on its own, but together they begin to add up to a new story.

Attention: talking about Arrival and making ourselves at home

> *Outlining the contours of what a non-growth society might look like is an essential preliminary to any programme for political actions that respects the ecological demands of the moment.* —*Serge Latouche* [50]

Adam Smith may have written the key book for free market economics, but he didn't much care for economic growth. It hadn't occurred to him or anyone else yet to use the size of the economy as a measure of success. Instead, Smith uses a disarmingly simple word for describing economic progress: improvement. All sorts of things are described this way, with roads and canals chosen as the 'greatest of improvements'.[51] The economy is *better*: improved, rather than bigger.

The words we use about the economy matter. They reinforce a view of the world, and a view of ourselves. They can paint a picture of selfish people grasping after their own interest, or cooperative individuals working together for a shared prosperity. They can portray a world of scarcity and competition for resources, or of abundance and the common good. The dominant narrative of today emphasises the first half of each of those equations, a view that is strengthened over and over through political speeches, media reporting and cultural bias. Use of such language builds a sort of 'cognitive scaffolding', in the words of Snricek and Williams.[52] It thus operates as an invisible power by which people internalise dominant explanations, constraining us to look at things in a narrow way or to ask only certain questions. Language is thus a part of what Gramsci described as the 'common sense' (the set of everyday assumptions about the world that people take for granted).[53] The established social order comes to be seen as natural and unchangeable: the 'only game in town'.

But, systems thinkers tell us that transformational change requires a paradigm shift: it is from mindsets that the system, with all its goals, structures, rules and boundaries, arises.[54] Shifts in mindsets will happen when frames of reference are transformed, breaking open new questions, new perspectives and new interpretations of events and outcomes.[55] To that end, the language people use will be key in overcoming the dominance of the growth paradigm and helping to shift to the paradigm of making ourselves at home. That's why we use terms such as Arrival and the notion of making ourselves at home. 'We begin by changing the stories we tell about ourselves,' says campaigner Chris Martenson. 'The narratives that we run at the individual, national and even global levels define the actions we take and what we prioritise'.[56] Arrival and making ourselves at home enable a different story about progress and appropriate priorities in the 21st century.

Beyond simply new words, frames and images, narratives and stories enable us to paint a picture of a very different economy from that of today. This is part of opening people's minds to an alternative. As Donella Meadows urges: 'keep speaking louder and with assurance from the new [paradigm]'. It is a key element in moving the so-called 'Overton Window'. This concept – named after Joseph P. Overton, a former vice-president of the Mackinac Center for Public Policy – describes a set of ideas that the public deem acceptable or even desirable. Overton's thesis was that for a policy or concept to gain political traction, it had to sit within the window. If it is in the Overton Window, it is unlikely that a policy maker will face public censure for advocating that policy. Overton described a six-step process as ideas move from the very margins of political thought to being implemented as policy:

1. unthinkable
2. radical
3. acceptable
4. sensible
5. popular
6. policy.

Of course, the process is unlikely to be so simple and linear in the real world, nor so neat or automatic. Events, shocks and powerful personalities play a role in moving the realm of acceptability, for good and for bad.* But education or even persuasion can be part of moving ideas and policy demands into the space of public and, eventually, political acceptability.

Of course, storytellers and artists have as much to say on this topic as political theorists. They may want to point out that all societies have their myths – a founding story of revolutionary courage or a fight for independence, for example. The Golden Age is another recurring myth – things were better in the past, and we should try and get back there. The idea of the frontier, of expanding westwards into endless virgin territory, is fundamental to the American dream. There is a big slice of frontier mythology in the narrative of infinite growth. Even progress itself is a form of mythology.[57] We don't have time to explore it in any depth, but the myth of progress has been a powerful one, calling on us to expect more and hope for more with each passing generation. For thousands of years, humanity believed that its lot was fixed in the world, ordained by the gods or the stars. Progress replaced that fixed view of the future. How does the notion need to adapt in a context of prosperity? We have detailed the idea of Arrival and making ourselves at home with reference to social, environmental and development theory, but it's also a more intuitive idea, a matter of the heart as well as the head. We are in some senses offering an alternative, a counter-narrative. Alex Evans, author of *The Myth Gap*, puts it this way: 'The key battles for the sort of world we want in the 21st century will not take place in Cabinet rooms, or Parliaments, or the corridors of the UN. Rather, they'll take place inside each of us, at the level of values, mind-sets, and the "deeper stories" that publics and politicians alike use to make sense of the world'.[58]

The importance of sketching, explaining, illuminating and championing a vision of the economy that is markedly different from that of today is an integral part of the task at hand. Meadows explains that one of 'the most powerful ways to influence the behaviour of a system is through its purpose or goal ... the goal

* Examples of things regressing include the contested use of torture by the CIA after 9/11. Similarly, pre-emptive strikes – attacks on a perceived aggressor without a declaration of war – were historically controversial, but have become a standard defence policy.

is the direction-setter of the system, the definer of discrepancies that require action'.[59] So articulating a new goal should be embraced as a vital element in a process of change – not simply an exercise in, as is often alleged, 'naivety' or 'romanticism', or 'idealism'. Just as Victor Hugo believed: 'utopia today, flesh and blood tomorrow'.

Measuring making ourselves at home

> *We may have eighty years' wisdom about the shortcomings of GDP, but it's a number that still carries far too much influence with many decision-makers. The need for discussion and debate about human development has never been greater. —Khalid Malik, Director of the Human Development Report Office*[60]

Just as an individual's DNA determines the colour of their eyes and their hair, the purpose of an economy determines the outcomes, whether it is GDP or something more pro-social and sustainable. Donella Meadows reminds us that 'high leverage' can be harnessed via 'articulating ... repeating, standing up for, [and] insisting upon, new system goals'.[61] Current metrics for success push the economy away from long-term objectives; they undermine the sort of prevention discussed on previous pages. Indeed, they often incentivise expensive downstream action. Ultimately, they undermine the possibility of making ourselves at home. An alternative set of metrics and measures of success to underpin global development are needed if the transition is going to be even remotely plausible: ones that better align the purpose of the economy with the goals of making ourselves at home. Without such change, if GDP still dominates policy making, the sort of systemic shifts required to make ourselves at home will be practically impossible. New measures are needed to define the new purpose of the economy, aligned to a new focus on its quality rather than quantity.

As such, a GDP lens patently does not fit the purpose of making ourselves at home. GDP adds up economic activity, essentially money changing hands via consumer, business and government spending.* Much of this spending, as we have seen, is often driven by failure and by misdirected efforts to meet people's real needs, or by the need to clean up what gets broken in the pursuit of more GDP growth. Yet, despite the perverse incentives inherent in GDP, it is used far beyond what it was designed for – in a 'maximalist' way by politicians, economists and the media as a proxy for how a nation is performing.[62]

Fortunately, a range of 'beyond GDP' measures are emerging – some developed via grassroots consultation, others from 'experts' listing what they believe a new notion of progress best encompasses. Some will be appropriate for different times and different circumstances – but it is worth noting some key features of a few of them (see Box 10.2). Collectively, these post-GDP indicators 'help break the institutional privileges granted by the GDP system and make the "invisible visible"'.[63] They are part of operationalising new goals for the economy – turning lofty visions into tangible and measurable benchmarks of the current state of affairs and assessments of progress.

Box 10.2: Alternatives to GDP

The Genuine Progress Indicator builds on the Index of Sustainable Economic Welfare constructed by Herman Daly and John Cobb (renamed the GPI in the mid-1990s). It recognises that communities benefit from several sources (such as care work or volunteering), not simply from the output of marketable commodities. It also recognises that income inequality lowers economic welfare. It encompasses household labour, public streets and highways, wetlands, rivers, public spending on health and education, and takes account of 'defensive consumption' such as commuting, insurance, pollution and personal expenditure on medical care. For example, household spending on water filters and bottled water is deemed a cost because it is a 'defensive expenditure'. It also captures crime and depletion of natural assets and extraction of non-renewable energy,

* GDP = consumption + investment + government spending + exports – imports.

recording this expenditure as a reduction of genuine progress.*[64] Researchers have compiled estimates of GPI over many years for 17 countries – the trends show that 1978 was the peak of international (genuine) prosperity and that since then there has been a downward trajectory due to growing inequality of incomes and environmental degradation.[65] In 2012 the Vermont legislature mandated the University of Vermont to prepare annual GPI reports. The State of Maryland has also adapted GPI as a planning tool.[66]

The Happy Planet Index, produced by the New Economics Foundation, assesses the ecological efficiency with which 'good lives' are attained for 140 countries. It takes 'happy life years' (life expectancy and life satisfaction) and divides them by the ecological footprint of a country. Its results show that a high level of resource consumption does not produce comparable levels of wellbeing. Costa Rica topped the Index in 2016, with long life expectancy, high life satisfaction and a per capita ecological footprint one quarter of that of the UK.

The United Nations Development Programme's *Human Development Index* (HDI) was created in 1990 by Amartya Sen and Mahbub ul Haq. It ranks nations by a composite measure of life expectancy, educational attainment (adult literacy and school enrolment) and income (via GDP per capita). The HDI is disaggregated to regions, sexes, urban and rural areas and ethnic groups, and its methodology has been adjusted for environment and inequality. Famously, when Sen told Haq that it is 'vulgar to capture in one number an extremely complex story, just as GDP is vulgar', Haq replied 'Amartya, you're exactly right, what I want you to do is produce an index as vulgar as GDP, but more relevant to our own lives'.[67]

The Social Progress Index is an aggregate index of 52 social and environmental indicators to capture three dimensions (basic human needs, foundations of wellbeing and opportunity). Social progress is defined as the 'capacity of a society to meet the basic human needs of its citizens, establish the building blocks that allow citizens and

* One of its potential limitations is that losses of natural capital could be offset by gains in human-built capital (for example, replacing a park with a school of the same value), or vice versa.

communities to enhance and sustain the quality of their lives, and create the conditions for all individuals to reach their full potential'. Because the index focuses on outcomes of success rather than measures of activity, it is possible for a country to 'overperform' or 'underperform' at turning wealth into progress. The 2016 index identifies the US as an underperformer, while Costa Rica, Uruguay and Ghana are examples of nations that deliver more progress than average for their GDP.[68]

The OECD Better Life Index comprises 11 dimensions of human wellbeing and focuses on people rather than the economic system. It includes objective and subjective measures to assess how current changes in assets will affect wellbeing in the future. The *How's Life?* 2015 report on aspects that shape people's lives included housing, health, work–life balance, education, social connections, civic engagement, governance, environment, personal security and subjective wellbeing. Related to the index is the OECD's Framework for Measuring Wellbeing and Progress. This is comprised of three areas: material conditions, quality of life and sustainability. The framework recognises that GDP captures only a portion of material conditions (as opposed to all the domains of wellbeing and progress) and shows that a sizable portion of GDP is 'regrettables' – negative forms of spending such as tackling pollution or crime.[69]

Oxfam's *Humankind Index for Scotland* puts people at the apex of policy making. Rather than adopting the views of think-tanks, academics or other 'experts', and rather than using arbitrary weightings for respective components, the Humankind Index is a direct reflection of the views and priorities of the people of Scotland. Oxfam asked almost 3,000 people what they needed in order to live well in their communities, making a particular effort to reach out to seldom-heard communities and creating time and space for deliberation, discussion and debate. This generated a set of priorities that were weighted to reflect the importance of each factor of prosperity relative to the others.

These indices are all abstractions of course. The point is that there are certainly better ways of measuring genuine progress than simple increase in economic activity.

Given the importance of rebalancing power for making ourselves at home, such measures are so much better if they encompass citizen participation. We have seen how one element of the multifaceted crisis facing the world is a democratic deficit, with people feeling that they cannot influence the decisions that impact on them. If 'beyond GDP' measures were merely to replace GDP with an alternative that, although well intentioned and more focused on sustainability and human needs, is nonetheless a product of remote decisions, there would be a risk of reinforcing power imbalances and the democratic deficit. Often the 'experts' who determine the composition of these indices are the same intellectuals and technocrats that held influential roles as the ecological, financial and human crises outlined above emerged. More than that, to the extent that the emerging initiatives formulate a product that is intuitively acceptable and plausible for the current growth-ist policy regime, they are unlikely to usher in a meaningful shift in the locus of power.

In 2009, when economists Amartya Sen, Joseph Stiglitz and Jean-Paul Fitoussi delivered their *Final Report for the Commission on the Measurement of Economic Performance and Social Progress* they called for a 'global debate ... [and] discussion of societal values, for what we, as a society, care about, and whether we are really striving for what is important'.[70] In the same vein, Canadian economist Mark Anielski declares that 'future wellbeing indicator work should have a firm foundation in quality of life values expressed by citizens in the community'.[71] A more metaphorical way of making the point is Khalid Malik's observation that

> Only the wearer may know where the shoe pinches, but pinch-avoiding arrangements cannot be effectively undertaken without giving voice to the people and giving them extensive opportunities for public discussion. The importance of various elements in evaluating wellbeing and freedom of people can be adequately appreciated and assessed only through persistent dialogue among the population.[72]

Many, though not all, beyond GDP initiatives have participation at their core, drawing on the results of public consultations of various forms.[73] This is generally to ensure that the measures are an accurate reflection of what a constituency wants, rather than aiming to address political capture and democratic deficits. Yet participation in the construction of measures of progress (such as the Humankind Index in Box 10.2 above) can act as a 'prefigurative' attempt to redress power imbalances and to involve people in decision making, rather than reinforcing elite dominance (no matter how benign the elite's intentions). A practical manifestation of this is devising measures of progress in a way that elevates the voices of the currently marginalised.

ELEVEN

Choosing Arrival – one step at a time

> *If you don't like the way the world is, you change it. You have an obligation to change it. You just do it one step at a time.* —*Marian Wright Edelman*[1]

Arrival and making ourselves at home are propositional concepts: they present a vision that is a marked contrast to the current state of affairs. We recognise that the range of changes we have outlined above – and in particular the new vision of the purpose of the economy – is ambitious and flies in the face of much dominant economic orthodoxy. Proponents of such changes are often scoffed at by those with a vested interest in the current system and their ideas are dismissed as 'unrealistic'. Calls for transformation are often derided as 'utopian' by those who seek to preserve business as usual. Their reaction is testimony to the challenges that concepts such as Arrival face, not least the extent of political capture, path dependency and the resilience of the current system. The growth economy will not go quietly. But we persevere because 'without the belief in a different future, radical political thinking will be excluded from the beginning'.[2]

Nevertheless, we are hopeful that Arrival will be recognised, and that in time the new goal of making ourselves at home will be embraced as a positive evolutionary step for society and the economy. That point is likely to be reached through a combination of push and pull factors: the push will come through ecological crisis and social pressure. The pull factors will flow from a vision of a fairer and more sustainable world, and changing conceptions of real wealth as the conditions of wellbeing. Already we can see that many are choosing this future, and not waiting for governments to lead. On the contrary, the macro economy and many national governments need to catch up with what is already happening in communities and businesses around the world.

Making ourselves at home is not a government-led vision. It is a broad societal shift that involves every level of society. We are not just presenting a list of suggested policies, although we of course recognise that policies can enable or constrain. To make ourselves at home there need to be changes in technology, institutions and laws, new cultures and social relations, new discourses, business models and mechanisms for sharing wealth, new approaches to the environment and ecosystems.[3] In other words, making ourselves at home is a multidimensional task. There are choices for all of us, decisions about how we live and how to do business. Everyone will have a role in making ourselves at home, co-creating a future that emphasises quality over quantity.

How can we be proactive in hastening this shift and ensuring it is a more positive pull, rather than a panicked result of push? We present here a small selection of changes that are happening to varying degrees somewhere in the world. Hence none of them should be deemed 'radical' in the sense that they are untested or utopian. As seen above, systems thinkers encourage us to see gradual changes as incremental steps that will eventually add up: 'radical incrementalism'. They erode the stability of the old system and unlock options for developing a new system. While no single project will change the system, many small steps over a long period of time just might do so.[4]

Steps for international institutions

- Prioritise the needs of the most disadvantaged, recognising that development does not mean the same thing for all countries (or even for all people within a country); do not impose a narrow GDP notion of development. Economic growth is important for low income countries, while richer countries need to prioritise social and environmental welfare via better distribution rather than growth. Create partnerships, dialogues and measures to encourage these dynamics.

- Use the framework of the SDGs to build common purpose across developing and developed countries. Stress that unlike the Millennium Development Goals, the SDGs are for all countries.
- Foster a new leadership and model of global governance fit for the 21st century by creating international institutions in which influence is no longer based on size of economy. This will counter the extent to which wealthier nations dictate policies to their own advantage. One scenario is to build an alliance of countries and regions (supported by progressive businesses and social groups) committed to fostering a development model that is focused on the quality of growth and wellbeing, rather than narrowly defined economic output. Such a group of governments will share common values and be able to exchange experiences and foster new forms of cooperation. It will also enable its members to have more influence on international politics and economic governance. Katherine has been involved in instigating such a group, the Wellbeing Economy Governments partnership.
- Ensure that there is sufficient finance to enable developing countries to take up low carbon technologies and sustainable practices. Source this from those countries that have profited from exploitation of the world's resources (for example, via the Green Climate Fund).
- Together with national governments, work towards a new understanding of international relations that is based on cooperation and mutual aid rather than competition between nation-states.
- Encourage equality between men and women; ensure that girls and boys have equal access to quality education; that women's rights are enshrined and upheld at national and local level; that women no longer face violence; and that they have an equal share in decision making.

Steps for governments

- Measure progress more holistically, developing a broader set of metrics and reducing the importance of GDP figures. Distinguish between healthy and unhealthy forms of growth.

Recognise the importance of development as meeting people's fundamental human needs.

- Address inequalities as a priority. This is a long-term, wide-ranging brief that should in time be incorporated into every department, with all policies and spending assessed on their potential impact on equality, including gender equality.
- Put in place standards that increase circularity in the materials economy, through targets for zero waste or making businesses responsible for end-of-life disposal.[5]
- Adopt a commons approach to natural resources, particularly the atmosphere. This could be done through individual carbon trading, which would allow individuals with smaller carbon footprints to sell some of their allocation to others. Rates of carbon emissions rise with affluence, so this would help to redistribute income. Managing water supplies could also benefit from a commons approach, with varying tariffs that rise with usage: it should be cheap to water a house plant, but relatively expensive to irrigate a golf course.
- Work to redress market failures, where social or environmental costs are externalised. For example, the car culture has multiple impacts on the environment, health and society that are not priced into the cost of motoring. Aviation is similar. Tools include taxation, air pollution targets, efficiency standards and regulating to make companies responsible.
- Move towards 'predistribution', creating a more inclusive economy and reducing the need for costly redistributive bureaucracy further down the line. Employee ownership, community-owned utilities, salary ratios or a maximum wage would all contribute to this and there are a range of other levers that government can pull to facilitate their introduction. Use government regulations, procurement, encouragement and largesse to promote pro-social businesses.
- Embrace Neva Goodwin's advice to 'use taxes to bring about the results we want, rather than the results we don't want'.[6] Price in a way that recognises human values, including equity, ecological realities and present and future needs. Sweep away perverse subsidies, such as tax breaks for fossil fuels. Redirect subsidies to support activities that meet the conditions

necessary to make ourselves at home, like high environmental quality and decent employment. This might entail:
- sumptuary or luxury taxes at a high enough level to discourage status consumption and encourage sustainable consumption;
- rebalancing the tax system away from income and towards wealth. Wealth taxes are economically preferable to taxing work; they are fairer and would tackle inequality more directly.[7] Wealth taxes should include inheritances and other windfall gains, land value taxes (which would be lower in deprived areas and so would operate as a spur to business activity), and perhaps in the future taxes on ownership of robots used in production processes;
- capital gains tax set at a level to ensure that unearned income is not taxed at a lower rate than earnings from work;
- corporate tax relief extended to those businesses that adopt purpose and practices conducive to making ourselves at home;
- taxes levied on carbon emissions and energy-intensive goods and services so they are more expensive and efficiency is incentivised,[8] but without relying on them for revenue, lest perverse incentives undermine necessary direction of travel;
- exploration of a frequent flyer levy.

• Develop and implement proposals for debt relief – for countries and for citizens.
• Plan for and adjust to the challenges of an ageing population, rather than delaying it through population growth.
• Commit to equal opportunities for women, including universal secondary education, removing gender bias in law, ensuring that unpaid care is recognised and redistributed. Commit to high-quality child care and reducing the gender pay gap.
• Investigate a participants' income, which would simplify benefits systems, reward unpaid work, reduce inequality and facilitate volunteering.
• Explore ways to shift remuneration so that it is correlated to social value.

- Support flexible working, part-time work and life-course savings. Government can encourage business in this by shifting tax and other associated employers' costs from number of workers to hours worked, changing the costs facing employers so they are rewarded rather than penalised for taking on more staff. Even better would be a shift to wealth and capital taxes rather than taxes on labour at all.[9]
- Increase democratic deliberation and participation, from regional devolution to electoral reform, giving people a greater voice in government and more opportunities to influence the decisions that affect them.

Steps for businesses

- Encourage employee ownership (for example, in the business itself and via its supply chain) and workplace democracy. Limit income inequality by setting a pay ratio, ensuring that success is shared with all employees, from the lowest-paid to the highest-paid.
- Allow flexible working, co-working and part-time work patterns wherever possible.
- Ensure that women are treated and remunerated equally with men and that women have an equal role in decision making.
- Redesign jobs so they are more meaningful, with parity between effort and reward, more worker autonomy, and ensure that tasks that cannot be made attractive are shared, rather than shunted to the lowest-paid.
- Phase out quarterly reporting and seek long-term, mission-orientated investors. Even better, transition to a stakeholder firm rather than seeking shareholders at all.
- If the business must be shareholder owned, issue different classifications of shares, with committed shareholders receiving favour in dividends or bonus shares and greater voting rights. For example, shareholder corporate governance rights should be subject to a minimum period of owning a share.
- Broaden measures of success to include triple bottom-line accounting, with social and environmental aspects considered alongside the financial. Rewrite the duties of executives to make these obligations rather than optional extras. Rank

employees, customers and society as beneficiaries of the corporation.
- Transition towards the circular economy by keeping ownership of equipment or moving to a leasing model.

Steps for cities and local communities

- Invest in public space, from streets to squares to parks, areas that are open to all and in a way that fosters local pride and a sense of place. Protect public space from over-commercialisation through advertising.
- Strive to widen access to facilities, keeping community sporting, artistic and cultural facilities as cheap as possible or free at the point of participation.
- Support volunteers and community participation. Sports clubs, amateur dramatics and choirs, scouts and guides, and thousands of charities and community groups are key building blocks of shared lives. Wherever possible, keep costs low for equipment, venue hire, travel and administration. Individual volunteers could be supported and thanked with benefits such as extensions to tax-free allowances or a participants' income.
- Facilitate slower lifestyles through planning. For example, by creating walkable neighbourhoods, cycling infrastructure, attractive higher-density mixed neighbourhoods and high quality green spaces.
- Create opportunities for people to co-create and co-own services, such as co-housing, community energy, community health trusts, co-ops, business hubs, and crowd-funding initiatives.
- Share resources through libraries, time-banking, car-pooling and so on. Libraries aren't just for books, but for tools, toys, leisure equipment and more. Encouraging sharing rather than private ownership reduces costs and widens access, while reducing ecological impact and encouraging care and repair. Call for shared goods to be encouraged by making them value-added tax exempt.
- Give citizens a wider say in the policies that affect them locally, through initiatives such as participatory budgeting, planning and referenda.

- Encourage life-long learning as a key element of wellbeing. This is partly about lowering obstacles to formal education through colleges and universities, but could also be through part-time college places, evening classes and skill sharing.
- Provide high-quality and sustainable public transport, transitioning away from the default mode of private car transport.

Steps for individuals

Some readers may have got this far and will be wondering if there is a role for individuals too, lifestyle choices that can contribute to this vision. We recognise that some steps will resonate primarily with those fortunate enough to not have to worry about meeting their basic needs, but others are arguably more universal.

- Recognise the full definition of wealth that includes health and relationships, meaningful work and participation in society. Strive to pursue this fullness of life rather than financial gain.
- Embrace experientialism over materialism, knowing that experiences are more likely to deliver satisfaction and build community.
- Take your time – work part time. If you get offered a pay rise, take the opportunity to work fewer hours rather than to earn more. Invest that time in what you value most, whether that is family, creative projects or volunteering.
- Buy fewer, better things. Aspire to own things that you love and value, not clutter that you resent.
- When spending is necessary, spend the world you want into reality by supporting companies that you believe in – from ethical fashion to fairly traded goods to local business.
- Participate in shared goods and services when you can. That includes community energy, community gardens, peer-to-peer finance and co-working spaces.
- Vote for recognition of Arrival, and if there's nobody standing for such things where you are, join political parties or campaigns to advocate for those policies.
- Talk about all of this, so that these attitudes and values become normal among families, neighbours and friends.

TWELVE

Conclusion

If you are lucky enough to drink wine by the sea, you're lucky enough. —*Unknown*

Humanity is a long way from where it was 100 years ago. There has been so much good news to report as people have lifted themselves out of poverty and prosperity has spread around the world. Many are able to live the kinds of lives their grandmothers could only dream of.

But material progress has been a mixed blessing, and it has brought profound social, political and environmental problems. Some of those are reaching critical turning points – climate change is certainly one such looming catastrophe. Persistent poverty alongside inequality and its corrosive effect on democracy is another, seen in the widespread disenchantment with political systems and the rise of more extreme politics.

We believe that we find ourselves at a key and unprecedented moment in history. The last few decades of growth have brought immense benefits, but those gains have been unevenly shared and are at risk of slipping away as the environment and society come under increasing pressure. The fruits of growth are rotting on the vine as economies remain geared to the pursuit of yet more growth.

The answer to this crisis is not to hark back to the past, whether that be a stalled vision of socialism or an imagined simpler time. Neither is it necessary to imagine some further destination, either a techno- or ecotopia just beyond the horizon, if we press on a little further. Humanity already has what it needs: it is, however, patently terrible at sharing and cherishing those riches. The world that previous generations worked so hard for is here. Today's generations are Keynes' proverbial grandchildren, the inheritors of their forebears' aspirations.

Keynes foresaw that future time of abundance. He also wondered if we would find it hard to adapt. Survival has been a primary goal since time immemorial. Keynes was thinking 'with dread of the readjustment of the habits and instincts of the ordinary man [sic], bred into him for countless generations, which he may be asked to discard within a few decades'.[1] That insight applies today – to avoid squandering their prosperity, individuals, societies and economies will have to change their habits.

'Enough' is impossible to define, but many nations have Arrived in a place where they have more than enough to meet basic material needs and secure a good life for all their citizens. It's time to get better at making ourselves at home with what we have, rather than trying to cram in more. Instead of growing more fruit, the invitation is to savour what has already been grown – and to share it better with those who have too little.

In the industrialised world, the great challenge is not to remain competitive, or to increase efficiency or production. It is to slow down without derailing, to reimagine progress beyond more of the same. The challenge is to make ourselves at home in the world. There is plenty more to do, infinite opportunities for progress – but what comes next is improvement, not enlargement.

Appendix

Further reading

Our purpose in this book has been two-fold. First, we wanted to sketch out the idea of Arrival – where the economy finds itself when the work of growth is done. Second, we have described what the priorities might be for an economy that has grown up, a process that we have compared to making ourselves at home.

Inevitably, this has been a starting point, not a comprehensive vision for the transformation of society. We haven't covered everything, and that's deliberate. For one thing, there was the simple practicality of keeping the book short. We're also suspicious of big manifestos describing alternative systems. Who are we to tell humanity what to do? It's better to offer ideas and invite people into a conversation, and we can decide together what the future holds.

That said, we're well aware of several big topics that we haven't covered in any detail, but that deserve more attention. So let us offer some pointers for further reading:

Money and finance

We've made only passing mention of finance, debt and money. A new economy will need solutions to the debt-based money system that we currently have, which, many argue, locks us into economic growth. The Positive Money campaign is worth looking up here, particularly its report *Escaping Growth Dependency*. While doing so, it is also worth examining some counter arguments such as those made by Tim Jackson and Peter Victor, or by Mark Burton, who question the notion of an iron-clad link between debt and growth. James Robertson's book *Future Money* is a useful starting point in understanding how money functions and why it works against sustainability. The Finance Innovation Lab is a useful source of new thinking on finance. Ann Pettifor's work on debt in a wealthy-country context is very useful, and David Graeber's book *Debt: The First 5,000 Years* is a remarkable overview. It would also be worth dipping into the IMF's *Chicago Plan Revisited* report. We also didn't have space to explore the potential of new mechanisms such as community currencies, social stock exchanges, social investment banks and community shares, but clearly these all offer a great deal to the agenda of making ourselves at home.

Housing and land

There is a whole school of economists, known as the Georgists (after the land activist Henry George), who see land as the key to an equitable society. This perspective is very relevant, especially in a country such as Britain, where land is poorly distributed and rising house prices are a major driver of inequality. The principal policy recommendation of Georgism, the Land Value Tax, is long overdue. See landvaluetax.org for more. Community land trusts are another way of including more people in the value of land. For ideas on different modes of housing, including social housing and co-ownership, see Chris Bird's book *Local Sustainable Homes*. Danny Dorling, an economist whom we have cited a couple of times, has written about housing and inequality in his book *All That Is Solid*. The New Economics Foundation has also done some useful work on land and housing (see, for example, the book by Josh Ryan-Collins and Laurie MacFarlane). On the buildings themselves, Jeremy has a particular interest in sustainable architecture and writes about it regularly on his blog: makewealthistory.org/category/architecture.

Technology

Writing about technology is difficult in a shifting landscape, and we have been reluctant to venture predictions on the role of robotisation and computerisation in the economy of the future. Ryan Avent's book *Wealth of Humans* has been helpful, and Erik Brynjolfsson is a leader in the field. See his book *The Second Machine Age*. Nick Srnicek is also a compelling voice on technology, and his books *Inventing the Future* (with Alex Williams) and *Platform Capitalism* combine an understanding of technological change with an awareness of inequality. The World Economic Forum is also a good repository of material on this matter (weforum.org). Some sustainability commentators see a future with less technology, and others see more technology as the solution. There are intelligent voices on both sides, such as The Simplicity Institute on the former and The Breakthrough Institute on the latter. Jeremy has worked on future scenarios with the Royal Society, which is a useful source of information on new and emerging technologies and how they will affect us. See royalsociety.org.

Trade

What is the role of international trade in a sustainable future? Where do we stand on the movement of goods, capital and people? These are questions we have not had time to explore, but for those who want to learn more, we would point to the work of Christian Felber and, of course, the Fair Trade movement. Trade does not always have to mean goods being shipped around the world: the work of organisations such as BALLE, the Institute for Local Self-Reliance, and the Centre for Local Economic Strategies shows that with attention to the circulation of goods within a smaller locality, a range of economic and social benefits can emerge.

Education

If we are talking about qualitative forms of progress and development, then education is one of the first things that comes to mind. Lifelong learning is a deeply rewarding non-material alternative to acquiring consumer goods. Jeremy has been inspired by Guy Claxton's work on this, such as his book *What's the Point of School?* Education for sustainability and citizenship are important movements. That includes Ecoschools, the world's largest education programme – see ecoschools.global. Lifelong learning and the conscientisation aspect of education can have a positive bearing on the scope to make ourselves at home – look, for example, at the development education movement or institutions such as Schumacher College.

Politics

Party politics is different in every country, and we did not want to get bogged down in the specifics of any one nation and its parties. Obviously, the kinds of changes that we describe in these pages will have to be fought for within existing systems, and that means party politics – at least at the outset. We would point to the work of London-based Compass for its critical but proactive efforts to change politics in the UK, and George Monbiot as one author who has given some thought to radical change within the British system (he writes about it in his book *Out of the Wreckage*). For American politics, see the work of Becky Bond and Zack Exley, and their book *Rules for Revolutionaries: How Big Organizing Can Change Everything*. As an advocate of better voting systems, Jeremy is a member of the Electoral Reform Society and we both recommend its work as showing how the structures of politics can work better for people and for democracy writ large.

Notes

Preface

1 Atwood (1980).

Chapter One

1 Marçal (2016 [2012]: 189.
2 Cancer Research UK (2016).
3 Keynes (1930).
4 Keynes (1930).
5 Skidelsky and Skidelsky (2013): 7.
6 Keynes (1930).
7 Mill (1909 [1848]).
8 Hayek (1947).
9 Okri (2014).

Chapter Two

1 Obama (2014).
2 Steffen et al (2015).
3 United Nations (2015).
4 You et al (2015).
5 World Health Organization (2015).
6 World Health Organization (2016).
7 Global Burden of Disease Study (2016).
8 United Nations (2015).
9 UNESCO Institute for Statistics (2015).
10 World Health Organization (2014).
11 UNESCO Institute for Statistics (2015).
12 Walton (2010).
13 Quoted in Mobertz (2017).
14 DfID (2008).
15 GAFI and IMF, cited in Shenker (2009).
16 Turner, Cilliers and Hughes (2015).
17 UNDP (1996).
18 Klump (2016).
19 Malik (2014).

[20] Skidelsky and Skidelsky (2013): 4 (italics in original).
[21] Skidelsky and Skidelsky (2013): 4.
[22] Raworth (2017): 245.

Chapter Three

[1] Illich (1973): 11.
[2] CK, Louis (2008).
[3] Galbraith (1999 [1st edn 1958]): 284.
[4] Dreze and Sen (1989).
[5] Childs and McLaren (2012).
[6] Tran (2013).
[7] Mortality Projections Committee (2017) and https://inequality.org/great-divide/whats-killing-white-folks/
[8] Max-Neef (1991): 31.
[9] Shiva (2013).
[10] Meadows et al (1972).
[11] Meadows (2008): 146.
[12] Turner (2014).
[13] Jackson and Webster (2016).
[14] Miller and Hopkins (2013).
[15] Wright (2006): 5.
[16] Klein (2014): 169.
[17] WWF (2014): 10.
[18] Slezak (2016).
[19] UNISDR and Centre for Research on the Epidemiology of Disasters (2015).
[20] WWF (2016).
[21] United Nations Food and Agriculture Organization (2016b): 6.
[22] Ceballos et al (2015).
[23] Hayhow et al (2016).
[24] DARA and Climate Vulnerable Forum (2015): 14.
[25] International Energy Agency (2016b).
[26] Winsemius et al (forthcoming) and Hallegatte et al (2013), cited in Hallegatte et al (2016).
[27] NASA (2016).
[28] Cited in Milman (2016).
[29] Quoted in Goldberg (2016).
[30] G20 (2016).
[31] International Bank for Reconstruction and Development and World Bank (2012): 2.
[32] Chancel and Piketty (2015).
[33] Sibaud (2013): 53 and Trucost (2013).
[34] Trucost (2013).
[35] Fioramonti (2017): 210.
[36] Jowitt (2010).

[37] Starr (2016).
[38] Kempf (2008): 23.
[39] de Sismondi (1991 [1819]).
[40] Alvaredo et al (2017): 5, 7.
[41] Hardoon, Ayele, and Fuentes-Nieva (2016). See also Atkinson (2015), Stiglitz (2012) and Milanovic (2016).
[42] Hickel (2017): 2.
[43] Hardoon, Ayele and Fuentes-Nieva (2016).
[44] World Bank and International Monetary Fund (2016): xv.
[45] Edward (2005).
[46] Hickel (2016).
[47] Hoy and Samman (2015).
[48] UNICEF and World Health Organization (2015): 24.
[49] Christie's (2017).
[50] International Energy Agency (2017): 11.
[51] Davies, R. (2016).
[52] World Bank (2016).
[53] United Nations Food and Agriculture Organization (2016a): 14.
[54] Gustavsson et al (2011).
[55] Gordon, Mack, Lansley et al (2013).
[56] Xue et al (2005).
[57] Case and Deaton (2017). See also Cribb, Hood and Joyce (2016): 3.
[58] de Sismondi (1991 [1819]).
[59] de Sismondi (1991 [1819]): 21.
[60] Kuznets (1934).
[61] Wallich (1972).
[62] ABC Radio National (2016).
[63] See for a good analysis of the dynamics of this relationship: http://www.un.org/esa/desa/papers/2015/wp145_2015.pdf
[64] Hickel (2015).
[65] See also Atkinson (2015); Piketty (2014 [2013]); Stiglitz (2012); and Milanovic (2016); Harvey (2005); Lansley (2006); and Dorling (2012).
[66] Piketty (2014 [2013]).
[67] ONS (2015).
[68] Lazonick and Mazzucato (2013).
[69] Lazonick and Mazzucato (2013).
[70] Bivens and Mishel (2015).
[71] Resolution Foundation (2012; 2013); Institute for Employment Research and Institute for Fiscal Studies (2012); Pennycook and Whittaker (2012); Lansley (2006); and Lansley (2009).
[72] Lansley (2009).
[73] Alvaredo et al (2017).
[74] Richard et al (2006).
[75] White (2006).
[76] Sjåfjell et al (2014).
[77] Dobbin and Jung (2011), cited in Birch (2015).

78 Williamson, Driver and Kenway (2014).
79 Deakin (2014).
80 Chang (2010).
81 The Resolution Foundation found that only 12p in every £1 of UK GDP goes to wages in the bottom half (down 25% in the three decades to 2012): Resolution Foundation (2012).
82 Prasad (2013), cited in Davies (2009).
83 Nicholas (2013).
84 Nicholas (2013).
85 Fuentes-Nieva and Galasso (2014); Callahan and Mijin Cha (2013); and Stoddart (2014).
86 Cited in Alperovitz (2013).
87 Stoddart (2014).
88 Morgan and Hewett (2015).
89 Meadows (2008): 156.
90 Ramesh (2012) and Hastings (2009).
91 Strauss-Kahn (2010).
92 Wilkinson and Pickett (2009).
93 Skidelsky and Skidelsky (2013 [2012]): 5.
94 Kabeer and Natali (2013).
95 International Labour Organisation (nd).
96 UN Women (2016).
97 Rhodes (2016).
98 Donald and Moussié (2016).
99 *Ethical Markets Magazine* (2013).
100 Dorling (2010).
101 Paskov, Gërxhani and van de Werfhorst (2013).
102 Paskov, Gërxhani and van de Werfhorst (2013).
103 Layte and Whelan (2013).
104 Smith and Harding (1997) and Link et al (2002), cited in McCartney et al (2013): 7.
105 Wilkinson and Pickett (2009).
106 McManus and Roberts (2014): 8.
107 Marmot (2004): 241.
108 Brooks (2011): 146.
109 Dorling (2010): 99; Hamilton and Catterall (2007; 2008); Chase and Walker (2012); Walker et al (2013).
110 Veblen (1925): 39.
111 Lothian and Unger (2012).
112 Federal Reserve Bank of New York (2016).
113 Crouch (2011): 114.
114 Lothian and Unger (2012).
115 Aldrick (2009).
116 Thomadakis (2015).
117 Lansley (2013).
118 Credit Suisse (2013): 51 and Davies (2009): 26.

[119] Lothian and Unger (2012).
[120] Di Muzio and Robbins (2017).
[121] Birch (2015).
[122] Eisenstein (2011): 106–7 and Townsend and Zarnett (2013): 21.
[123] Davies (2009): 61.
[124] Preston (2007).
[125] World Bank (1993) and Borowy, I. (2011), cited in McCartney et al (2013): 7.
[126] See summary of this material in McCartney et al (2013): 7.
[127] Kubiszewski et al (2013).
[128] www.socialprogressimperative.org/ (accessed 27 February 2018).
[129] Social Progress Imperative (2016).
[130] *The Economist* (2016).
[131] Dorling (2010): 129.
[132] Schor (2011): 177; Shaw and Taplin (2007); Michaelson et al (2012): 53.
[133] Schor (2011): 177.
[134] Kahneman and Deaton (2010). NB This was based on a sample of over 450,000 respondents and defined wellbeing as 'affect'. There is no breakdown when wellbeing is defined as life evaluation.
[135] See Layard (2005).
[136] World Health Organization (2017).
[137] National Institute for Mental Health (2017).
[138] Quoted in Esfahani (2013).
[139] Bachmann et al (2016): 411–19.
[140] Marsh (2018).
[141] Sane, quoted in Kennedy (2016).
[142] Lessof et al (2016): 65.
[143] NHS Digital (2016): 295.
[144] UK Association of School and College Leaders and the National Children's Bureau (2016).
[145] Saad (2014).
[146] Cited in Randall and Corp (2014).
[147] Bowles and Park (2005): 397–412.
[148] Wilson and Moulton (2010).
[149] Griffin (2010).
[150] Orr (2014).
[151] Brooks (2011): 385.
[152] Schor (2011): 140–1.
[153] Marmot (2004): 14.
[154] Aglietta (1987), cited in Lee (2000): 255 and Zamagni (2014): 202.
[155] Polanyi (2001 [1944]).
[156] Harvey (2005): 167.
[157] Mental Health Foundation (nd).
[158] House of Commons (2016).
[159] Investors in People (2015).
[160] Chartered Institute for Personnel and Development (2016).

[161] Dahlgreen (2015).
[162] Oxfam UK doughnut report calculations based on ONS (2014a; 2014b).
[163] Adkins (2016).
[164] Davies W. (2016): 86.
[165] Department for Business, Energy and Industrial Strategy (2016).
[166] Western and Rosenfeld (2011).
[167] Western and Rosenfeld (2011) and Blanchflower and Freeman (1992), cited in Lawlor et al (2011): 35.
[168] Pennycook and Whittaker (2012): 14.
[169] Broughton, Biletta and Kullander (2010).
[170] House of Commons Library (2015).
[171] Chu (2014).
[172] Galloway and Danson (2016): 1.
[173] Corlett and Clarke (2017): 23.
[174] Quoted in Latouche (2009): 82.
[175] Bender and Theodossiou (2017).
[176] Trebeck (2011).
[177] Eisenstein (2011): 84–85.
[178] Fioramonti (2013): 56.
[179] Eisenstein (2011): 127, 131; Standing (2016).
[180] Quoted in Gopel (2016): 114.
[181] *Sunday Times* (2017).
[182] Poortinga, Sautkina and Thomas (2016).
[183] Sandel (2012).
[184] Waring (1999): 25.
[185] Nirmalananda (1986).
[186] Schor (2011): 27.
[187] Cited in McLaren and Childs (2013): 16.
[188] Smith (1790).
[189] Dickerson and Kemeny (2004).
[190] Schor (2011): 177.
[191] Walker et al (2013).
[192] Levine, Frank and Dijk (2010).
[193] Frank (2007): 3.
[194] Mill (1909 [1848]).
[195] Schor (1999).
[196] Walasek and Brown (2016).
[197] Kasser (2002): 12–13; 72.
[198] Walasek and Brown (2016).
[199] Latouche (2009): 17; Henderson and Capra quoted in Alexander, Crompton and Shrubsole (2011): 18; Lee (2000): xix.
[200] Ofcom (2008).
[201] Advertising Association (2017).
[202] Ilvashov (2015).
[203] *Women's Wear Daily* (2015).
[204] Horyn (2015).

[205] Gardener and Burnley (2015).
[206] Waste and Resources Action Programme (2012).
[207] Datamonitor research in Davis (2013): 46.
[208] OfferUp (2016).
[209] Self Storage Association (2015).
[210] Steuver (2004): 122.
[211] Schor (2011): 102.
[212] Moss (2012).
[213] Latouche (2009): 20.
[214] Latouche (2009): 55.
[215] Smith and Max-Neef (2011).
[216] Galbraith (1999 [1958]): 32.
[217] Kopnina (2016), in Washington and Twomey (2016): 76.
[218] Sharma (2016): 25.
[219] SPERI (2014).
[220] Cohen (2008 [1996]: 166.
[221] WWF (2014).
[222] Engelman (2012): 121.

Chapter Four

[1] Whitby et al (2014): 3.
[2] Latouche (2009): 16.
[3] OECD (2008) quoted in Fioramonti (2013): 3; see also Rees (2014): 86.
[4] Whitby et al (2014): 11.
[5] Brown (2010).
[6] Cameron (2010).
[7] Jackson (2009).
[8] Harvey (1989): 180. Emphasis added.
[9] Gramsci (1971).
[10] Assadourian (2012).
[11] Jackson (2017): xxviii.
[12] Mullainathan and Shafir (2013).
[13] Jameson (2010).
[14] Fioramonti (2013): 9.
[15] Kuznets (1934).
[16] Michaelson et al (2009).
[17] European Commission, IMF, OECD and UN (2009).
[18] Berik et al (2009).
[19] Fioramonti (2013): 3.
[20] *Der Spiegel* (2009).
[21] May (2016).
[22] Quoted in IMF (2015).
[23] Obama (2015).
[24] Quoted in Wright (2015).
[25] Quoted in Jericho (2016).

26 See, for example, Eisenstein (2011): 83; and Rees (2014): 86.
27 Harvey, D. (1989): 180.

Chapter Five

1 Soper (2011).
2 Slater (1997): 73.
3 Molenaar (2011).
4 Seddon (1992).
5 Christie Commission (2011): 7.
6 McCartney, Taulbut et al (2013): 3.
7 Christie Commission (2011): p. 27.
8 Bramley et al (2016).
9 Eden Project (2017).
10 Pretty, Barton et al (2015).
11 Barford and Pickett (2014).
12 National Institute on Alcohol Abuse and Alcoholism (2017).
13 Centers for Disease Control (2017).
14 Bowles and Jayadev (2014). The authors provide their sources here: http://tuvalu.santafe.edu/~bowles/gloped.pdf (accessed 5 March 2018).
15 *The Economist* (2017).
16 Perdue, cited in Zuckerman (2017).
17 Coady et al (2015): 5.
18 World Bank, quoted in Coote (2012): 11.
19 Daly (2015).
20 Smith and Max-Neef (2011): 146. See also Christie Commission (2011).
21 Fioramonti (2013): 16.
22 Galbraith (1999): 148.

Chapter Six

1 Quoted in Simms and Potts (2012): 10.
2 Mill (1909 [1848]).
3 Gudynas (2013): 174.
4 Fioramonti (2017): 11.
5 Monbiot (2017): 87.
6 Living Well Within Limits, see: https://lili.leeds.ac.uk/
7 Raworth (2012).
8 O'Neill et al (2018).
9 Kroll (2015): 5–6.
10 Kroll (2015): 5.
11 Sachs (1992): xv.
12 Smith (1776): Book 1, chapter 9.
13 Korten (2016); Senft (2016).
14 Van de Bergh (2017).
15 Postwachstum (2010).

16 Lohmann (2014).
17 Schumacher (1993): 129.
18 Quoted in Hirsch (2014).
19 Polanyi Levitt (2013): 109.
20 Pouw and McGregor (2014); and Haidt (2001).
21 Nussbaum (2011): 18, 185.
22 Smith and Max-Neef (2011): 142.
23 Max-Neef (1991): 16.
24 Skidelsky and Skidelsky (2013).
25 Shaw and Taplin (2007); and Huppert and Cooper (2014): 17.
26 Michaelson et al (2009).
27 Gleibs (2013).
28 Quoted in *Ethical Markets Magazine* (2013).
29 Strang and Park (2016).
30 Michaelson et al (2009).
31 See, for example, Antonovsky (1993).
32 Marmot (2004): 112.
33 See, for example, Morrison (2003).
34 Skidelsky and Skidelsky (2013): 148.
35 Deci and Ryan (2008).
36 The Qur'an, Surat I-gasas *The Stories* 28:76; The Bible, 1 Timothy 6:10.
37 Quoted by Segal, J. (2014): 21.
38 Gandhi (1997): 36.
39 Rundle (2015).
40 Buffett (2010).
41 Steiner (2012).
42 Oguz, Merad and Snape (2013).
43 United Nations (2013): 3.
44 Sen (2000): 36.
45 Mill (1909 [1848]).
46 Honoré (2013): 15.
47 Fukuoka (1978): 18.
48 Galbraith (1999): 148.
49 Fred Block in Polanyi (2001 [1944]): xxv.
50 Wilkinson and Pickett (2009).
51 Coote (2012): 8.
52 Lowitja Institute International Indigenous Health and Wellbeing Conference, Melbourne, 8–10 November 2016: https://conference2016.lowitja.org.au/statement/
53 Coote (2012): 21.
54 10 Year Plan for Oregon: http://www.oregon.gov/COO/Ten/docs/10YearCollateralSinglePage.pdf (accessed 18 September 2015).
55 See: https://voyager.jpl.nasa.gov/
56 Newcastle City Council (2017).
57 Widely attributed to Jonas Salk.
58 Buffett (2013).

59 Coote (2012): 5.
60 Raskin et al (2002): 62.
61 World Bank (2012a): 5.
62 Jackson (2009): 8.
63 Sorrell (2007).
64 Gillingham, Rapson and Wagner (2014).
65 Kyba et al (2017).
66 Magee and Devezas (2017).
67 Wiedmann et al (2015).
68 Monbiot (2011).
69 Wiedmann et al (2015).
70 Cames et al (2015).
71 Ward, Sutton et al (2016).
72 Jackson (2009): 80.
73 Wiedmann et al (2015).
74 Ward, Sutton et al (2016).

Chapter Seven

1 Molenaar (2011).
2 Francis (2015).
3 Raworth (2017): 269.
4 Internet meme, attributed to the anonymous user 6/803399 of the Reddit forum.
5 Ferreira and Ravallion (2008).
6 See Piketty (2014 [2013]).
7 Fix (2017).
8 Branko Milanovic, cited in Glennie (2011).
9 TUC (2011).
10 Lustig (2012).
11 Verbist, Förster and Vaalavuo (2012): 35.
12 Hills, Sefton and Stewart (2009).
13 White and Anderson (2001).
14 Hoy and Sumner (2016).
15 Woodward (2015).
16 Wanninski (1978).
17 Hills (2004), cited in Horton and Gregory (2009): 44.
18 Hacker (2011).
19 Gorbis (2017).
20 Woolf (2016).
21 Anderson (2016).
22 Mill (1909 [1848]).
23 Thomas (2017).
24 *Time* Magazine (1966).
25 TUC (2018).
26 Modern Families (2017): 6.

27 Cited in Dietz and O'Neill (2013): 131.
28 ONS (2016).
29 Carers UK (2012).
30 UN Women (2015).
31 Woetzel et al (2015).
32 Schor (2013), in Coote and Franklin (2013): 12.
33 Riechmann y Recio (1997): 34, cited in Ecuador (2009): 22.
34 Schor (2013), in Coote and Franklin (2013): 12.
35 Schor (2011): 114.
36 Rosnick (2013).
37 Cited in Schor (2013): 11.
38 Bentham et al (2013).
39 Simms and Potts (2012): 24.
40 Goodwin (2014).
41 Rai and Waylen (2014): 7.
42 Wainwright (2015).
43 Jackson (2017): 144.
44 Steger, Dik and Duffy (2012).
45 Dunlop and Trebeck (2012).
46 Lawlor, Kersley and Steed (2009).
47 Binder (2016).
48 Saunders and Lawson (2016).
49 Graefe (2016).
50 Avent (2016).
51 Chafkin (2016).
52 OECD (2015).
53 Brynjolfsson and McAfee (2012).
54 See Ethics in Action: https://ethicsinaction.ieee.org/ (accessed 30 December 2017).
55 Avent (2016): 235.
56 Soper (2011).
57 GlobeScan (2012).
58 Havas Worldwide (2014).
59 Wallman (2015): 272.
60 Wakefield et al (2017); see also: http://healthingroups.wixsite.com/healthingroups
61 Xue (2005).
62 Mill (1909 [1848]).
63 Simms and Potts (2012): 14.
64 Simms and Potts (2012): 22, 14.
65 National Trust (2017): 5.
66 Wallman (2015): 161.
67 Schor (2011): 178.
68 Pretty et al (2015).
69 Rosnick (2013).
70 www.iFixit.com

71 www.therestartproject.org
72 See: www.edinburghremakery.org.uk
73 Unwin (2016).
74 Simms and Potts (2012):10.
75 Dupre and Boulbry (2016).
76 Helfrich (2017).
77 Daly (1990).
78 See Alaska Permanent Fund website: https://pfd.alaska.gov/
79 Doyle (2014).
80 Stern (2010): 11.
81 Bill H-385, Vermont Senate: http://www.leg.state.vt.us/docs/2012/bills/Intro/H-385.pdf (accessed 8 October 2015).
82 Quoted in Allen (2014): 246.
83 Wall (2017): 28.
84 Ecuador (2009).
85 Vidal (2011).
86 Davison (2017).
87 *Times of India* (2017).
88 Smith (2016).
89 Montgomery (2012).
90 Mill (1909 [1848]).
91 MacArthur (2014).
92 Benton and Hazell (2013): 4, 22.
93 Benton and Hazell (2013): 22.
94 Thomas (2012).
95 Thomas (2012).
96 Wender et al (2014).
97 Agency of Design (2013) *Design out Waste project:* www.agencyofdesign.co.uk
98 Scottish Government (2010).
99 Ellen MacArthur Foundation (2014): 18.
100 Ellen MacArthur Foundation (2014): 20.
101 Philips (2015).
102 Kostakis et al (2015).
103 Srnicek (2016).
104 Maclurcan and Hinton (2014).
105 Selvanathan (2015).
106 Mara et al (2017).
107 White (2006): 8.
108 Jackson (2017): 141.
109 Kay (2012).
110 Hughes (2013).
111 Davis, Offenbach and Grant (2014): 32.
112 Smithers (2014): 10.
113 Stout (2013).
114 Polman (2014).

[115] Deakin (2014): 39.
[116] Smithers (2014): 78–9 and Deakin (2014).
[117] See: http://www.pluralistcommonwealth.org/
[118] Gregory (2012); and Webb and Novkovic (2014): 2.
[119] Webb and Novkovic (2014): 2.
[120] Birchall and Hammond Ketilson (2009) cited in Sanchez Bajo (2014): 274.
[121] Davies (2009): 93.
[122] Davies (2009): 17.
[123] Jones and Kalmi (2009) cited in Lawlor et al (2011): 38.
[124] Erdal (2014): 214–16.
[125] Cited in Erdal (2014): 218.
[126] Fitch (1996): 18–21.
[127] O'Sullivan (2001).
[128] Zamagni (2014).
[129] Smith and Rothbaum (2014): 234.
[130] Altman (2014): 181–2.
[131] Zamagni (2014): 205.
[132] Erdal (2014): 211.
[133] Sanchez Bajo (2014): 275 and Webb and Novkovic (2014): 4.
[134] Employee Ownership Index (2015).
[135] Oakland City Council Supporting the Development of Worker Cooperatives in Oakland, viewed online 12 April 2018.
[136] See: https://www.scottish-enterprise.com/services/develop-your-organisation/employee-ownership/overview
[137] Lynn (2005): 16
[138] Maclurcan and Hinton (2014).
[139] Mill (1909 [1848]).
[140] Widely attributed to Aristotle.
[141] See for example Held, (1986): 7; and Young (2000): 18.
[142] Mansbridge, J. (1980), cited in Young (2000): 19 and Graeber (2013): 155.
[143] See, for example, Young (2000): 1; and Pateman (1970).
[144] The Hansard Society (2016).
[145] Roßteutscher (2000): 172.
[146] Walker (2002); Pateman (1970): 3; Held, D. (1986): 1; Hirst (1994): 9.
[147] Dryzek (1996): 71–2. See for a discussion of these processes and effects: Hirst (1999).
[148] Korten (2001): 12.
[149] Bertelsman Stiftung (2013).
[150] See, for example, Barber (1984): xiv and Hirst (1994): 3.
[151] Burchardt (2012).
[152] Bell (1987).
[153] McKenzie (2014): 73.
[154] McKenzie (2014): 73; see also: http://www.participatorybudgeting.org/participatory-budgeting-white-paper/
[155] Fanon (1961): 312.

156 Nykvist et al (2013): 11, 46, 77; and Chancel and Piketty (2015); Gore (2015).
157 Hickel (2017).
158 UNDP (2011).
159 WWF (2016): 75.
160 Simms (2009).
161 Porritt (2008): 35.
162 Victor (2014): 109–12; Victor and Rosenbluth (2006); and Victor (2011).
163 See the regular Prosumer Reports from Havas International. http://mag.havas.com/prosumer-reports/ and also Fioramonti (2017).
164 WAVES (2015).

Chapter Eight

1 Alperovitz (2013): 140.
2 For more examples of projects, policies and initiatives that manifest the ethos of making ourselves at home, see: https://goodanthropocenes.net/; https://www.thesolutionsjournal.com/ ; http://www.goethe.de/ins/cz/prj/fup/enindex.htm and https://solutions.thischangeseverything.org/
3 Cohen (2014).
4 Collins (2015).
5 Prada (2013): 146.
6 Gudynas (2013): 36.
7 Gudynas (2013): 35.
8 Prada (2013): 148.
9 Morales (2011).
10 Ecuador (2008).
11 Solon (2014).
12 Ecuador (2009): 20.
13 Ecuador (2009): 20.
14 Hengrasmee (2013): 202.
15 Kroll (2015): 35.
16 Jahan (2015): 47.
17 Pilling (2018): 14–15.
18 Kato (2013).
19 Kato (2010).
20 Cited in Cohen (2012).
21 OECD (2017).
22 Laudicinia (2017).
23 Kroll (2015).
24 Dolan (2013).
25 Latouche (2009): 8.
26 See: www.happyplanetindex.org
27 Cota (2012).
28 Freedom House (2018). See: https://freedomhouse.org/report/freedom-world/2018/costa-rica (accessed 6 February 2018).
29 Madrigal (2018).

30 Participatory Budgeting Project (2016) https://www.participatorybudgeting.org/white-paper/
31 Luton Borough Council (2018).
32 Lamb and Stephanson (2014).
33 Quoted in Lamb and Stephanson (2014).
34 Newcastle City Council (2013).
35 New York City Council (nd).
36 Urban Justice Center (2015).
37 Montreal Urban Ecology Centre (2015).
38 Majale (2009).
39 Majale (2009).
40 World Bank (2012b).
41 NHSSP (2016).
42 Open Government Partnership (2016).)
43 Iceland Constitutional Council (2011).
44 Jónsdóttir (2016).
45 MacFadyen (2014). See also: http://www.flatpackdemocracy.co.uk/
46 Harris (2015).
47 OECD (2016).
48 Eurostat (2018).
49 Delsen and Smits (2014).
50 Silim (2013): 5.
51 Silim (2013): 18.
52 Felongco (2014); BBC News (2013).
53 Xinhua/ECNS (2015).
54 Semler (1993).
55 Varoufakis (2012).
56 Zhang (2015).
57 Haier Group (2017).
58 Alperovitz (2013): 47.
59 Altman (2014): 177.
60 Duda (2016).
61 The Carl Zeiss Foundation, https://www.zeiss.com/corporate/int/about-zeiss/the-carl-zeiss-foundation.html (accessed 28 February 2018).
62 Greencity Wholefoods, Glasgow, https://www.greencity.coop/about-us/ (accessed 28 February 2018).
63 Whittam and Talbot (2014).
64 Fedecovera Guatemala, Guatemala City, http://www.fedecovera.com/ (accessed 28 February 2018).
65 Cumbers (2014).
66 Cumbers (2014).
67 See: https://www.fourthsector.net/
68 Network for Business Innovation and Sustainability (2012).
69 See updates at: http://benefitcorp.net/policymakers/state-by-state-status (accessed 28 February 2018).

70 Ishack Project: www.ishackproject.co.za/about-us/ (accessed 28 February 2018).
71 Lubberman (2007).
72 Quoted in Wang (2015).
73 See: www.natura.com/
74 Forbes (2017).
75 Felber and Hagelberg (2016).
76 Felber and Hagelberg (2016).
77 Lessem and Schieffer (2010): 68.
78 See: www.alrayanbank.co.uk
79 Welby (2017): 108.
80 See: www.reliancebankltd.com
81 Duckles (2016).
82 See: www.triodos.co.uk and www.ecology.co.uk
83 See https://www.ecotricity.co.uk/about-ecotricity (accessed 20 December 2016).
84 See: www.zopa.com ; www.seedrs.com ; www.crowdcube.com.
85 See: www.unbound.com
86 Quoted in Eventbright (nd).
87 UK Music (2015).
88 Roberts (2015).
89 For a good introduction to New York City's volunteering schemes, see Chapter Five, 'A City of Citizens' in Tisch (2010).
90 See: www.nycservice.org
91 Nesta (2014).
92 IPSOS Mori (2014): 53.
93 Packard (1961): 29.
94 Dietz and O'Neill (2013): 160.
95 See: www.slowfood.com
96 Wells (2015).
97 BBC News (2012).
98 National Gardening Association (2014).
99 Williams (2016).
100 Crossan et al (2015).
101 Blair (2009).
102 Warhurst (2012).
103 Gipe (2012).
104 Ministry of Foreign Affairs of Denmark (nd).
105 Torkington (2016).
106 See: Ethiopia's Climate Resilient Green Economy plan, www.ethcrge.info (accessed 20 March 2018).
107 Coupeau (2016).
108 Parkinson (2016).
109 Gregory (2011) and City of Freiburg im Breisgau (2017).
110 See, for example, Garcia et al (2017).
111 International Energy Agency (2016a).

112 Klingbeil (2016).
113 McEvoy (2014).
114 Ellen MacArthur Foundation (nd).
115 See: www.bakeys.com
116 Ellen MacArthur Foundation (2016).
117 Ellen MacArthur Foundation (2016).
118 Ocean Conservancy (2015).
119 See: www.ecovativedesign.com
120 *The Scotsman* (2004).
121 Green Building News (2015).
122 APPSRG and APPMG (2014).
123 APPSRG (2014).
124 Business Wire (2009).
125 Volvo (2015).
126 European Commission (2015).
127 Rreuse (2016).
128 European Parliament (2016).
129 Tatum (2016).
130 McAuley (2016).
131 Orange (2016).
132 See: www.retuna.se/ and Len (2015).
133 Bourne and Zeri (2013).
134 Bourne and Zeri (2013).
135 The Circular Awards (2017).
136 Welsh Assembly Government (2010).
137 Allwood and Cullen (2015): 64.
138 Tearfund (2016).
139 Coats and Benton (2016).
140 Botsman and Rogers (2011): xv.
141 Share Tawe (nd) 'Swansea City of Sanctuary', https://swansea.cityofsanctuary.org/share-tawe
142 See: www.couchsurfing.com; www.streetbank.com; www.bookmooch.com, respectively.
143 Creative Commons (2016).
144 Johnson (2013).
145 Johnson (2013).
146 For Amsterdam see: www.sharenl.nl/amsterdam-sharing-city/; Sharing Cities network see: www.sharingcities.eu

Chapter Nine

1 Quoted in Skidelsky and Skidelsky (2013): 218.
2 Practical Action (2016).
3 Goodall (2016): 12.
4 Allwood and Cullen (2015): 63.
5 Rees and Moore (2013): 15; Vale (2013): 15
6 Oxford Poverty and Human Development Initiative (2012).

7 See: www.fairlimits.nl for more detail.
8 Woodward and Abdallah (2012).
9 Woodward and Abdallah (2012).
10 Kahneman and Deaton (2010).
11 Kubiszewski, Costanza et al (2013).
12 GDP data from World Bank (2017), GDP per capita (current US$). Marks & Spencer market capitalisation from Y Charts, https://ycharts.com/companies/MAKSY/market_cap (accessed 20 March 2018).
13 GDP data from World Bank (2017) GDP per capita (current US$).
14 CIA (2016).
15 GDP data from World Bank (2017) GDP per capita (current US$).
16 Saddler (2013).
17 Wiedmann et al (2015).

Chapter Ten

1 Gopel (2016): 7.
2 Gopel (2016); Green (2016).
3 Gopel (2014).
4 Geels and Schot (2007).
5 For a good discussion of this see The Finance Innovation Lab (2015): 28.
6 Mersmann et al (2014).
7 Meadows (2010).
8 Kuhn (1996).
9 See, for example, the Common Cause Handbook.
10 Mersmann et al (2014).
11 Musk (2006).
12 Institute of Chartered Accountants England and Wales (2014).
13 Social Cognitive Networks Academic Research Center at Rensselaer Polytechnic Institute (2011), cited in Gopel (2016): 156.
14 Rogers (2003 [1962]).
15 Quoted in Srnicek and Williams (2015): 25.
16 Bendell (2000).
17 For a fuller discussion see Trebeck (2007).
18 Srnicek and Williams (2015): 75.
19 Mersmann et al (2014).
20 Gopel (2014).
21 See, for example, chapters in Sabatier and Jenkins-Smith (1993); Weible, Sabatier and McQueen (2009); and Mayne (forthcoming).
22 Kingdon (1984) and Kingdon (2002).
23 Bandura (1977) and Braithwaite and Drahos (2000).
24 Lindblom (1959) and John (2003).
25 Lindblom (1977) and Wright Mills (1956).
26 Trebeck (2007).
27 Rowlands (1997): 13.
28 Keane (1988) and Tarrow (1994).
29 See, for example, Gramsci (1971).

30 de Sismondi (1991 [1819]): 434.
31 The Dhammapada (1994): 3.
32 Kasser (2014).
33 Schwartz (1992).
34 Monbiot (2017).
35 DEFRA (2017).
36 See, for example, Haidt (2001).
37 See Kahneman (2011).
38 Kasser (2011).
39 Frijda, Manstead and Bern (2000).
40 Lakoff, Dean and Hazen (2004).
41 Kahneman (2011): 53.
42 Dolan, Hallsworth et al (2010).
43 Ajzen (1988).
44 Kahneman (2011): 42, 60.
45 Darnton and Horne (2013).
46 Thaler and Sunstein (2008).
47 See, for example, Freire (1993 [1970]).
48 Ajzen (1988).
49 Hahnel (2016).
50 Latouche (2009): 32.
51 Smith (2007): 164.
52 Srnicek and Williams (2015): 81.
53 Anderson (1976).
54 Gopel (2014).
55 Gopel (2014) and Meadows (2010).
56 Martenson (2011): 12.
57 See Gray (2014).
58 Evans (2013).
59 Meadows (2008): 138.
60 Malik (2014).
61 Meadows (2008): 162.
62 Whitby, Seaford and Berry (2014): 11.
63 Fioramonti (2017): 214.
64 Fioramonti (2013): 89.
65 Kubiszewski et al (2013).
66 Maryland Genuine Progress Indicator, see: http://dnr.maryland.gov/mdgpi/Pages/default.aspx (accessed 27 March 2017).
67 Cited in Gertner (2010).
68 See: www.socialprogressimperative.org/help (accessed 28 February 2018).
69 OECD (nd).
70 Stiglitz, Sen and Fitoussi (2009).
71 Anielski (2007).
72 Malik (2013).
73 McGregor (2015).

Chapter Eleven

1 Quoted in Traver (1987).
2 Srnicek and Williams (2015): 139.
3 Mersmann et al (2014).
4 Mersmann et al (2014).
5 Dietz and O'Neill (2013): 146.
6 Goodwin (2014).
7 Nicholas (2013): 3.
8 Robertson (1998): 158.
9 Coote, Franklin and Simms (2010): 29.

Chapter Twelve

1 Keynes (1930 [1963]).

References

ABC Radio National (2016) 'The Goldilocks question: How much economic growth is just right?', Australian Broadcasting Corporation, Sydney, http://www.abc.net.au/radionational/programs/themoney/the-goldilocks-question:-how-much-economic-growth-is-just-right/7248760 (from 4:47 minutes) (accessed 4 March 2018).

Adkins, A. (2016) 'Employee Engagement in U.S. Stagnant in 2015', *Employee Engagement Gallup*, 13 January 2016. http://news.gallup.com/poll/188144/employee-engagement-stagnant-2015.aspx (accessed 10 April 2018).

Advertising Association (2017) *Expenditure report Q3*, London. https://www.adassoc.org.uk/advertising-association-warc-expenditure-report/expenditure-report-q3-2017-uk-adspend-sees-record-2017/ (accessed 27 February 2018).

Agency of Design (2013) *Design out waste project*, London. www.agencyofdesign.co.uk.

Ajzen, I. (1988) *Attitudes, personality, and behavior*, Chicago: Dorsey Press.

Aldrick, P. (2009) 'HSBC Chairman Stephen Green says banks owe debt to society', *The Telegraph*, 8 September. https://www.telegraph.co.uk/finance/newsbysector/banksandfinance/6157413/HSBC-chairman-Stephen-Green-says-banks-owe-debt-to-society.html (accessed 3 March 2018).

Alexander, J., Crompton, T. and Shrubsole, G. (2011) *Think of me as evil? Opening the ethical debates in advertising,* Public Interest Research Centre, Godalming: WWF UK. https://www.globalpolicy.org/images/pdfs/think_of_me_as_evil.pdf (accessed March 4, 2018).

Alexander, S. and Macleod, A. (eds) (2014) *Simple living in history*, Melbourne: Simplicity Institute.

Allen, B. (2014) 'A role for co-operatives in governance of common-pool resources and common property systems'. In: Novkovic, S. and Webb, T. (eds) *Co-operatives in a post-growth era: creating co-operative economics*, London: Zed Books.

Allwood, J.M. and Cullen, J.M. (2015) *Sustainable Materials Without the Hot Air*, Cambridge: UIT.

Alperovitz, G. (2013) *What Then Must We Do? Straight Talk About the Next American Revolution,* White River Junction: Green Press Initiative.

Altman, M. (2014) 'Are Co-operatives a Viable Business Form? Lessons from Behavioural Economics'. In: Novkovic, S. and Webb, T. (eds) *Co-operatives in a post-growth era: creating co-operative economics*, London: Zed Books.

Alvaredo, F., Chancel, L., Piketty, T., Saez, E. and Zucman, G. (2017) *World Inequality Report*, Paris: World Inequality Lab. http://wir2018.wid.world/ (accessed 4 March 2018).

Anderson, P. (1976) 'The Antinomies of Antonio Gramsci', *New Left Review*, 1: 100. https://newleftreview.org/I/100/perry-anderson-the-antinomies-of-antonio-gramsci (5 September 2017).

Anderson, S. (2016) *Portland's path to CEO pay reform*, Washington, DC: Institute for Policy Studies.

Anielski, M. (2007) *The economics of happiness: building genuine wealth*, Gabriola Island: New Society Publishers.

Antonovsky, A. (1993) 'The structure and properties of the sense of coherence scale', *Social Science & Medicine*, 36 (6): 725–33.

APPSRG (2014) *Remanufacturing: towards a resource efficient economy*, London: All Party Parliamentary Sustainable Resource Group.

APPSRG and APPMG (2014) *Triple win: the social, economic and environmental case for remanufacturing*, London: All Party Parliamentary Sustainable Resource Group and All Party Parliamentary Manufacturing Group.

Assadourian, E. (2012) 'The path to degrowth in overdeveloped countries', in *State of the world 2012*, Washington, DC: World Watch Institute.

Atkinson, T. (2015) *Inequality*, Cambridge: Harvard University Press.

Atwood, M. (1980) 'An end to an audience?', lecture at Dalhousie University as part of the Dorothy J. Killam Lecture Series, 8 October. https://dalspace.library.dal.ca/bitstream/handle/10222/60268/dalrev_vol60_iss3_pp415_433.pdf?sequence=1 (accessed 1 March 2018).

Avent, R. (2016) *The wealth of humans: work and its absence in the twenty-first century*, London: Allen Lane.

Bachmann, C.J., Aagaard, L., Burcu, M., Glaeske, G., Kalverdijk, L.J., Petersen, I., Schuiling-Veninga, C., Wijlaars, L., Zito, M.J. and Hoffmann, F. (2016) 'Trends and patterns of antidepressant use in children and adolescents from five western countries, 2005–2012', *European Neuropsychopharmacology*, 26 (3): 411–19.

Bandura, A. (1977) 'Self-efficacy: towards a unifying theory of behavioural change', *Psychological Review*, 84 (2): 191–215.

Barber, B. (1984) *Strong democracy: participatory politics for a new age*, Berkeley: University of California Press.

Barford, A. and Pickett, K. (2014) 'How to build a more equal American society: lessons from successful experiences', *The Solutions Journal*, 5 (4): 60–71.

BBC News (2012) 'Rising number of Britons growing own food', 17 May. http://www.bbc.co.uk/news/uk-18094945 (accessed 20 December 2016).

BBC News (2013) 'Yahya Jammeh gives Gambians an extra day off', 1 February. http://www.bbc.co.uk/news/world-africa-21280766 (accessed 10 March 2018).

Bell, D. (1987) 'The world and the United States in 2013', *Daedalus*, 116 (3): 1–32.

Bendell, J. (2000) *Terms for endearment: business, NGOs and sustainable development*, Sheffield: Greenleaf.

Bender, K. and Theodossiou, I. (2017) 'The unintended consequences of flexicurity: the health consequences of flexible employment', *Review of Income and Wealth*, 10.111/roiw. 12316.

Bentham, J., Bowman, A., de le Cuesta, M., Engelen, E., Erturk, I., Folkman, P., Froud, J., Johal, S., Law, J., Leaver, A., Moran, M. and Williams, K. (2013) 'Manifesto for the Foundational Economy', Working Paper no 131, Manchester: Centre for Research on Socio-Cultural Change.

Benton, D. and Hazell, J. (2013) *Resource resilient UK: a report from the Circular Economy Task Force*, London: Green Alliance.

Berik, G., van der Meulen Rodgers, Y. and Seguino, S. (2009) 'Feminist economics of inequality, development and growth', *Feminist Economics*, 15 (3): 1–33.

Bertelsman Stiftung (2013) *Intergenerational justice in aging societies*, Gütersloh: Bertelsman Stiftung.

Binder, M. (2016) '"Do it with joy!" Subjective wellbeing outcomes of working in non-profit organisations', *Journal of Economic Psychology*, 54: 64–84.

Birch, K. (2015) *We have never been neoliberal: a manifesto for a doomed youth*, Arlesford: Zero Books.

Bivens, J. and Mishel, L. (2015) *Understanding the historic divergence between productivity and a typical worker's pay: why it matters and why it's real*, Washington, DC: Economic Policy Institute.

Blair, D. (2009) 'The child in the garden: an evaluative review of the benefits of school gardening', *The Journal of Environmental Education*, 40 (2): 15–38.

Botsman, R. and Rogers, R. (2011) *What's mine is yours: how collaborative consumption is changing the way we live*, New York: Harper Collins.

Bourne, T. and Zeri, A. (2013) 'Scotland proposes a more resource efficient and circular economy', *The Guardian*, 23 October. https://www.theguardian.com/sustainable-business/scotland-proposes-resource-efficient-circular-economy (accessed 28 October 2013).

Bowles, S. and Jayadev, A. (2014) 'One nation under guard', *Opinionator*, 15 February. https://opinionator.blogs.nytimes.com/2014/02/15/one-nation-under-guard/ (accessed 27 February 2018).

Bowles, S. and Park, Y. (2005) 'Emulation, inequality, and work hours: was Thorsten Veblen right?', *The Economic Journal*, 115 (November): 397–412.

Braithwaite, J. and Drahos, P. (2000) *Global business regulation*, Cambridge: Cambridge University Press.

Bramley, G., Hirsch, D., Littlewood, M. and Watkins, D. (2016) *Counting the cost of UK poverty*, York: Joseph Rowntree Foundation.

Brooks, D. (2011) *The social animal: a story of how success happens*, New York: Random House.

Broughton, A., Biletta, I. and Kullander, M. (2010) *Flexible forms of work: 'very atypical' contractual arrangements*, Dublin: European Observatory of Working Life.

Brown, G. (2010) Speech at The Work Foundation, 8 January. http://www.number10.gov.uk/Page22085 (accessed 9 January 2010) .

Brynjolfsson, E. and McAfee, A. (2012) *Race against the machine: how the digital revolution is accelerating innovation, driving productivity, and irreversibly transforming employment and the economy*, Research Briefing, Cambridge, MA: MIT Research Centre for Digital Business.

Buffett, P. (2013) 'The charitable-industrial complex', 26 July, *New York Times*. http://www.nytimes.com/2013/07/27/opinion/the-charitable-industrial-complex.html (accessed 29 July 2013).

Buffett, W. (2010) 'My philanthropic pledge', *Fortune Magazine*, 16 June. http://archive.fortune.com/2010/06/15/news/newsmakers/Warren_Buffett_Pledge_Letter.fortune/index.htm (accessed 5 March 2018).

Burchardt, T. (2012) *Deliberative research as a tool to make value judgements*, Working Paper 159, London: Centre for Analysis of Social Exclusion.

Business Wire (2009) '1.5 billion single-use cameras and counting: Kodak's recycling program marks record milestone, leaving little to waste', 7 April, *Business Wire*. https://www.businesswire.com/news/home/20090407005176/en/1.5-Billion-Single-Use-Cameras-Counting (accessed 10 March 2018).

Callahan, D. and Mijin Cha, J.M. (2013) *Stacked deck: how the dominance of politics by the affluent and business undermines economic mobility in America*, New York: Demos.

Cameron, D. (2010) 'PM's speech on creating new economic dynamism', speech to the Confederation of British Industry, 25 October. https://www.gov.uk/government/speeches/pms-speech-on-creating-a-new-economic-dynamism (accessed 25 September 2015).

Cames, M., Graichen, J., Siemons, A. and Cook, V. (2015) *Emission reduction targets for international aviation and shipping PE 569.964*, Brussels: Directorate General for Internal Policies & European Parliament.

Cancer Research UK (2016) *Cancer survival for all cancers combined*, London: Cancer Research UK. http://www.cancerresearchuk.org/health-professional/cancer-statistics/survival (accessed 12 October 2016).

Carers UK (2012) *Valuing carers 2011: calculating the value of carers' support*, London: Carers UK and University of Leeds.

Case, A. and Deaton, A. (2017) 'Mortality and morbidity in the 21st century', Brookings Papers on Economic Activity, spring.

Ceballos, G., Ehrlich, P., Barnosky, A., García, A., Pringle, R. and Palmer, T. (2015) 'Accelerated modern human-induced species losses: entering the sixth mass extinction', *Science Advances*, 1: 5.

Centers for Disease Control (2017) *Adult obesity facts*, Atlanta, GA: Centers for Disease Control. http://www.cdc.gov/obesity/data/adult.html (accessed 27 February 2018).

Chafkin, M. (2016) 'Uber's first self-driving fleet arrives in Pittsburgh this month', *Bloomberg Business Week*, 18 August. https://www.bloomberg.com/news/features/2016-08-18/uber-s-first-self-driving-fleet-arrives-in-pittsburgh-this-month-is06r7on (accessed 28 February 2018).

Chancel, L. and Piketty, T. (2015) *Carbon and inequality: from Kyoto to Paris. Trends in the global inequality of carbon emissions (1998–2013) and prospects for an equitable adaptation fund*, Paris: Paris School of Economics.

Chang, H.J. (2010) *23 things they don't tell you about capitalism*, London: Allen Lane.

Chartered Institute for Personnel and Development (2016) 'Employee outlook spring 2016: employee views on working life', London: CIPD/Halogen.

Chase, E. and Walker, R. (2012) 'The co-construction of shame in the context of poverty: beyond a threat to the social bond', *Sociology*, 47 (4): 739–54.

Childs, M. and McLaren, D. (2012) *Mapping a route from a planet in peril to a world of wellbeing*, London: Friends of the Earth.

Christie Commission (2011) *Commission on the Future Delivery of Public Services*, Edinburgh: Scottish Government. www.scotland.gov.uk/Publications/2011/06/27154527/2 (accessed 29 June 2011).

Christie's (2017) 'Leonardo's Salvator Mundi makes auction history', 15 November, New York: Christie's. http://www.christies.com/features/Leonardo-and-Post-War-results-New-York-8729-3.aspx (accessed 5 December 2017).

Chu, B. (2014) 'Is this the death of the traditional employee?', *The Independent*, 23 April. http://www.independent.co.uk/news/business/analysis-and-features/is-this-the-death-of-the-traditional-employee-9279083.html (accessed 12 March 2016).

CIA (2016) *World factbook*, Washington, DC: Central Intelligence Agency. https://www.cia.gov/library/publications/the-world-factbook/ (accessed 11 March 2018).

The Circular Awards (2017) See https://thecirculars.org/2017-finalists#award-for-circular-economy-public-program (accessed 28 February 2018).

City of Freiburg im Breisgau (2017) 'Approaches to sustainability: green city Freiburg', Freiberg: City of Freiburg im Breisgau. http://www.freiburg.de/pb/site/Freiburg/get/params_E-1350553581/640888/GreenCity_E2017.pdf (accessed 10 March 2018).

CK, L. (2008) Louis CK interview (episode 147), *Late Night with Conan O'Brien*. https://www.youtube.com/watch?v=akiVi1sR2rM (viewed 12 October 2016).

Coady, D., Parry, I., Sears, L. and Shang, B. (2015) *How big are global energy subsidies?*, Washington, DC: International Monetary Fund. http://www.imf.org/en/Publications/WP/Issues/2016/12/31/How-Large-Are-Global-Energy-Subsidies-42940 (accessed 29 December 2017).

Coats, E. and Benton, D. (2016) *Job quality in a circular economy*, London: Green Alliance.

Cohen, J. (2008 [1996]) *How many people can the earth support?*, London: W.W. Norton and Company.

Cohen, M. (2012) 'Transitioning to a postconsumerist future', *Green European Journal*, vol 3. Common Cause Handbook.

Cohen, M. (2014) *The decline and fall of consumer society?*, Boston, MA: The Great Transition Initiative.

Collins, B. (2015) *Intentional whole health system redesign: Southcentral Foundation's Nuka system of care*, London: The King's Fund.

Coote, A. (2012) *The wisdom of prevention: long-term planning, upstream investment and early action to prevent harm*, London: New Economics Foundation. http://www.neweconomics.org/publications/entry/the-wisdom-of-prevention (accessed 18 August 2014).

Coote, A. and Franklin, J. (eds) (2013) *Time on our side: why we all need a shorter working week*, London: New Economics Foundation.

Coote, A., Franklin, J. and Simms, A. (2010) *21 hours: why a shorter working week can help us all to flourish in the 21st century*, London: New Economics Foundation.

Corlett, A. and Clarke, S. (2017) *Living standards 2017*, London: Resolution Foundation.

Cota, I. (2012) 'Sun, sand and root canal: medical tourism booms in Costa Rica', Reuters, 26 November. https://www.reuters.com/article/us-costarica-tourism/sun-sand-and-root-canal-medical-tourism-booms-in-costa-rica-idUSBRE8AP17X20121126 (accessed 28 February 2018).

Coupeau, C. (2016) 'Road paved with solar panels powers French town', AFP, 22 December. https://www.yahoo.com/news/road-paved-solar-panels-powers-french-town-153838381.html (accessed 10 March 2018).

Coyle, D. (2013) *GDP: A brief but affectionate history*, Princeton, NJ: Princeton University Press.

Creative Commons (2016) *State of the commons report,* Mountain View: Creative Commons. https://stateof.creativecommons.org/ (accessed 10 March 2018).

Credit Suisse (2013) *Global wealth report 2013*, Zurich: Credit Suisse.

Cribb, J., Hood, A. and Joyce, R. (2016) *The economic circumstances of different generations: the latest picture*, IFS Briefing Note BN187, London: Institute for Fiscal Studies.

Crossan, J., Shaw, D., Cumbers, A. and McMaster, R. (2015) *Glasgow's community gardens: sustainable communities of care*, University of Glasgow: Adam Smith Business School.

Crouch, C. (2011) *The strange non-death of neoliberalism*, Cambridge: Polity Press.

Cumbers, A. (2014) *Renewing public ownership: constructing a democratic economy in the twenty-first century*, London: CLASS.

Dahlgreen, W. (2015) '37% of British workers think their job is meaningless', YouGov, 12 August. https://yougov.co.uk/news/2015/08/12/british-jobs-meaningless/ (accessed 27 February 2018).

Dale, G. (2012) 'The growth paradigm: a critique', *International Socialism*, 134. http://isj.org.uk/the-growth-paradigm-a-critique/ (accessed 5 September 2018)

Daly, H. (1990) 'Towards some operational principles for sustainable development', *Ecological Economics*, 2 (1): 1–6.

Daly, H. (2015) *Economics for a full world*, Cambridge: Great Transition Initiative.

Danis, M., Clancy, C.M. and Churchill, L. (eds) (2002) *Ethical dimensions of health policy*, Oxford: Oxford University Press.

DARA and Climate Vulnerable Forum (2015) *Climate vulnerability monitor: a guide to the cold calculus of a hot planet* (2nd edition), Madrid. http://daraint.org/wp-content/uploads/2012/09/CVM2ndEd-FrontMatter.pdf (accessed 9 December 2015).

Darnton, A. and Horne, J. (2013) *Influencing behaviours: moving beyond the individual*, Edinburgh: The Scottish Government. http://www.gov.scot/Publications/2013/06/8511/0 (accessed 1 January 2018).

Davies, R. (2016) 'Rolls-Royce unveils first driverless car complete with silk "throne"', *The Guardian*, 16 June. https://www.theguardian.com/business/2016/jun/16/rolls-royce-unveils-first-driverless-car-vision-next-100 (accessed 16 October 2016).

Davies, W. (2009) *Reinventing the firm*, London: Demos.

Davies, W. (2016) *The happiness industry: how the government and big business sold us wellbeing*, London: Verso Books.

Davis, A., Offenbach, D. and Grant, N. (2014) 'Rethinking corporate governance: a question of representation'. In: Williamson, J., Driver, C. and Kenway, P. (eds), *Beyond shareholder value: the reasons and choices for corporate governance reform*, London: Trades Union Congress, New Policy Institute, SOAS.

Davis, M. (2013) 'Hurried and alone: time and technology in the consumer society'. In: Coote, A. and Franklin, J. (eds), *Time on our side: why we all need a shorter working week*, London: New Economics Foundation.

Davison, I. (2017) 'Whanganui River given legal status of a person under unique Treaty of Waitangi settlement', *New Zealand Herald*, 15 March. http://www.nzherald.co.nz/nz/news/article.cfm?c_id=1&objectid=11818858 (accessed 28 February 2018).

Deakin, S. (2014) 'Against shareholder empowerment'. In: Williamson, J., Driver, C. and Kenway, P. (eds), *Beyond shareholder value: the reasons and choices for corporate governance reform*, London: Trades Union Congress, New Policy Institute, SOAS.

Deci, E. and Ryan, R. (2008) 'Self-determination theory: a macrotheory of human motivation, development, and health', *Canadian Psychology/Psychologie Canadienne*, 49 (3): 182–5.

DEFRA (2014) *UK biodiversity indicators*, London: DEFRA.

DEFRA (2017) *Local authority collected waste management statistics*, London: DEFRA. https://data.gov.uk/dataset/local_authority_collected_waste_management_statistics (accessed 11 March 2018).

Delsen, L. and Smits, J. (2014) *The rise and fall of Dutch savings schemes*, Network for Studies on Pensions, Aging, and Retirement (Netspar). Discussion Paper 02/2014-008, Tilburg.

Department for Business, Energy and Industrial Strategy (2016) *Trade union membership*, statistical bulletin, London. https://www.gov.uk/government/uploads/system/uploads/attachment_data/file/616966/trade-union-membership-statistical-bulletin-2016-rev.pdf (accessed 27 February 2018).

Der Spiegel (2009) 'Economic crisis is Germany's biggest challenge since reunification', *Der Spiegel*, 10 November. http://www.spiegel.de/international/germany/merkel-addresses-parliament-economic-crisis-is-germany-s-biggest-challenge-since-reunification-a-660424.html (accessed 12 October 2016).

de Sismondi, J.C.L. Simonde (1991 [1819]) *New principles of political economy*, trans. R. Hyse, New Brunswick, NJ and London: Transaction Publishers.

DfID (2008) *Growth: building jobs and prosperity in developing countries*, London: Department for International Development. http://www.oecd.org/derec/unitedkingdom/40700982.pdf (accessed 12 October 2016).

Dickerson, S. and Kemeny, M. (2004) 'Acute stressors and cortisol responses: a theoretical integration and synthesis of laboratory research', *Psychological Bulletin*, 130 (3): 355–91.

Dietz, R. and O'Neill, D. (2013) *Enough is enough: building a sustainable economy in a world of finite resources*, Abingdon: Routledge.

Di Muzio, T. and Robbins, R. (2017) *An anthropology of money*, New York: Routledge.

Dobbs, R., Madgavkar, A., Manyika, J., Woetzel, J., Bughin, J., Labaye, E. and Kashyap, P. (2006) *Poorer than their parents? A new perspective on income inequality*, London: McKinsey Global Institute.

Dolan, E. (2013) 'Growth and quality of life: what can we learn from Japan?', *Economonitor*, 15 February. http://www.economonitor.com/dolanecon/2013/02/15/growth-and-quality-of-life-what-can-we-learn-from-japan/ (accessed 28 February 2018).

Dolan, P., Hallsworth, M., Halpern, D., King, D. and Vlaev, I. (2010) *MINDSPACE: influencing behaviour through public policy*, London: Cabinet Office and Institute for Government.

Donald, K. and Moussié, R. (2016) *Redistributing unpaid care work: why tax matters for women's rights*, Brighton: Institute of Development Studies. http://www.ids.ac.uk/publication/redistributing-unpaid-care-work-why-tax-matters-for-women-s-rights (accessed 16 October 2016).

Dorling, D. (2010) *Injustice: why social inequality persists*, Bristol: The Policy Press.

Dorling, D. (2012) *The no-nonsense guide to equality*, Oxford: The New Internationalist.

Doyle, A. (2014) 'All Norwegians become crown millionaires', Reuters, 9 January. https://www.reuters.com/article/us-norway-millionaires/all-norwegians-become-crown-millionaires-in-oil-saving-landmark-idUSBREA0710U20140108?irpc=932 (accessed 28 February 2018).

Dreze, J. and Sen, A. (1989) *Hunger and public action*, Oxford: Oxford University Press.

Dryzek, J. (1996) *Democracy in capitalist times*, New York: Oxford University Press.

Duckles, J. (2016) 'Christians urged to help the poor keep warm', Diocese of Oxford, 26 November. http://www.oxford.anglican.org/christians-urged-help-poor-keep-warm/ (accessed 20 December 2016).

Duda, J. (2016) 'The Italian region where co-ops produce a third of its GDP', *Yes Magazine*, 5 July. http://www.yesmagazine.org/new-economy/the-italian-place-where-co-ops-drive-the-economy-and-most-people-are-members-20160705 (accessed 28 February 2018).

Dunlop, S. and Trebeck, K. (2012) *The Oxfam humankind index for Scotland: first results*, Oxford: Oxfam GB.

Dupre, M. and Boulbry, G. (2016) 'Sales increase by up to 56% when shoppers know a product will last', *The Conversation France*, 17 May. https://theconversation.com/sales-increase-by-up-to-56-when-shoppers-know-a-product-will-last-57149/ (accessed 28 February 2018).

Ecuador (2008) *Constitution of the Republic of Ecuador*. http://pdba.georgetown.edu/Constitutions/Ecuador/english08.html (accessed 28 February 2018).

Ecuador (2009) *National plan for good living, 2009–2013*, Republic of Ecuador. http://www.planificacion.gob.ec/wp-content/uploads/downloads/2016/03/Plan-Nacional-Buen-Vivir-2009-2013-Ingles.pdf (accessed 28 February 2018).

Eden Project (2017) *The cost of disconnected communities*, Boldeva: Eden Project Communities and CEBR.

Edward, P. (2005) 'The Ethical Poverty Line as a tool to measure global absolute poverty', *Journal of Radical Statistics*, 89: 53–66.

Eisenstein, C. (2011) *Sacred economics: money, gift and society in the age of transition,* Berkeley: Evolver Editions.

Ellen MacArthur Foundation (nd) 'Maersk Line case study', Cowes. https://www.ellenmacarthurfoundation.org/case-studies/using-product-passports-to-improve-the-recovery-and-reuse-of-shipping-steel (accessed 28 February 2018).

Ellen MacArthur Foundation (2014) *Towards the circular economy*, vol 3, Cowes. https://www.ellenmacarthurfoundation.org/assets/downloads/publications/Towards-the-circular-economy-volume-3.pdf (accessed 5 March 2018).

Ellen MacArthur Foundation (2016) *The new plastics economy: rethinking the future of plastics*, Cowes. https://www.ellenmacarthurfoundation.org/publications/the-new-plastics-economy-rethinking-the-future-of-plastics (accessed 10 March 2018).

Employee Ownership Index (2015), London: Capital Strategies. http://www.employeeownershipindex.co.uk/wiki/index.php5?title=Performance (accessed 28 February 2018).

Engelman, R. (2012) 'Nine population strategies to stop short of 9 billion'. In *State of the world 2012*, Washington, DC: World Watch Institute.

Erdal, D. (2014) 'Employee ownership and health: an initial study'. In: Novkovic, S. and Webb, T. (eds) *Co-operatives in a post-growth era: creating co-operative economics*, London: Zed Books.

Esfahani, E. (2013) 'There's more to life than being happy', *The Atlantic*, 9 January. http://m.theatlantic.com/health/archive/2013/01/theres-more-to-life-than-being-happy/266805/ (accessed 4 October 2015).

Ethical Markets Magazine (2013) 'Beyond GDP: Robert Manchin, managing director of the Gallup Organisation Europe, on measuring wellbeing and social progress', *Ethical Markets Magazine*, July. http://www.ethicalmarkets.com/beyond-gdp-robert-manchin-managing-director-of-the-gallup-organisation-europe-on-measuring-wellbeing-and-social-progress/ (accessed 1 April 2018).

European Commission (2015) *Closing the loop: an EU action plan for the circular economy*, Brussels: European Commission.

European Commission, IMF, OECD and UN (2009) *System of national accounts 2008*, New York: United Nations. http://unstats.un.org/unsd/nationalaccount/docs/SNA2008.pdf (accessed 5 March 2018).

European Parliament (2016) *Planned obsolescence: exploring the issue*, Brussels: European Parliament briefing. http://www.europarl.europa.eu/RegData/etudes/BRIE/2016/581999/EPRS_BRI%282016%29581999_EN.pdf (accessed 10 March 2018).

Eurostat (2018) *Employment statistics June 2017*, Luxembourg: European Commission. http://ec.europa.eu/eurostat/statistics-explained/index.php/Employment_statistics#Part-time_work (accessed 10 March 2018).

Evans, A. (2013) 'Finding a myth for the 21st century', presentation to the Modern Church Conference. http://www.globaldashboard.org/wp-content/uploads/Modern-Church-presentation.pdf (accessed 11 March 2018).

Eventbright (nd) 'Hardcore festies: the driving force behind today's growth in music festivals', San Francisco: Eventbrite. https://www.eventbrite.com/blog/academy/hardcore-festies-most-valuable-fan-driving-todays-growth-in-music-festivals/ (accessed 10 March 2018).

Fanon, F. (1961) *The wretched of the earth*, trans. C. Farrington, New York: Grove Weidenfeld.

Federal Reserve Bank of New York (2016) *Quarterly report on household debt and credit*, New York: Federal Reserve Bank of New York. https://www.newyorkfed.org/medialibrary/interactives/householdcredit/data/pdf/HHDC_2016Q1.pdf (accessed 16 October 2016).

Felber, C. and Hagelberg, G. (2016) 'What would an economy for the common good look like?', *Tikkun Daily*, 4 September. http://www.tikkun.org/tikkundaily/2016/09/04/what-would-an-economy-for-the-common-good-look-like/ (accessed 28 February 2018).

Felongco, G.P. (2014) 'Manila announces 4-day week', *Gulf News Philippines*, 26 September. http://gulfnews.com/news/asia/philippines/manila-announces-4-day-work-week-1.1390500 (accessed 10 March 2018).

Ferreira, F. and Ravallion, M. (2008) *Global poverty and inequality: a review of the evidence*. Policy Research, Working Paper 4623, Washington, DC: The World Bank.

The Finance Innovation Lab (2015) *A strategy for systems change*, London. http://financeinnovationlab.org/wp-content/uploads/2015/04/FIL_SystemsChange-Web-Final.pdf (accessed 30/102016).

Fioramonti, L. (2013) *Gross domestic problem*, London: Zed Books.

Fioramonti, L. (2017) *The world after GDP: economics, politics and international relations in the post-growth era*, Cambridge: Polity Press.

Fitch, R. (1996) 'The cooperative economics of Italy's Emilia-Romagna holds a lesson for the U.S.', *The Nation*, 13 May: 18–21. http://www.uwcc.wisc.edu/info/bologna.html (accessed 5 March 2018).

Fix, B. (2017) *Evidence for a power theory of personal income distribution*, Working Papers on Capital as Power, no 2017/03.

Forbes (2017) 'Why Natura might be the ideal buyer for the Body Shop brand', *Forbes*, 13 June. https://www.forbes.com/sites/greatspeculations/2017/06/13/why-natura-might-be-the-ideal-buyer-for-the-body-shop-brand/#1441629f27e0 (accessed 28 February 2018).

Francis (2015) Encyclical Letter *Laudato Si*, The Vatican. See https://laudatosi.com (accessed 4 September 2018).

Frank, R. (2007) *Falling behind: how rising inequality harms the middle class*, Berkeley: University of California Press.

Freedom House (2018): see https://freedomhouse.org/report/freedom-world/2018/costa-rica (accessed 6 February 2018).

Freire, P. (1993 [1970]) *Pedagogy of the oppressed*, trans. M.B. Ramos, London: Penguin Books.

Frijda, N., Manstead, A. and Bern, S. (2000) *Emotions and beliefs: how feelings influence thoughts*, Cambridge: Cambridge University Press.

Fuentes-Nieva, R. and Galasso, N. (2014) *Working for the few: political capture and economic inequality*, Oxford: Oxfam International.

Fukuoka, M. (1978) *The one straw revolution*, New York: New York Review of Books.

G20 (2016) 'G20 Leaders' Communique Hangzhou Summit'. Hangzhou Summit, 4–5 September. http://www.g20.org/English/Dynamic/201609/t20160906_3396.html (accessed 12 October 2016).

Galbraith, J.K. (1999 [1958]) *The affluent society*, London: Penguin Books.

Galloway, L. and Danson, M. (2016) *In-work poverty and enterprise: self-employment and business ownership as contexts of poverty*, Edinburgh: Heriot-Watt University. https://pureapps2.hw.ac.uk/ws/portalfiles/portal/9934375 (accessed 3 March 2018).

Gandhi, M. (1997) *Hind Swaraj and other Writings*, Cambridge: Cambridge University Press.

Garcia, I., Leidreiter, A., Fünfgelt, J., Mwanga, S. and Onditi, M. (2017) 'Policy roadmap for 100% renewable energy and poverty eradication in Tanzania', Hamburg: World Future Council. https://www.worldfuturecouncil.org/file/2017/05/Policy-Roadmap-Tanzania.pdf (accessed 10 March 2018).

Gardener, D. and Burnley, J. (2015) *Made in Myanmar: entrenched poverty or decent jobs for garment workers?*, Oxford: Oxfam International.

Geels, F. and Schot, J. (2007) 'Typology of sociotechnical transition pathways', *Research Policy*, 36: 399–417.

Gertner, J. (2010) 'The rise and fall of the G.D.P.', *New York Times*, 13 May. www.nytimes.com/2010/05/16/magazine/16GDP-t... (accessed 19 August 2013).

Gillingham, K., Rapson, D. and Wagner, G. (2014) *The rebound effect and energy efficiency policy*, Resources for the Future, Discussion Paper 14–39, November, Washington, DC.

Gipe, P. (2012) 'Iceland: a 100% renewables example in the modern era', 7 November, Mullumbimby. http://reneweconomy.com.au/2012/iceland-a-100-renewables-example-in-the-modern-era-56428 (accessed 10 March 2018).

Gleibs, I. (2013) 'Does money buy happiness? It depends on the context', *LSE blogs*. http://blogs.lse.ac.uk/politicsandpolicy/does-money-by-happiness-a-dynamic-analysis-of-relationships-between-financial-and-social-capital-on-life-satisfaction/ (accessed 5 August 2013).

Glennie, J. (2011) 'Global inequality: tackling the elite 1% problem', *The Guardian*, 28 November. www.guardian.co.uk/global-development/poverty-matters/2011/nov/28/... (accessed 21 May 2013).

Global Burden of Disease, Study (2016) 'Global, regional and national life expectancy, 1980–2015: a systematic analysis for the Global Burden of Disease Study 2015', *The Lancet*, 388: 1459–544.

GlobeScan (2012) *Rethinking consumption: consumers and the future of sustainability*, BBMG, Toronto: Globescan and SustainAbility. https://globescan.com/rethinking-consumption-consumers-and-the-future-of-sustainability/ (accessed 28 February 2018).

Goldberg, J. (2016) 'The Obama doctrine: the U.S. president talks through his hardest decisions about America's role in the world', *The Atlantic*, April. http://www.theatlantic.com/magazine/archive/2016/04/the-obama-doctrine/471525/ (accessed 12 October 2016).

Goodall, C. (2016) *The switch*, London: Profile Books.

Goodwin, N. (2014) *Prices and work in the new economy*, Global Development and Environment Institute, Boston, MA: Tufts University.

Gopel, M. (2014) *Navigating a new agenda: questions and answers on paradigm shifts and transformational change*, Berlin: Wuppertal Institute for Climate, Environmental and Energy.

Gopel, M. (2016) *The great mindshift: how a new economic paradigm and sustainability transformations go hand in hand*, Berlin: Springer Open and Wuppertal Institut.

Gorbis, M. (2017) *Universal basic assets: manifesto and action plan*, Palo Alto, CA: Institute for the Future.

Gordon, D., Mack, J., Lansley, S. et al (2013) *The impoverishment of the UK: PSE UK first results – living standards*, Swindon: ESRC.

Gore, T. (2015) *Extreme Carbon inequality: why the Paris climate deal must put the poorest, lowest emitting and most vulnerable people first*, Oxford: Oxfam International.

Graeber, D. (2013) *The democracy project*, London: Allen Lane.

Graefe, A. (2016) *Guide to automated journalism*, Tow Centre for Digital Journalism, New York: Tow Foundation. https://academiccommons.columbia.edu/catalog/ac:s4mw6m907n (accessed 28 February 2018).

Gramsci, A. (1971) *Selections from the prison notebooks of Antonio Gramsci*, New York: International Publishers.

Gray, J. (2014) *The silence of animals: on progress and other myths*, London: Penguin.

Green, D. (2016) *How change happens*, Oxford: Oxford University Press.

Green Building News (2015) 'Biogas technology at Khangezile school', *Green Building News,* 9 June. http://www.greenbusinessguide.co.za/biogas-technology-at-khangezile-school/ (accessed 10 March 2018).

Gregory, D. (2012) *Is there a cooperative alternative to capitalism?*, Essay prize winner, www.ethicalconsumer.org/cooperativealternative.aspx (accessed 28 February 2018).

Gregory, R. (2011) 'Germany – Freiburg – Green City', *EcoTipping Points*, January. http://www.ecotippingpoints.org/our-stories/indepth/germany-freiburg-sustainability-transportation-energy-green-economy.html

Griffin, J. (2010) *The lonely society*, London: The Mental Health Foundation. https://www.mentalhealth.org.uk/sites/default/files/the_lonely_society_report.pdf (accessed 27 February 2018).

Gudynas, E. (2013) 'Debates on development and its alternatives in Latin America: a brief heterodox guide'. In: Lang, M. and Mokrani, D. (eds) *Beyond development: alternative visions from Latin America.* Quito: Transnational Institute and Rosa Luxemburg Foundation.

Gustavsson, J., Cederberg, C., Sonesson, U., van Otterdijk, R. and Meybeck, A. (2011) *Global food losses and food waste: extent, prevention and causes*, Rome: United Nations Food and Agriculture Organization.

Hacker, J. (2011) 'The institutional foundations of middle-class democracy, in priorities for a new political economy: memos to the left', *Progressive Governance Conference*, Oslo, pp 33–7.

Haidt, J. (2001) 'The emotional dog and its rational tail: a social intuitionist approach to moral judgment', *Psychological Review,* 108 (4): 814–34.

Haier Group (2017) http://www.haier.net/en/about_haier/ (accessed 28 February 2018).

Hahnel, R. (2016) 'Participatory economics and the next system', *The Next System Project*. http://thenextsystem.org/participatory-economics-and-the-next-system/ (accessed 11 September 2016).

Hallegatte, S., Bangalore, M., Bonzanigo, L., Fay, M., Kane, T., Narloch, U., Rozenberg, J., Treguer, D. and Vogt-Schilb, A. (2016) *SHOCK WAVES: managing the impacts of climate change on poverty*, Washington, DC: World Bank.

Hamilton, K. and Catterall, M. (2007) 'Keeping up appearances: low-income consumers' strategies aimed at disguising poverty', *Asian Pacific Advances in Consumer Research.*

Hamilton, K. and Catterall, M. (2008) '"I can do it!" Consumer coping and poverty', *Advances in Consumer Research*, 35: 551–56.

Happy Planet Index (2016) New Economics Foundation. http://happyplanetindex.org/

Hansard Society (2016) *Audit of political engagement 13, the 2016 report*, London: Hansard.

Hardoon, D., Ayele, S. and Fuentes-Nieva, R. (2016) *An economy for the 1%: how privilege and power in the economy drive extreme inequality and how this can be stopped*, Oxford: Oxfam.

Harris, J. (2015) 'How flatpack democracy beat the old parties in the People's Republic of Frome', *The Guardian*, 22 May. https://www.theguardian.com/politics/2015/may/22/flatpack-democracy-peoples-republic-of-frome (accessed 10 March 2018).

Harvey, D. (1989) *The condition of postmodernity*, Oxford: Blackwell Publishers.

Harvey, D. (2005) *A brief history of neoliberalism*, Oxford: Oxford University Press.

Hastings, A. (2009) 'Poor neighbourhoods and poor services: evidence on the "rationing" of environmental service provision to deprived neighbourhoods', *Urban Studies*, 46: 2907–27.

Havas Worldwide (2014) 'The new consumer and the sharing economy', *Prosumer Report*, 18.

Hayek, F. (1947) Mont Pelerin address, quoted in Nik-Khah, E. and Van Horn, R. (2016) *The ascendancy of Chicago neoliberalism: The Handbook of Neoliberalism*, London: Routledge.

Hayhow, D.B. et al (2016) *The state of nature*, The State of Nature Partnership. https://www.rspb.org.uk/globalassets/downloads/documents/conservation-projects/state-of-nature/state-of-nature-uk-report-2016.pdf (accessed 27 February 2018).
Held, D. (1986) 'Introduction: New Forms of Democracy?', In: Held, D. and Pollitt, C. (eds), *New forms of democracy*, London: SAGE Publications.
Helfrich, S. (2017) 'Commons as a way of working and living together', P2P Foundation, 2 March. https://blog.p2pfoundation.net/silke-helfrich-on-the-commons-as-a-way-of-working-and-living-together/2017/03/02 (accessed 8 April 2018).
Hengrasmee, S. (2013) 'A study of suburban Thailand'. In: Vale, R. and Vale, B. (eds), *Living within a fair share ecological footprint*, Abingdon: Routledge.
Hickel, J. (2015) 'It will take 100 years for the world's poorest people to earn $1.25 a day', *The Guardian*, 30 March. http://www.theguardian.com/global-development-professionals-network/2015/mar/30/it-will-take-100-years-for-the-worlds-poorest-people-to-earn-125-a-day (accessed 26 December 2015).
Hickel, J. (2016) 'The true extent of global poverty and hunger: questioning the good news narrative of the Millennium Development Goals', *Third World Quarterly*, 37: (5): 749–67.
Hickel, J. (2017) *The Divide: A Brief Guide to Global Inequality and its Solutions*, London: Penguin Random House.
Hills, J., Sefton, T. and Stewart, K. (2009) *Towards a more equal society*, Bristol: Policy Press.
Hirsch, A. (2014) 'Maya Angelou appreciation – "The ache for home lives in all of us"' in *The Guardian*, 1 June, https://www.theguardian.com/books/2014/jun/01/maya-angelou-appreciation-afua-hirsch (accessed 29 September 2018).
Hirst, P. (1994) *Associative democracy*, Cambridge: Polity Press.
Hirst, P. (1999) 'Has globalisation killed social democracy?', *The Political Quarterly*, 70 (1): 84–96.
Honoré, C. (2013) *The slow fix*, San Francisco: HarperOne.
Horton, T. and Gregory, J. (2009) *The solidarity society: why we can afford to end poverty, and how to do it with public support*, London: Fabian Society.

Horyn, C. (2015) 'Why Raf Simons is leaving Christian Dior', *The Cut*, 22 October. http://nymag.com/thecut/2015/10/raf-simons-leaving-christian-dior.html (accessed 27 February 2018).

House of Commons (2016) *Employment practices at Sports Direct*, Business, Innovation and Skills Committee, Report of Third Session, 2016–17, London: UK Parliament.

House of Commons Library (2015) *The self-employment boom: key issues for 2015*, Briefing Paper, London: UK Parliament.

Hoy, C. and Samman, E. (2015) *What if growth had been as good for the poor as everyone else?*, London: Overseas Development Institute.

Hoy, C. and Sumner, A. (2016) *Gasoline, guns, and giveaways: is there new capacity for redistribution to end three quarters of global poverty?*, Working Paper 443, London: Center for Global Development.

Hughes, A. (2013) *Short-termism, impatient capital and finance for manufacturing innovation in the UK. Future of Manufacturing Project: evidence paper 16*, London: Government Office for Science.

Huppert, F. and Cooper, C. (eds) (2014) *Interventions and policies to enhance wellbeing,* Chichester: Wiley Blackwell.

Iceland Constitutional Council (2011) Stjórnlagaráð, a Constitutional Council. *A proposal for a new constitution for the Republic of Iceland* (March). http://stjornlagarad.is/other_files/stjornlagarad/Frumvarp-enska.pdf (accessed 19 December 2016).

Illich, I. (1973) *Tools for conviviality*, New York: Harper & Row.

Ilvashov, A. (2015) 'Mango is making fast fashion even faster', *Refinery 29 magazine*, 4 December. http://www.refinery29.com/2015/12/98878/mango-fast-fashion-cycle (accessed 27 December 2018).

Institute for Employment Research and Institute for Fiscal Studies (2012) *Who gains from growth? Living standards to 2020*, London: Resolution Foundation.

Institute of Chartered Accountants England and Wales (2014) *Keywords: building a language of systems change*, London: ICAEW & School, Said Business.

International Bank for Reconstruction and Development and World Bank (2012) *Inclusive green growth: the pathway to sustainable development*, Washington, DC.

International Energy Agency (2016a) *Germany: energy system overview*, Paris: IEA. https://www.iea.org/media/countries/Germany.pdf (accessed 8 April 2018).

International Energy Agency (2016b) *Special report on energy and air pollution*, Paris: IEA.

International Energy Agency (2017) *Energy access outlook 2017*, Paris: IEA.

International Labour Organisation (nd) *Gender and employmen*t, Geneva: ILO.

IMF (2015) 'IMF survey: Lagarde calls for new recipe for stronger growth', *IMF Survey*, Washington, DC: International Monetary Fund. http://www.imf.org/external/pubs/ft/survey/so/2015/NEW100815A.htm (accessed 12 October 2016).

Investors in People (2015) '60% of people not happy in their jobs', press release, 19 January. https://www.investorsinpeople.com/press/60-cent-uk-workers-not-happy-their-jobs (accessed 27 February 2018).

IPSOS Mori (2014) *Global trends 2014*, London: IPSOS Mori. https://www.ipsos.com/sites/default/files/publication/1970-01/ipsos-mori-global-trends-2014.pdf (accessed 10 March 2018).

Jackson, T. (2009) *Prosperity without growth? The transition to a sustainable economy*, London: Sustainable Development Commission.

Jackson, T. (2017) *Prosperity without growth: foundations for the economy of tomorrow* (2nd edn), Abingdon: Routledge.

Jackson, T. and Webster, R. (2016) *Limits to growth revisited: a review of the limits to growth debate*, Guildford: All-Party Parliamentary Group on Limits to Growth.

Jacobsen, M.Z. et al (2017) '100% clean and renewable wind, water, and sunlight all-sector energy roadmaps for 139 countries of the world', *Joule*, 1 (1): 108–21.

Jahan, S. (2015) *Human development report 2015: work for human development*, New York: UNDP.

Jameson, C. (2010) 'The "short step" from love to hypnosis: a reconsideration of the Stockholm Syndrome', *Journal for Cultural Research*, 14 (4): 337–55.

Jericho, G. (2016) 'Harping on about economic growth makes politicians seem out of touch', *The Guardian*, 14 November. https://www.theguardian.com/commentisfree/2016/nov/15/harping-on-about-economic-growth-makes-politicians-seem-out-of-touch (accessed 27 February 2018).

John, P. (2003) 'Is there life after policy streams, advocacy coalitions, and punctuations: using evolutionary theory to explain policy change', *Policy Studies Journal*, 31 (4): 481–498.

Johnson, C. (2013) 'Is Seoul the next great sharing city?', *Shareable*. www.shareable.net/blog/is-seoul-the-next-great-sharing-city (accessed 24 July 2013).

Joint Nature Conservation Committee (2015) *Biodiversity indicators*, London: Defra. http://jncc.defra.gov.uk/page-4244-theme=print (accessed 12 January 2015).

Jónsdóttir, B. (2016) 'Meet Birgitta Jónsdóttir: the ex-WikiLeaks volunteer who has helped the Pirate Party reshape Iceland', interview with *Democracy Now*, 1 November. https://www.democracynow.org/2016/11/1/meet_birgitta_jonsdottir_the_ex_wikileaks (accessed 10 March 2018).

Jowitt, J. (2010) 'World's top firms cause $2.2 tn of environmental damage, report estimates', *The Guardian*, 18 February. https://www.theguardian.com/environment/2010/feb/18/worlds-top-firms-environmental-damage accessed (27 February 2018).

Kabeer, N. and Natali, L. (2013) 'Working paper: Gender equality and economic growth: is there a win-win?', *Institute of Development Studies*, 417.

Kahneman, D. (2011) *Thinking, fast and slow*, London: Penguin.

Kahneman, D. and Deaton, A. (2010) 'High income improves evaluation of life but not emotional wellbeing', *PNAS*, 107 (38): 16489–16493.

Kasser, T. (2002) *The high price of materialism*, Cambridge, MA: MIT Press.

Kasser, T. (2011) *Values and human wellbeing*, The Bellagio Initiative. http://www.bellagioinitiative.org/wp-content/uploads/2011/10/Bellagio-Kasser.pdf (accessed 2 February 2012).

Kasser, T. (2014) 'Teaching about values and goals: applications of the circumplex model to motivation, wellbeing, and prosocial behavior', *Teaching of Psychology*, 41 (4): 365–71.

Kato, N. (2010) 'Japan and the ancient art of shrugging', *New York Times*, 22 August. http://www.nytimes.com/2013/12/03/opinion/kato-japan-in-a-post-growth-age.html (accessed 7 March 2018).

Kato, N. (2013) 'Japan in a post-growth age', *New York Times*, 2 December. http://www.nytimes.com/2013/12/03/opinion/kato-japan-in-a-post-growth-age.html (accessed 7 March 2018).

Kay, J. (2012) *UK equity markets and long-term decision making*, London: Department for Business, Innovation and Skills.

Keane, J. (1988) *Civil society and the state: new European perspectives*, London: Verso.

Kempf, H. (2008) *How the rich are destroying the earth*, Totnes: Green Books.

Kennedy, M. (2016) 'More than third of teenage girls in England suffer depression and anxiety', *The Guardian*, 22 August. https://www.theguardian.com/society/2016/aug/22/third-teenage-girls-depression-anxiety-survey-trend-truant (accessed 3 September 2017).

Keynes, J.M. (1930) 'Economic possibilities for our grandchildren', *Essays in persuasion*, New York: W. W. Norton & Co.

Kingdon, J. (1984) *Agendas, alternatives and public policy*, Boston, MA: Little, Brown & Co.

Kingdon, J. (2002) 'The Reality of Public Policy Making'. In: Danis, M., Clancy, C.M. and Churchill, L. (eds), *Ethical dimensions of health policy*, Oxford: Oxford University Press.

Klein, N. (2014) *This changes everything: capitalism vs the climate*, New York: Simon and Schuster.

Klingbeil, C. (2016) *A dream scenario*, Berlin: Futurzwei. http://www.goethe.de/ins/cz/prj/fup/en15749294.htm (accessed 10 March 2018).

Klump, R. (2016) 'Pro-poor growth in Vietnam: miracle or model?', cited in Besley, T. and Cord, L. (eds) *Delivering on the promise of pro-poor growth: insights and lessons from country experiences*, Washington: The World Bank.

Korten, D. (2001) *When corporations rule the world*, Oakland: Berrett-Koehler.

Korten, D. (2016) 'Why the economy should stop growing – and just grow up', *Yes Magazine*, 4 May 4. http://www.yesmagazine.org/planet/why-the-economy-should-stop-growing-and-just-grow-up-20160504 (accessed 8 April 2018).

Kostakis, V., Niaros, V., Dafermos, G. and Bauwens, M. (2015) *Design global, manufacture local: exploring the contours of an emerging productive model.* Futures 73.

Kroll, C. (2015) *Sustainable development goals: are the rich countries ready?*, Gutersloh: Bertlesmann Stiftung. https://www.bertelsmann-stiftung.de/en/publications/publication/did/sustainable-development-goals-are-the-rich-countries-ready/ (accessed 6 March 2018).

Kubiszewski, I., Costanza, R., Franco, C., Lawn, P., Talberth, J., Jackson, T. and Aylmer, C. (2013) 'Beyond GDP: measuring and achieving global genuine progress', *Ecological Economics*, 3 (C): 57–68.

Kuhn, T. (1996) *The structure of scientific revolutions*, Chicago: The University of Chicago Press.

Kuznets, S. (Acting Secretary of Commerce) (1934) *National income, 1929–1932: letter from the Acting Secretary for Commerce transmitting in response to Senate Resolution No. 220 (72nd Cong.).*

Kyba, C.M., Kuester, T., Sánchez de Miguel, A., Baugh, K., Jechow, A., Hölker, F., Bennie, J., Elvidge, C.D., Gaston, K.J. and Guanter, L. (2017) 'Artificially lit surface of Earth at night increasing in radiance and extent', *Science Advances*, 3 (1): article e1701528.

Lakoff, G., Dean, H. and Hazen, D. (2004) *Don't think of an elephant! Know your values and frame the debate: the essential guide for progressives*, White River Junction: Chelsea Green.

Lamb, A. and Stephanson, H. (2014) 'Building relationships through participatory budgeting', Open Democracy, 4 April. https://www.opendemocracy.net/participation-now/alison-lamb-hilde-c-stephansen/building-relationships-through-participatory-budget (accessed 28 February 2018).

Lansley, S. (2006) *Rich Britain: the rise and rise of the new super-wealthy*, London: Politico's Publishing.

Lansley, S. (2009) *Life in the middle*, Touchstone Pamphlet no 6, London: Trades Union Congress. https://www.tuc.org.uk/sites/default/files/documents/lifeinthemiddle.pdf (accessed 3 September 2017).

Lansley, S. (2013) *How to boost the wage share*, London: Trades Union Congress https://www.tuc.org.uk/sites/default/files/tucfiles/How%20to%20Boost%20the%20Wage%20Share.pdf (accessed 3 September 2017).

Latouche, S. (2009 [2007]) *Farewell to growth*, Cambridge: Polity Press.

Laudicinia, P. (2017) *Wages have fallen 43% for millennials. No wonder they've lost hope*, World Economic Forum, 15 January. https://www.weforum.org/agenda/2017/01/wages-have-fallen-43-for-millennials-no-wonder-they-ve-lost-hope (accessed 28 February 2018).

Lawlor, E., Kersley, H. and Steed, S. (2009) *A bit rich: calculating the real value to society of different professions*, London: New Economics Foundation.

Lawlor, E., Spratt, S., Shaheen, F. and Beitler, D. (2011) *Why the rich are getting richer: the determinants of economic inequality*, London: New Economics Foundation.

Layard, R. (2005) *Happiness*, London: Allen Lane.

Layte, R. and Whelan, C.T. (2013) *Who feels inferior? A test of the status anxiety hypothesis of social inequalities in health*, GINI Discussion Paper 78, August, Amsterdam: Amsterdam Institute for Advanced Labour Studies.

Lazonick, W. and Mazzucato, M. (2013) 'The risk-reward nexus in innovation-inequality relationship', *Industrial and Corporate Change*, Spring.

Lee, M.J. (ed) (2000) *The consumer society reader*, Malden, MA: Blackwell Publishers.

Len, M. (2015) *Improving product repairability: policy options at EU level*, Brussels: Rreuse. http://www.rreuse.org/wp-content/uploads/Routes-to-Repair-RREUSE-final-report.pdf (accessed 28 February 2018).

Lessem, R. and Schieffer, A. (2010) *Integral economics*, Aldershot: Gower Publishing.

Lessof, C., Ross, A., Brind, R., Bell, E. and Newton, S. (2016) *Longitudinal study of young people in England cohort 2: health and wellbeing at wave 2*, London: Department of Education of England.

Levine, A., Frank, R. and Dijk, O. (2010) 'Expenditure cascades'. https://papers.ssrn.com/sol3/papers.cfm?abstract_id=1690612 (accessed 27 February 2018).

Lindblom, C. (1959) 'The science of muddling through', *Public Administration Review*, 19 (2): 79–88.

Lindblom, C. (1977) *Politics and markets: the world political-economic systems*, New York: Basic Books.

Lohmann, L. (2014) 'An alternative to "alternatives"', *Corner House*, World Rainforest Movement Bulletin. http://www.thecornerhouse.org.uk/resource/alternative-alternatives (accessed 5 March 2018).

Lothian, T. and Unger, R. (2012) 'Stimulus, slump, superstition and recovery: thinking and acting beyond vulgar Keynesianism', *Juncture*, London: IPPR.

Lubberman, U. (2007) 'Uwe Lubberman talks to PSFK about Premium Cola'. http://www.psfk.com/2007/11/uwe-lubbermann-talks-to-psfk-about-premium-cola.html (accessed 20 December 2016).

Lustig, N. (2012) 'Taxes, transfers, and income redistribution in Latin America', *Inequality in Focus*, 1 (2): 1-5.

Luton Borough Council (2018) 'Your say, your way'. http://www.luton.gov.uk/yoursay (accessed 28 February 2018).

Lynn, B.C. (2005) *The end of the line: the rise and coming fall of the global corporation*, New York: Crown/Archetype.

MacArthur, E. (2014) Interview with McKinsey. https://www.mckinsey.com/business-functions/sustainability-and-resource-productivity/our-insights/navigating-the-circular-economy-a-conversation-with-dame-ellen-macarthur (accessed 28 February 2018).

McAuley, J. (2016) 'France becomes the first country to ban plastic plates and cutlery', *Washington Post*, 19 September. https://www.washingtonpost.com/news/worldviews/wp/2016/09/19/france-bans-plastic-plates-and-cutlery/?utm_term=.cb405588a254 (accessed 10 March 2018).

McCartney, G., Taulbut, M., Scott, E., Macdonald, W., Burnett, D. and Fraser, A. (2013) 'Response to the Scottish Government's Expert Working Group on Welfare (EWGW) call for evidence, from NHS Health Scotland', December, Glasgow: NHS Health Scotland.

McEvoy, P. (2014) 'Circular economy: re-use, re-cycle, Renault!', Renault Group, 5 June. https://group.renault.com/en/news/blog-renault/circular-economy-recycle-renault/ (accessed 28 February 2018).

MacFadyen, P. (2014) *Flatpack democracy: a guide to creating independent politics*, Bath: Eco-Logic.

McGregor, J.A. (2015) *Global initiatives in measuring human wellbeing: convergence and difference*, CWiPP Working Paper Series, no 2. Sheffield: Centre for Wellbeing in Public Policy, University of Sheffield.

McKenzie, K. (2014) 'Using participatory budgeting to improve mental capital at the local level'. In: *If you could do one thing … Nine local actions to reduce health inequalities*, London: British Academy. http://www.britac.ac.uk/policy/health_inequalities.cfm (accessed 12 March 2016).

McLaren, D. and Childs, M. (2013) *Consumption and identity: a review of literature which is relevant to the question: 'what is a better foundation for people's identity than consumption?'*, London: Friends of the Earth. https://www.foe.co.uk/sites/default/files/downloads/consumption-identity-18135.pdf (accessed 10 October 2015).

Maclurcan, D. and Hinton, J. (2014) 'Beyond capitalism: not-for-profit business ethos motivates sustainable behavior', *The Guardian*, 1 October. https://www.theguardian.com/sustainable-business/2014/oct/01/for-profit-capitalism-selfish-unsustainable-behaviour-inequality (accessed 10 April 2018).

McManus, J. and Roberts, J. (2014) 'Executive summary'. In: *If you could do one thing … Nine local actions to reduce health inequalities*, London: British Academy. http://www.britac.ac.uk/policy/health_inequalities.cfm (accessed 12 March 2016).

Madrigal, A. (2018) 'Costa Rica's children vote too', *Tico Times*, 5 February. http://www.ticotimes.net/2018/02/05/costa-ricas-children-voted-too (accessed 7 March 2018).

Magee, C.L. and Devezas, T.C. (2017) 'A simple extension of dematerialization theory: incorporation of technical progress and the rebound effect', *Forecasting and Social Change*, 117: 196–205.

Majale, M. (2009) 'Developing participatory planning process in Kitale, Kenya', case study prepared for *Planning Sustainable Cities: Global Report on Human Settlements 2009*, Nairobi: UN Habitat.

Malik, K. (2013) *Human development report 2013: the rise of the South*, New York: United Nations Development Programme. http://hdr.undp.org/en/2013-report (accessed 22 July 2014).

Malik, K. (2014) *Measuring human progress in the 21st century*, New York: United Nations Development Programme.

Mara, B., Erinch, S., West, C., Irani, I. and Nash, R. (2017) *Impact investing: who are we serving? A case of mismatch between supply and demand*, discussion paper, Oxford: Oxfam GB.

Marçal, K. (2016 [2012]) *Who cooked Adam Smith's dinner? A story about women and economics*, trans. by S. Vogel, New York: Pegasus Books.

Marmot, M. (2004) *The status syndrome: how social standing affects our health and longevity*, New York: Holt Paperbacks.

Marsh, S. (2018) 'Eating disorders: NHS reports surge in hospital admissions,' *The Guardian*, 12 February. https://www.theguardian.com/society/2018/feb/12/eating-disorders-nhs-reports-surge-in-hospital-admissions (accessed 2 March 2018).

Martenson, C. (2011) *The crash course: the unsustainable future of our economy, energy and environment*, Hoboken, NJ: John Wiley and Sons.

Max-Neef, M. (1991) *Human scale development: conception, application, and further reflections*, New York: The Apex Press.

May, T. (2016) 'New cabinet committee to tackle top government economic priority', press release, 2 August, London: Prime Minister's Office. https://www.gov.uk/government/news/new-cabinet-committee-to-tackle-top-government-economic-priority (accessed 27 February 2018).

Mayne, R. (forthcoming) *Achieving system change*, Oxford: Oxfam GB.

Meadows, D. (2008) *Thinking in systems: a primer*, edited by Diana Wright, Sustainability Institute, White River Junction: Chelsea Green Publishing.

Meadows, D. (2010) 'Leverage points: places to intervene in a system', *Solutions Journal,* 1 (1): 41–9.

Meadows, D., Meadows, D.L., Randers, J. and Behrens III, W. (1972) *The limits to growth*, London: Potomac Associates/ Earth Island.

Mental Health Foundation (nd) *Work life balance*, London: Mental Health Foundation. https://www.mentalhealth.org.uk/a-to-z/w/work-life-balance (accessed 27 February 2018).

Mersmann, F., Wehnert, T., Gopel, M., Arens, S. and Ujj, O. (2014) *Shifting paradigms: unpacking transformation for climate action: a guidebook for climate finance and development practitioners*, Berlin: Wuppertal Institute.

Michaelson, J., Abdallah, S., Steuer, N., Thompson, S. and Marcs, N. (2009) *National accounts of wellbeing: bringing real wealth onto the balance sheet*, London: New Economics Foundation.

Milanovic, B. (2016) *Global inequality: a new approach for the age of globalization*, Cambridge, MA: Belknap Press.

Mill, J.S. (1909 [1848]) 'Book IV, chapter vi of the stationary state', *Principles of political economy with some of their applications to social philosophy*, edited by William J. Ashley, London: Longmans, Green and Co.

Miller, A. and Hopkins, R. (2013) *Climate after growth: why environmentalists must embrace post-growth economics and community resilience,* Santa Rosa, CA: Post Carbon Institute and Transition Network.

Milman, O. (2016) 'Nasa: Earth is warming at a pace "unprecedented in 1,000 years"', *The Guardian*, 30 August. https://www.theguardian.com/environment/2016/aug/30/nasa-climate-change-warning-earth-temperature-warming (accessed 12 October 2016).

Ministry of Foreign Affairs of Denmark (nd) *Independent from fossil fuels by 2050*, official website for Denmark. http://denmark.dk/en/green-living/strategies-and-policies/independent-from-fossil-fuels-by-2050/ (accessed 10 March 2018).

Mobertz, L. (2017) Interview: '"Renegade" economist Kate Raworth on future-proofing business', 18 July, Boulder: Conscious Company Media. https://consciouscompanymedia.com/the-new-economy/interview-renegade-economist-kate-raworth-future-proofing-business/ (accessed 4 March 2018).

Modern Families (2017) *The modern families index*, London: Working Families. https://www.workingfamilies.org.uk/wp-content/uploads/2017/01/Modern-Families-Index_Full-Report-1.pdf (accessed 2 March 2018).

Molenaar, H. (2011) 'The nature of development lies in social integration', *The Broker*, 5 October. http://www.thebrokeronline.eu/Blogs/Bellagio-Initiative/The-nature-of-development-lies-in-social-integration (accessed 8 April 2018).

Monbiot, G. (2011) 'Peak stuff?', *The Guardian*, 3 November. http://www.monbiot.com/2011/11/03/peak-stuff/ (accessed 4 October 2015).

Monbiot, G. (2017) *Out of the wreckage: a new politics for an age of crisis*, London: Verso.

Montgomery, D.R. (2012) *Dirt: the erosion of civilizations*, Berkeley: University of California Press.

Montreal Urban Ecology Centre (2015) 'Montréal Urban Ecology Centre releases new placemaking tool', 3 December. https://www.pps.org/article/muec-participatory-planning-guide (accessed 10 March 2018).

Morales, E. (2011) Preface to *Vivir bien: paradigmo no capitalista*, ed, Farah, I. and Vasapollo, L. CIDES-UMSA. (Author's translation).

Morgan, J. and Hewett, C. (2015) 'Broken instruments', *RSA Journal*, London: RSA. https://www.thersa.org/discover/publications-and-articles/journals/issue-2-2015 (accessed 7 September 2016).

Morrison, K. (2003) *Marx, Durkheim, Weber: formations of modern social thought*, London: SAGE Publications.

Mortality Projections Committee (2017) *Summary of Working Paper 97: CMI mortality projections model: CMI_2016*, March, Working Paper 97. https://www.actuaries.org.uk/news-and-insights/news/cmi-publishes-cmi2016-mortality-projections-model (accessed 27 August 2017).

Moss, S. (2012) *Natural childhood report*, Rotherham: National Trust. https://www.nationaltrust.org.uk/documents/read-our-natural-childhood-report.pdf (accessed 5 March 2018).

Mullainathan, S. and Shafir, E. (2013) *Scarcity: why having too little means so much*, New York: Henry Holt & Company.

Musk, E. (2006) *The secret Tesla Motors MASTER PLAN (just between you and me)*, Tesla.com https://www.tesla.com/en_GB/blog/secret-tesla-motors-master-plan-just-between-you-and-me (accessed 27 March 2018).

NASA (21 July 2016) *Global climate breaks new records January to June 2016.* https://climate.nasa.gov/news/2618/july-2017-equaled-record-july-2016/ (accessed 2 January 2018).

National Gardening Association (2014) 'Garden to table: a five year look at food gardening in America'. https://garden.org/special/pdf/2014-NGA-Garden-to-Table.pdf (accessed 10 March 2018).

National Institute on Alcohol Abuse and Alcoholism (2017) *Alcohol facts and statistics.* https://www.niaaa.nih.gov/alcohol-health/overview-alcohol-consumption/alcohol-facts-and-statistics (accessed 27 February 2018).

National Institute for Mental Health (2017) *Major depression among adults*, Bethesda, MD: US Department of Health and Human Services. https://www.nimh.nih.gov/health/statistics/prevalence/major-depression-among-adults.shtml (accessed 27 February 2018).

National Trust (2017) *Places that make us*, National Trust and University of Surrey. https://www.nationaltrust.org.uk/documents/places-that-make-us-research-report.pdf (accessed 30 December 2017).

Nesta (2014) 'Seven cities to galvanise thousands of volunteers as US launches in the UK', Nesta press release, 10 September. https://www.nesta.org.uk/blog/seven-uk-cities-unveil-plans-engage-volunteers (accessed 10 March 2018).

Network for Business Innovation and Sustainability (2012) *B corporations, benefit corporations and social purpose corporations: launching a new era of impact-driven companies*, October, Washington, DC. http://nbis.org/wp content/uploads/2012 October ImpactDrivenCompanies_NBIS_Whitepaper_Oct2012.pdf (accessed 10 March 2018).

New York City Council (nd) 'Participatory budgeting'. https://council.nyc.gov/pb/ (accessed 28 February 2018).

Newcastle City Council (2013) 'UDecide'. https://www.newcastle.gov.uk/communities-and-neighbourhoods/where-you-live/udecide#what (accessed 28 February 2018).

Newcastle City Council (2017) 'Parks trust set to take another step forward', 9 September. https://www.newcastle.gov.uk/news/parks-trust-set-take-another-step-forward (accessed 18 September 2017).

NHS Digital (2016) *Adult psychiatric morbidity survey*, Leeds: NHS Digital, 29 September.

NHSSP (2016) *Innovative good practices in Nepal's health sector*, Pulse Information and Advocacy brief. http://www.nhssp.org.np/pulse/Pulse_social_audit_good_practices_february2016.pdf (accessed 16 November 2017).

Nicholas, C. (2013) *Fairer tax for a better economy*, London: Institute for Public Policy Research.

Nirmalananda, S. (1986) *Enlightened anarchism*, Karnataka: Viswa Shanti Nikethana.

Nussbaum, M. (2011) *Creating capabilities: the human development approach*, Cambridge, MA: First Harvard University Press.

Nykvist, B., Persson, A., Moberg, F., Persson, L., Cornell, S. and Rockstrom, J. (2013) *National environmental performance on planetary boundaries*, Stockholm: Stockholm Resilience Centre for Swedish Environmental Protection Agency.

Obama, B. (2014) Address to the UN General Assembly, New York, 24 September. https://www.washingtonpost.com/politics/full-text-of-president-obamas-2014-address-to-the-united-nations-general-assembly/2014/09/24/88889e46-43f4-11e4-b437-1a7368204804_story.html?utm_term=.fd5c36dd38ab (accessed 5 December 2018).

Obama, B. (2015) 'Remarks by the President at the APEC CEO Summit'. In: *APEC*, ed. Asia-Pacific Economic Cooperation (APEC) CEO Summit, 18 November. Manilla. https://www.whitehouse.gov/the-press-office/2015/11/18/remarks-president-ceo-summit (accessed 12 October 2016).

Ocean Conservancy (2015) *Stemming the tide: land-based strategies for a plastic-free ocean*, Ocean Conservancy and McKinsey Center for Business and Environment. https://oceanconservancy.org/wp-content/uploads/2017/04/full-report-stemming-the.pdf (accessed 10 March 2018).

OECD (nd) *Measuring wellbeing and progress*, Paris: OECD. http://www.oecd.org/statistics/measuring-wellbeing-and-progress.htm (accessed 28 February 2018).

OECD (2008) 'Statistics, policy and knowledge 2007: measuring and fostering the progress of societies'. OECD iLibrary, https://doi.org/10.1787/9789264043244-en (accessed 5 September 2018)

OECD (2015) *Urban mobility system upgrade: how shared self-driving cars could change city traffic*, Paris: International Transport Forum. https://www.itf-oecd.org/urban-mobility-system-upgrade-1 (accessed 28 February 2018).

OECD (2016) *Average annual hours worked per worker*, Paris: OECD. https://stats.oecd.org/Index.aspx?DataSetCode=ANHRS (accessed 28 February 2018).

OECD (2017) *Better life index*, Paris: OECD. http://www.oecdbetterlifeindex.org/countries/japan/ (accessed 28 February 2018).

Ofcom (2008) *Review of television advertising and teleshopping regulation, Stage Two*, London: Office of Communications.

OfferUp (2016) *Buried: the state of stuff and stress*, Bellevue: OfferUp and ClearVoice Research. http://share.snacktools.com/FA87BBD569B/b7uj298n (accessed 27 February 2018).

Oguz, S., Merad, S. and Snape, D. (2013) *Measuring national wellbeing: what matters to personal wellbeing?* Newport: Office for National Statistics.

Okri, B. (2014) *A way of being free*, London: Head of Zeus.

O'Neill, D., Fanning, A., Lamb, W. and Steinberger, J. (2018) 'A good life for all within planetary boundaries', *Nature Sustainability*, 1 (February): 88–95.

ONS (2014a) *Labour market statistics August to October 2014–December 2014 release*, Table A. Newport: Office of National Statistics.

ONS (2014b) *Measuring national wellbeing domains and measures: March 2014 release*, Table 4.2. Newport: Office for National Statistics.

ONS (2015) *Ownership of UK quoted shares: 2014*, Newport: Office for National Statistics.

ONS (2016) *Household satellite accounts, 2005–2014*, Newport: Office for National Statistics.

Open Government Partnership (2016) 'What is the Open Government Partnership?' https://www.opengovpartnership.org/about/about-ogp (accessed 28 February 2018).

Orange, R. (2016) 'Waste not want not: Sweden to give tax breaks for repairs', *The Guardian*, 19 September. https://www.theguardian.com/world/2016/sep/19/waste-not-want-not-sweden-tax-breaks-repairs (accessed 10 March 2018).

Orr, G. (2014) 'Britain has been voted the loneliness capital of Europe', *The Independent*, 26 June. http://www.independent.co.uk/life-style/health-and-families/features/britain-has-been-voted-the-loneliness-capital-of-europe-so-how-did-we-become-so-isolated-9566617.html (accessed 27 February 2018).

O'Sullivan, T. (2001) *Tower of strength: the story of Tyrone O'Sullivan and Tower Colliery*, Edinburgh: Mainstream Publishing.

Oxford Poverty and Human Development Initiative (2012) *A short guide to GNH index*, Oxford: OPHI.

Packard, V. (1961) *The waste makers*, London: Longmans.

Parkinson, G. (2016) 'ACT lifts 2020 target to 100% renewable energy, as Australia stalls', Mullumbimby, 29 April. http://reneweconomy.com.au/2016/act-lifts-2020-target-to-100-renewable-energy-as-australia-stalls-86177 (accessed 10 March 2018).

Participatory Budgeting Project (2016) *White Paper: Next Generation Democracy*. https://www.participatorybudgeting.org/white-paper/

Paskov, M., Gërxhani, K. and van de Werfhorst, H.G. (2013) *Income inequality and status anxiety*, Amsterdam: GINI.

Pateman, C. (1970) *Participation and democratic theory*, Cambridge: Cambridge University Press.

Pennycook, M. and Whittaker, M. (2012) *Low pay Britain*, London: Resolution Foundation.

Philips (2015) 'Philips provides light as a service to Schiphol Airport', Philips press release, 16 April. https://www.philips.com/a-w/about/news/archive/standard/news/press/2015/20150416-Philips-provides-Light-as-a-Service-to-Schiphol-Airport.html (accessed 28 February 2018).

Piketty, T. (2014) *Capital in the twenty-first century*, trans. A. Goldhammer, Cambridge, MA: Belknap Press.

Pilling, D. (2018) *The growth delusion: the wealth and wellbeing of nations*, London: Bloomsbury.

Polanyi, K. (2001 [1944]) *The great transformation: the political and economic origins of our time*, Boston, MA: Beacon Press.

Polanyi Levitt, K. (2013) *From the great transformation to the great financialisation: on Karl Polanyi and other essays*, Black Point: Fernwood Publishing.

Polman, P. (2014) 'Business, society and the future of capitalism', *McKinsey Quarterly*, May. http://www.mckinsey.com/insights/sustainability/business_society_and_the_future_of_capitalism (accessed 28 February 2018).

Poortinga, W., Sautkina, E. and Thomas, G. (2016) 'The 5p carrier bag charge has paved the way for other waste reduction policies', *The Conversation*, 29 September. https://theconversation.com/the-5p-carrier-bag-charge-has-paved-the-way-for-other-waste-reduction-policies-64911 (accessed 27 February 2018).

Porritt, J. (2008) *Globalism and regionalism*, London: Black Dog Publishing.

Postwachstum (2010) '12 Lines of flight for just degrowth'. https://postwachstum.net/2010/11/23/12-lines-of-flight-for-a-just-degrowth-economy/ (accessed 27 February 2018).

Pouw, N. and McGregor, A. (2014) *An economics of wellbeing. What would economics look like if it were focused on human wellbeing?*, Brighton: Institute of Development Studies.

Practical Action (2016) *Poor people's energy outlook 2016*, Rugby: Practical Action Publishing Ltd.

Prada, R. (2013) 'Buen Vivir as a model for state and economy'. In: Lang, M. and Mokrani, D. (eds), *Beyond development: alternative visions from Latin America*. Quito: Transnational Institute and Rosa Luxemburg Foundation.

Preston, S. (2007) 'The changing relation between mortality and level of economic development', *International Journal of Epidemiology*, 36: 484–90.

Pretty, J., Barton, J., Pervez Bharucha, Z., Bragg, R., Pencheon, D., Wood, C. and Depledge, M. (2015) 'Improving health and wellbeing independently of GDP: dividends of greener and prosocial economies', *International Journal of Environmental Health Research*, 26 (1): 11–36.

Rai, S.M. and Waylen, G. (2014) *New frontiers in feminist political economy*, Abingdon: Routledge.

Ramesh, R. (2012) 'Council cuts "targeted towards deprived areas"', *The Guardian*, 14 November. https://www.theguardian.com/society/2012/nov/14/council-cuts-targeted-deprived-areas (accessed 12 October 2016).

Randall, C. and Corp, A. (2014) *Measuring national wellbeing: European comparisons*, Newport: Office of National Statistics.

Raskin, P., Banuri, T., Gallopin, G., Gutman, P., Hammond, A., Kates, R. and Swart, R. (2002) *The great transition: the promise and lure of the times ahead*, Boston, MA: Global Scenario Group.

Raworth, K. (2012) *A safe and just space for humanity: can we live within the doughnut?* Oxford: Oxfam International.

Raworth, K. (2017) *Doughnut economics: seven ways to think like a 21st century economist*, London: Penguin Random House.

Rees, W. (2014) 'Are prosperity and sustainability compatible?'. In: Novkovic, S. and Webb, T. (eds) *Co-operatives in a post-growth era: creating co-operative economics*, London: Zed Books.

Rees, W. and Moore, J. (2013) 'Ecological footprints, fair earth-shares and urbanisation'. In: Vale, R. and Vale, B. (eds), *Living within a fair share ecological footprint*, Abingdon: Routledge.

Resolution Foundation (2012) *Gaining from growth: the final report of the Commission on Living Standards*, London: Resolution Foundation.

Resolution Foundation (2013) *Squeezed Britain 2013*, London: Resolution Foundation.

Rhodes, F. (2016) *Women and the 1%: how extreme economic inequality and gender inequality must be tackled together*, Oxford: Oxfam International.

Roberts, G. (2015) 'How ParkRun became a global phenomenon', *The Independent*, 28 December. https://www.independent.co.uk/life-style/health-and-families/features/how-parkrun-became-a-global-phenomenon-the-free-activity-that-has-changed-millions-of-peoples-lives-a6788731.html (accessed 10 March 2018).

Robertson, J. (1998) *Beyond the dependency culture: people, power and responsibility*, London: Adamantine Press.

Rogers, E.M. (2003 [1962]) *Diffusion of innovations*, New York: Simon and Schuster.

Rosnick, D. (2013) *Reduced work hours as a means of slowing climate change*, Washington, DC: Center for Economic and Policy Research.

Roßteutcher, S. (2000) 'Associative Democracy: fashionable slogan or constructive innovation?'. In Saward, M. (ed) (2003) *Democratic innovation*, London: Routledge.

Rowlands, J. (1997) *Questioning empowerment: working with women in Honduras*, Oxford: Oxfam GB.

Rreuse (2016) 'Spain first country to stop reusable goods ending up in landfill', 28 April. http://www.rreuse.org/spain-first-country-to-set-target-to-stop-reusable-goods-ending-up-in-landfill/ (accessed 28 February 2018).

Rundle, M. (2015) 'Minecraft creator Notch says his billions have made him miserable', *Wired UK*, 30 August. http://www.wired.co.uk/article/notch-net-worth-isolation-twitter-outburst (accessed 5 March 2018).

Saad, L. (2014) 'The "40-hour" workweek is actually longer – by seven hours', Gallup Economy series, Washington, DC. http://www.gallup.com/poll/175286/hour-workweek-actually-longer-seven-hours.aspx (accessed 3 September 2017).

Sabatier, P. and Jenkins-Smith, S. (1993) *Policy change and learning: an advocacy coalition approach*, Boulder, CO: Westview Press.

Sachs W. (ed) (1992) *The development dictionary: a guide to knowledge as power*, London: Zed Books.

Saddler, H. (2013) *Power down*, Canberra: The Australia Institute. http://www.tai.org.au/content/power-down (accessed 11 March 2018).

Sanchez Bajo, C. (2014) 'Is the debt trap avoidable?'. In: Novkovic, S. and Webb, T. (eds), *Co-operatives in a post-growth era: creating co-operative economics*, London: Zed Books.

Sandel, M.J. (2012) *What money can't buy: the moral limits of markets*, New York: Farrar, Straus and Giroux.

Saunders, P. and Lawson, T. (2016) *Developing legal talent: stepping into the future law firm*, London: Deloitte Insights. https://www2.deloitte.com/content/dam/Deloitte/uk/Documents/audit/deloitte-uk-developing-legal-talent-2016.pdf (accessed 28 February 2018).

Sayers, M. and Trebeck, K. (2015) *The UK doughnut: a framework for environmental sustainability and social justice*, Oxford: Oxfam GB.

Schor, J. (1999) 'The new politics of consumption', *Boston Review*. http://bostonreview.net/BR24.3/schor.html (accessed 12 October 2012).

Schor, J. (2011) *True wealth: how and why millions of Americans are creating a time-rich, ecologically light, small-scale, high satisfaction economy*, New York: Penguin.

Schor, J. (2013) 'Why we need a shorter working week'. In: Coote, A. and Franklin, J. (eds) (2013) *Time on our side: why we all need a shorter working week*, London: New Economics Foundation.

Schumacher, E.F. (1993) *Small is beautiful*, London: Vintage.

Schwartz, S. (1992) 'Universals in the content and structure of values: theoretical advances and empirical tests in 20 countries'. In Zanna, M. (ed), *Advances in experimental social psychology*, 25: 1–65.

Scottish Government (2010) *Scotland's zero waste plan*, Edinburgh: The Scottish Government. http://www.gov.scot/Resource/Doc/314168/0099749.pdf (accessed 9 October 2015).

Seddon, J. (1992) *I want you to cheat: the unreasonable guide to service and quality in organisations*, Buckingham: Vanguard Consulting Limited.

Segal, J. (2014) 'Aristotle'. In: Alexander, S. and McLeod, A. (eds), *Simple living in history*, Melbourne: Simplicity Institute.

Self Storage Association (2015) 'Self storage industry fact sheet', Alexandria: Self Storage Association. www.selfstorage.org (accessed 27 October 2018).

Selvanathan, P. (2015) *Open letter from Puvan Selvanathan to President of the UN Human Rights Council*, 16 December. https://www.globalpolicy.org/home/270-general/52832-puvan-selvanathan-resigns-from-un-working-group-on-business-a-human-rights-calling-for-a-binding-treaty.html (Accessed 28 February 2018).

Semler, R. (1993) *Maverick: the success story behind the world's most unusual workplace*, New York: Arrow Books.

Sen, A. (2000) *Development as freedom*, New York: Random House.

Senft, J. (2016) 'Adultum – a critical narrative at the end of growth and a name for the coming age'. https://www.degrowth.info/en/2016/10/adultum-a-critical-narrative-at-the-end-of-growth-and-a-name-for-the-coming-age/ (accessed 27 February 2018).

Sharma, R. (2016) *The rise and fall of nations: ten rules of change in the post-crisis world*, London: Allen Lane.

Shaw, I. and Taplin, S. (2007) 'Happiness and mental health policy: a sociological critique', *Journal of Mental Health*, 16: 3, 359–73.

Shenker, J. (2009) 'And the rich got richer', *The Guardian*, 8 November. https://www.theguardian.com/commentisfree/2009/nov/08/egypt-imf (accessed 12 October 2016).

Shiva, V. (2013) 'How economic growth has become anti-life', *The Guardian*, 1 November 2013. https://www.theguardian.com/commentisfree/2013/nov/01/how-economic-growth-has-become-anti-life (accessed 10 April 2018).

Sibaud, P. (2013) *Short Circuit: the lifecycle of our electronic gadgets and the true cost to earth*, London: The Gaia Foundation.

Silim, A. (2013) *Job creation: lessons from abroad*, London: Trades Union Congress.

Simms, A. (2009) *Ecological debt: global warming and the wealth of nations*, London: Pluto Press.

Simms, A. and Potts, R. (2012) *The new materialism: how our relationship with the material world can change for the better*, London: Bread, print, roses.

Sjåfjell, B., Johnston, A., Anker-Sørensen, L. and Millon, D. (2014) *Shareholder primacy: the main barrier to sustainable companies*, Oslo: University of Oslo.

Skidelsky, R. and Skidelsky, E. (2013) *How much is enough? Money and the good life*, London: Penguin Books.

Slater, D. (1997) *Consumer culture and modernity*, Cambridge: Polity Press.

Slezak, M. (2016) 'World's carbon dioxide concentration teetering on the point of no return', *The Guardian*, 11 May. https://www.theguardian.com/environment/2016/may/11/worlds-carbon-dioxide-concentration-teetering-on-the-point-of-no-return (accessed 12 October 2016).

Smith, A. (1790) *An inquiry into the nature and causes of the wealth of nations*, Metalibri Edition, (2007).

Smith, P. and Max-Neef, M. (2011) *Economics unmasked: from power and greed to compassion and the common good*, Totnes: Green Books.

Smith, S. and Rothbaum, J. (2014) 'Co-operatives in a global economy: key issues, recent trends and potential for development'. In: Novkovic, S. and Webb, T. (eds), *Co-operatives in a post-growth era: creating co-operative economics*, London: Zed Books.

Smith, T. (2016) 'Why the International Criminal Court is right to focus on the environment', *The Conversation*, https://theconversation.com/why-the-international-criminal-court-is-right-to-focus-on-the-environment-65920 (accessed 23 October 2016).

Smithers, A. (2014) 'The change in management behaviour'. In: Williamson, J., Driver, C. and Kenway, P. (eds), *Beyond shareholder value: the reasons and choices for corporate governance reform*, London: Trades Union Congress, New Policy Institute, SOAS.

Social Progress Imperative (2016) 'News release: GDP "no guarantee" of quality of life: major new report'. http://www.socialprogressimperative.org/news-release-gdp-no-guarantee-of-quality-of-life-major-new-report/ (accessed 8 September 2016).

Solon, P. (2014) *Systemic alternatives: vivir bien: notes for the debate*, La Paz: Systemic Alternatives http://systemicalternatives.org/2014/07/30/1099/ (accessed 29 August 2015).

Soper, K. (2011) 'Relax: alternative hedonism and a new politics of pleasure', *Red Pepper*, 20 August. https://www.redpepper.org.uk/relax-alternative-hedonism/ (accessed 8 April 2018).

Sorrell, S. (2007) *The rebound effect: an assessment of the evidence for economy-wide energy savings from improved energy efficiency*, Sussex Energy Group, London: UK Energy Research Centre.

SPERI (2014) *The relationship between population growth and economic growth*, British Political Economy Brief No. 7. Sheffield: SPERI.

Srnicek, N. (2016) *Platform capitalism*, Cambridge: Polity Press.

Srnicek, N. and Williams, A. (2015) *Inventing the future: postcapitalism and a world without work*, London: Verso.

Standing, G. (2016) *The corruption of capitalism: why rentiers thrive and work does not pay*, London: Biteback Books.

Starr, D. (2016) 'Just 90 companies are to blame for most climate change, this "carbon accountant" says', *Science Magazine*, 25 April. http://www.sciencemag.org/news/2016/08/just-90-companies-are-blame-most-climate-change-carbon-accountant-says?mc_cid=0b39ed1297&mc_eid=777bb32305 (accessed 2 September 2017).

Steffen, W., Broadgate, W., Deutsch, L., Gaffney, O. and Ludwig, C. (2015) 'The trajectory of the anthropocene: the great acceleration', *The Anthropocene Review*, 2 (1): 81–98.

Steger, M., Dik, B. and Duffy, R. (2012) 'Measuring meaningful work: the work and meaning inventory', *Journal of Career Assessment*, 00: (0) 1–16.

Steiner, S. (2012) 'Top five regrets of the dying', *The Guardian*, 1 February. http://www.theguardian.com/lifeandstyle/2012/feb/01/top-five-regrets-of-the-dying (accessed 27 February 2018).

Stern, N. (2010) *A blueprint for a safer planet*, London: Vintage.

Steuver, H. (2004) *Off-ramp: adventures and heartache in the American elsewhere*, London: Picador.

Stiglitz, J. (2012) *The price of inequality: how today's divided society endangers our future*, New York: W.W. Norton and Company.

Stiglitz, J., Sen, A. and Fitoussi, JP (2009) *Report by the Commission on the Measurement of Economic Performance and Social Progress*, Paris: Commission on the Measurement of Economic Performance and Social Progress.

Stoddart, H. (2014) *Food, fossil fuels and filthy finance*, Oxford: Oxfam International.

Stout, L. (2013) 'The shareholder value myth', *The European Financial Review*, 30 April. http://www.europeanfinancialreview.com/?p=883 (accessed 28 February 2018).

Strang S. and Park, S.Q. (2016) 'Human cooperation and its underlying mechanisms'. In: Wöhr, M. and Krach, S. (eds), *Social behavior from rodents to humans. Current topics in behavioral neurosciences*, vol 30. Springer, Cham.

Strauss-Kahn, D. (2010) 'Human development and wealth distribution', International Monetary Fund, 1 November.

Sunday Times (2017) 'Could modern eating habits kill the kitchen cupboard?', *Sunday Times*, 11 June. https://www.thetimes.co.uk/article/could-modern-eating-habits-kill-the-kitchen-cupboard-zv3dd066j (accessed 27 February 2018).

Tarrow, S. (1994) *Power in movement: social movements, collective action and politics*, Cambridge and New York: Cambridge University Press.

Tatum, M. (2016) 'How France is leading the way on food waste', *The Grocer*, 20 May. https://www.thegrocer.co.uk/home/topics/waste-not-want-not/how-france-is-leading-the-way-on-food-waste/536447.article (10 March 2018).

Tearfund (2016) *Virtuous circle: how the circular economy can create jobs and save lives in low and middle income countries*, London: Tearfund and Institute of Development Studies.

Thaler, R. and Sunstein, C. (2008) *Nudge: improving decisions about health, wealth, and happiness*, New Haven: Yale University Press.

The Dhammapada (1994) *The Dhammapada: The Sayings of the Buddha*, trans. T. Byron, Boulder, CO: Shambala Publications.

The Economist (2016) 'Measuring a progressive society', 29 June. http://www.economist.com/blogs/graphicdetail/2016/06/daily-chart-20 (accessed 8 September 2016).

The Economist (2017) 'New York has record numbers of homeless people: but relatively few of them are sleeping rough', 23 March. https://www.economist.com/news/united-states/21719516-relatively-few-them-are-sleeping-rough-new-york-has-record-numbers-homeless (accessed 6 April 2018).

The Scotsman (2004) 'Bowmore distillery proves a fine malt can be green', *The Scotsman*, 4 February. https://www.scotsman.com/news/bowmore-distillery-proves-a-fine-malt-can-be-green-1-512311 (accessed 28 February 2018).

Thomadakis, S. (2015) *Growth, debt and sovereignty prolegomena to the Greek crisis*, London: LSE. http://eprints.lse.ac.uk/62081/ (accessed 16 October 2016).

Thomas, A. (2017) 'A shorter working week would revolutionise city life', *The Guardian*, 4 January. https://www.theguardian.com/sustainable-business/2017/jan/04/shorter-working-week-revolutionise-city-life (accessed 28 February 2018).

Thomas, S. (2012) 'The great recovery', *RSA blog*. https://www.thersa.org/action-and-research/rsa-projects/economy-enterprise-manufacturing-folder/the-great-recovery (accessed 25 July 2013).

Time Magazine (1966) 'Essay: the futurists – looking forward to AD 2000', 25 February. http://content.time.com/time/magazine/article/0,9171,835128-1,00.html (accessed 6 October 2015).

Times of India (2017) 'Uttarakhand High Court accords status of "living entitites" to Ganga, Yamuna', 20 March. http://timesofindia.indiatimes.com/india/uttarakhand-high-court-accords-status-of-living-entities-to-ganga-yamuna/articleshow/57738570.cms (accessed 28 February 2018).

Tisch, J.M. (2010) *Citizen you: doing your part to change the world*, New York: Random House.

Torkington, S. (2016) 'Scientists say 2014 was a turning point for climate change', World Economic Forum, 27 September. https://www.weforum.org/agenda/2016/09/china-peak-coal-climate-change/ (accessed 10 March 2018).

Townsend, M. and Zarnett, B. (2013) *A journey in search of capitalism 2.0. Part 1: blueprints for a sustainable economy*, Toronto: Earthshine.

Tran, M. (2013) 'Wellbeing of the poor has deteriorated over past 15 years, says Cafod', *The Guardian*, 30 July. www.theguardian.com/global-development/2013/jul/30/wellbeing-poor-casford/print (accessed 30 July 2013).

Traver, N. (1987) 'They cannot fend for themselves', *Time Magazine*, 23 March 23.

Trebeck, K. (2007) 'Tools for the disempowered? Indigenous leverage over mining companies', *Australian Journal of Political Science*, 42 (4): 541–62.

Trebeck, K. (2011) *Whose Economy? The winners and losers in the new Scottish economy*, Oxford: Oxfam.

Trucost (2013) *Natural capital at risk: the top 100 externalities of business*, London http://www.trucost.com/published-research/99/natural-capital-at-risk-the-top-100-externalities-of-business (accessed 21 October 2015).

TUC (2011) *Poverty myth buster: ten common false beliefs about poverty*, Trades Union Congress, 28 July. www.tuc.org.uk/social/tuc-19872-f0.cfm (accessed 3 August 2011).

TUC (2018) *Worksmart*. https://worksmart.org.uk/work-your-proper-hours-day (accessed 28 February 2018).

Turner, G. (2014) 'Is global collapse imminent?', MSSI Research Paper no 4, Melbourne Sustainable Society Institute, The University of Melbourne.

Turner, S., Kamfer Cilliers, J. and Hughes, B. (2015) *Reasonable goals for reducing poverty in Africa: targets for the post-2015 MDGs and Agenda 2063*, Pretoria: Institute for Security Studies.

UK Association of School and College Leaders and the National Children's Bureau (2016) *Document summary – ASCL and NCB survey briefing*, Leicester: ASCL, February. http://www.ascl.org.uk/utilities/document-summary.html?id=D91C5B0A-72A6-4117-96A9B343E51FB296 (accessed 3 March 2018).

UK Music (2015) *Measuring Music 2015 report*. https://www.ukmusic.org/assets/general/Measuring_Music_2015.pdf (accessed 10 March 2018).

UNDP (1996) *Human development report 1996*, New York: United Nations Development Programme.

UNDP (2011) *Human development reports*, New York: United Nations Development Programme.

UNESCO Institute for Statistics (2015) *Adult and youth literacy*, Montreal: UNESCO Institute for Statistics.

UNICEF and World Health Organization (2015) *25 years progress on sanitation and drinking water: 2015 update and MDG assessment*, Geneva.

UNISDR and Centre for Research on the Epidemiology of Disasters (2015) *The human cost of weather-related disasters 1995–2015*, United Nations Office for Disaster Risk Reduction: Geneva.

United Nations (2013) *My world: The United Nations Global Survey for a Better World. Summary of results*, New York: UN.

United Nations (2015) *The Millennium Development Goals report*, New York: UN. http://www.un.org/millenniumgoals/ (accessed 12 October 2016).

United Nations Food and Agriculture Organization (2016a) *FAO statistical pocketbook*, Rome: FAO. http://www.fao.org/docrep/014/mb060e/mb060e00.pdf (accessed 7 September 2016).

United Nations Food and Agriculture Organization (2016b) *The state of the world fisheries and aquaculture*, Rome: FAO. http://www.fao.org March a-i5555e.pdf (accessed 12 October 2016).

Unwin, S. (2016) 'Remade in Edinburgh, and the vision of creating a network of community reuse and repair centres', *CommonSpace*, 26 October. https://www.commonspace.scot/articles/9727/sophie-unwin-remade-edinburgh-and-vision-creating-network-community-reuse-and-repair (accessed 5 March 2018).

UN Women (2016) *Progress of the world's women 2015–2016: transforming economies, realizing rights*, New York: UN Women.

Urban Justice Center (2015) 'A people's budget: a research and evaluation report on participatory budgeting in New York City cycle 4: key research findings', New York: Urban Justice Center and the PBNYC Research Team. https://cdp.urbanjustice.org/sites/default/files/CDP.WEB.doc_Report_PBNYC_cycle4findings_20151021.pdf (accessed 7 March 2018).

Vale, R. and Vale, B. (eds) (2013) *Living within a fair share ecological footprint*, Abingdon: Routledge.

Van de Bergh, J. (2017) 'A third option for climate policy within potential limits to growth', *Nature Climate Change*, 7: 107–13.

Varoufakis, Y. (2012) 'Why Valve?', *Valve Economics*, 3 August. http://blogs.valvesoftware.com/economics/ (accessed 28 February 2018).

Veblen, T. (1925) *The theory of the leisure class: an economic study of institutions*, London: Allen and Unwin.

Verbist, G., Förster, M.F. and Vaalavuo, M. (2012) *The impact of publicly provided services on the distribution of resources: review of new results and methods*, OECD Social, Employment and Migration Working Papers, No. 130, Paris: OECD Publishing.

Victor, P. (2011) 'Growth, degrowth and climate change: a scenario analysis', *Ecological Economics*, 84: 206–12.

Victor, P. (2014) 'Living well: explorations into the end of growth'. In: Novkovic, S. and Webb, T. (eds) *Co-operatives in a post-growth era: creating co-operative economics*, London: Zed Books.

Victor, P. and Rosenbluth, G. (2006) 'Managing without growth', *Ecological Economics*, 61: 492–504.

Vidal, J. (2011) 'Bolivia enshrines natural world's rights with equal status for Mother Earth', *The Guardian*, 20 April. https://www.theguardian.com/environment/2011/apr/10/bolivia-enshrines-natural-worlds-rights (accessed 5 March 2018).

Volvo (2015) *Volvo Group sustainability report 2015*, Gothenburg: Volvo. http://www.volvogroup.com/en-en/events/2016/feb/annual-and-sustainability-report-2015.html (accessed 10 March 2018).

Wainwright, H. (2015) 'More than equality: reasons to be a feminist socialist', *Open Democracy*, 7 December. https://www.opendemocracy.net/transformation/hilary-wainwright/how-i-became-feminist-socialist (accessed 28 February 2018).

Wakefield, J.R.H., Sani, F., Madhok, V. et al (2017) 'The relationship between group identification and satisfaction with life in cross cultural community sample', *Journal of Happiness Studies*, 18 (3): 785–807. Also see: http://healthingroups.wixsite.com/healthingroups.

Walasek, L. and Brown, G.D.A. (2016) 'Income inequality, income, and internet searches for status goods: a cross-national study of the association between inequality and wellbeing', *Social Indicators Research*, 129 (3): 1001–14.

Walker, P. (2002) *We, the people: developing a new democracy*, London: New Economics Foundation.

Walker, R., Kyomuhendo, G.B., Chase, E., Choudhry, S., Gubrium, E.K., Yongmie Nicola, J., Lødemel, I., Mathew, L., Mwiine, A., Pellissery, S. and Ming, Y. (2013) 'Poverty in global perspective: is shame a common denominator?', *Journal of Social Policy*, 42 (2): 215–33.

Wall, D. (2017) *Elinor Ostrom's rules for radicals*, London: Pluto Press.

Wallich, H. (1972) 'Zero growth', *Newsweek*, vol 79: 24 January.

Wallman, J. (2015) *Stuffocation: living less with more*, London: Penguin Random House.

Walton, M. (2010) *Capitalism, the state, and the underlying drivers of human development*, New York: UNDP.

Wang, C. (2015) 'How to sell clothes to women who don't want to be sold to', *Refinery29*, 26 September 26. https://www.refinery29.com/apiece-apart-eileen-fisher (accessed 10 April 2018).

Wanninski, J. (1978) 'Taxes, revenues, and the Laffer curve', *The Public Interest 50*, posted by National Affairs, Washington. https://www.nationalaffairs.com/storage/app/uploads/public/58e/1a4/c54/58e1a4c549207669125935.pdf (accessed 28 February 2018).

Ward, J.D., Sutton, P.C., Werner, A.D., Costanza, R., Mohr, S.H. and Simmons, C.T. (2016) 'Is decoupling GDP growth from environmental impact possible?' *PLoS One*, 11 (10): e0164733.

Warhurst, P. (2012) 'How we can eat our landscapes', talk to TED conference. https://www.ted.com/speakers/pam_warhurst (accessed 28 February 2018).

Waring, M. (1999) *Counting for nothing: what men value and what women are worth*, 2nd edn, Toronto: University of Toronto Press.

Washington, H. and Twomey, P. (eds) (2016) *A future beyond growth*, Abingdon: Routledge.

Waste and Resources Action Programme (2012) 'Valuing our clothes: the true cost of how we design, use and dispose of clothing in the UK', Oxon: WRAP. http://www.wrap.org.uk/sites/files/wrap/VoC%20FINAL%20online%202012%2007%2011.pdf (accessed 5 March 2018).

WAVES (2015) *Natural capital accounting in brief*, Washington, DC: World Bank.

Webb, T. and Novkovic, S. (2014) 'Introduction: co-operative economics, why our world needs it'. In: Novkovic, S. and Webb, T. (eds) *Co-operatives in a post-growth era: creating co-operative economics*, London: Zed Books.

Weible, C., Sabatier, P., and McQueen, K. (2009) 'Themes and variations: taking stock of the advocacy coalition framework', *The Policy Studies Journal*, 37 (1): 121–40.

Welby, J. (2017) *Dethroning Mammon: making money serve grace*, London: Bloomsbury.

Wells, J. (2015) 'How Britain became hooked on homebrew', *The Telegraph*, 20 August 2015. https://www.telegraph.co.uk/men/the-filter/11803139/How-Britain-became-hooked-on-homebrew.html (accessed 10 March 2018).

Welsh Assembly Government (2010) *Towards zero waste, the overarching waste strategy document for Wales*, Cardiff: Welsh Assembly Government.

Wender, B. et al (2014) 'Anticipatory life-cycle assessment for responsible research and innovation', *Journal of Responsible Innovation*, 1 (2): 200–7.

Western, B. and Rosenfeld, J. (2011) 'Unions, norms, and the rise in US wage inequality', *American Sociological Review*, 76 (4): 513–37.

Whitby, A., Seaford, C. and Berry, C. (2014) *The BRAINPOol Project final report: beyond GDP – from measurement to politics and policy, BRAINPOol deliverable 5.2*, World Future Council.

White, A. (2006) *Transforming the corporation*, Boston, MA: Tellus Institute. http://www.gtinitiative.org/documents/PDFFINALS/5Corporations.pdf (accessed 23 December 2014).

White, H. and Anderson, E. (2001) 'Growth versus distribution: does the pattern of growth matter?', *Development Policy Review*, 19 (3) 267–89.

Whittam, G. and Talbot, S. (2014) 'A review of social and employee-owned co-operative business models and their potential to reduce poverty', Glasgow: UWS-Oxfam Partnership. http://uwsoxfampartnership.org.uk/wp-content/uploads/2014/10/Co-op-Business-Model-Report-final.pdf (accessed 28 February 2018).

Wiedmann, T., Schandl, H., Lenzen, M., Moran, D., Suh, S., West, J. and Kanemoto, K. (2015) 'The material footprint of nations', *PNAS*, 112 (20): 6271–6.

Wilkinson, R. and Pickett, K. (2009) *The spirit level – why more equal societies almost always do better*, London: Allen Lane.

Williams, C. (2016) 'The science is in: gardening is good for you', *The Conversation*, 26 September. https://theconversation.com/the-science-is-in-gardening-is-good-for-you-65251 (accessed 20 December 2016).

Williamson, J., Driver, C. and Kenway, P. (eds) (2014) *Beyond shareholder value: the reasons and choices for corporate governance reform*, London: Trades Union Congress, New Policy Institute, SOAS. http://www.tuc.org.uk/sites/default/files/BSV.pdf (accessed 23 December 2014).

Wilson, C. and Moulton, B. (2010) 'Loneliness among older adults: a national survey of adults 45+', prepared by Knowledge Networks and Insight Policy Research, Washington, DC: AARP. http://assets.aarp.org/rgcenter/general/loneliness_2010.pdf (accessed 3 September 2017).

Woetzel, J., Madgavkar, A., Ellingrud, K., Labaye, E., Devillard, S., Kutcher, E., Manyika, J., Dobbs, R. and Krishnan, M. (2015) *The power of parity, how advancing women's equality could add to global growth*, McKinsey Global Institute.

Women's Wear Daily (2015) 'Overheated! Is fashion headed for a burnout?', *WWD*, 27 October 2015. http://wwd.com/fashion-news/fashion-features/fashion-designers-karl-lagerfeld-marc-jacobs-10269092/ (accessed 27 February 2018).

Woodward, D. (2015) 'Incrementum ad absurdum: global growth, inequality and poverty eradication in a carbon-constrained world', *World Social and Economic Review*, no 4.

Woodward, D. and Abdallah, S. (2012) *Global Inequality*, London: Stakeholder Forum.

Woolf, N. (2016) 'Portland City Council passes tax on CEOs who earn 100 times more than staff', *The Guardian*, 8 December. https://www.theguardian.com/us-news/2016/dec/08/portland-oregon-ceo-pay-tax-passes-income-inequality (accessed 28 February 2018).

World Bank (1993) *World development report*, Washington DC: World Bank.

World Bank (2012a) *Inclusive green growth: the pathway to sustainable development*, Washington, DC: World Bank.

World Bank (2012b) *Social audits in Nepal's community schools: measuring policy against practice*, Budget Transparency Initiative, Washington, DC: World Bank.

World Bank (2016) *Transport overview*, Washington DC: World Bank. http://www.worldbank.org/en/topic/transport/overview (accessed 16 October 2016).

World Bank (2017) World Bank national accounts data. http://data.worldbank.org/ (accessed 26 February 2018).

World Bank and International Monetary Fund (2016) *Global monitoring report 2015/2016: development goals in an era of demographic change*, Washington DC: World Bank. https://openknowledge.worldbank.org/handle/10986/22547 (accessed 4 March 2018).

World Health Organization (2014) *Global status report on violence prevention*, Geneva: WHO. http://apps.who.int/iris/bitstream/10665/145087/3/WHO_NMH_NVI_14.2_eng.pdf?ua=1&ua=1 (accessed 12 October 2016).

World Health Organization (2015) *Trends in maternal mortality: 1990 to 2015 estimates by WHO, UNICEF, UNFPA, World Bank Group and the United Nations Population Division*, Geneva: WHO.

World Health Organization (2016) *Poliomyelitis fact sheet*, Geneva: WHO. http://www.who.int/mediacentre/factsheets/fs114/en/ (accessed 12 October 2016).

World Health Organization (2017) *Depression fact sheet*, Geneva: WHO. http://www.who.int/mediacentre/factsheets/fs369/en/ (accessed 3 September 2017).

Wright, O. (2015) 'Human rights are no longer a "top priority" for the government, says Foreign Office chief', *The Independent*, 2 October. http://www.independent.co.uk/news/uk/politics/human-rights-are-no-longer-a-top-priority-for-the-government-says-foreign-office-chief-a6677661.html (accessed 14 October 2016).

Wright, R. (2006) *A short history of progress*, Edinburgh: Canongate.

Wright Mills, C. (1956) *The power elite*, Oxford: Oxford University Press.

WWF (2014) *Living Planet report 2014*, Geneva: WWF. http://wwf.panda.org/about_our_earth/all_publications/living_planet_report/ (accessed 28 June 2015).

WWF (2016) *Living Planet report 2016: Risk And Resilience In A New Era*, Gland: WWF. https://www.footprintnetwork.org/content/documents/2016_Living_Planet_Report_Lo.pdf (accessed 4 April 2018).

Xinhua/ECNS (2015) 'Work 4.5 days a week, government tells firms', *The Telegraph*, 17 August. https://www.telegraph.co.uk/sponsored/china-watch/business/11808004/china-government-urges-shorter-work-week.html (accessed 10 March 2018).

Xue, Y., Leventhal, T., Brooks-Gunn, J. and Earls, F.J. (2005) 'Neighbourhood residence and mental health problems of 5- to 11-year-olds', *Archives of General Psychiatry*, 62 (5): 554–63.

You, D., Hug, L., Ejdemyr, S., Idele, P., Hogan, D., Mathers, C., Gerland, P., New, J.R. and Alkema, L. (2015) 'Global, regional, and national levels and trends in under-5 mortality between 1990 and 2015, with scenario-based projections to 2030: a systematic analysis by the UN Inter-agency Group for Child Mortality Estimation', *The Lancet,* 386: 10010, 2275–86.

Young, I. (2000) *Inclusion and democracy*, New York: Oxford University Press.

Zamagni, S. (2014) 'Choices, incentives and co-operative organisation'. In: Novkovic, S. and Webb, T. (eds) *Co-operatives in a post-growth era: creating co-operative economics*, London: Zed Books.

Zhang, R. (2015) 'Rendanheyi 2.0: building an ecosystem to co-create and win together', speech to 2nd Haier Global Forum on Business Model Innovation, Beijing, 19 September.

Zuckerman, L. (2017) 'Cost of fighting US wildfires topped $2 billion in 2017', Reuters, 15 September. https://uk.reuters.com/article/us-usa-wildfires/cost-of-fighting-u-s-wildfires-topped-2-billion-in-2017-idUKKCN1BQ01F (accessed 27 February 2018).

Index

G

H

V

W

Y

Z

Printed in Great Britain
by Amazon